AMERICAN LITERATURE AND SOCIAL CHANGE

American Literature and Social Change

William Dean Howells to Arthur Miller

Michael Spindler

Indiana University Press
Bloomington

Reprinted 1985

Manufactured in Hong Kong

Library of Congress Cataloging in Publication Data

Spindler, Michael.
   American literature and social change.

   Bibliography: p.
   Includes index.
   1. American literature – History and criticism.
2. Social problems in literature.   3. Economics in
literature.   4. Capitalism in literature.   5. Consumption (Economics) in literature.   I. Title.
PS169.S57S74   1983   810'.9'355   83–47514
ISBN 0–253–30645–0
1 2 3 4 5   87 86 85 84 83

For Jean

Contents

Acknowledgements

I should especially like to acknowledge my indebtedness to Dr Robert Young (formerly of King's College, Cambridge) who first introduced me to the value of interdisciplinary study, and to Dr David Craig (of Lancaster University) who acted as friendly mentor and critical reader during the research which forms the basis of this book. My gratitude is also due to the editors of the *Journal of American Studies*, Professors Howard Temperley and Arnold Goldman, whose constructive criticism and publication of my submitted work have been of considerable benefit and encouragement to me. Chapter 7 of this book first appeared in that journal. Professor Dennis Welland and Dr Alison Easton read an earlier version of this study and made valuable comments which I gratefully bore in mind later. Whatever qualities there may be in the following pages I owe to the influence of these various people; the defects, unfortunately, are all my own. Finally, I must thank my wife for her patience and untiring moral support, without which this project would never have been completed.

Introduction: Production to Consumption

Nothing, it seems, could be more foreign to the modern American mind than the idea of a society in stasis. 'Standing still' on a social scale (as on the individual scale) has come to carry unfair implications of failure, decay, a radical loss of energy and direction. 'Change', 'transformation', 'development', 'progress', 'renewal', these are the affirmative terms that pepper debates, magazine reports, political pronouncements. Of course, the rhetoric and vocabulary of change are often used to mystify, to hold out the promise of a better tomorrow while cloaking a deeply conservative inertia within the social structure, but they also inculcate a potentially liberating conception – albeit a unidirectional and insufficiently dialectical conception – of America in a permanent process of becoming. At one level then, the immediate level of occupational and geographical mobility, of new towns in the Sun Belt, dying towns in Appalachia, technical and product innovation, the idea of social change as applied to the United States is a truism, a cliché. But at a deeper level, in the identification of the secular trends and powerful forces underlying the surface phenomena, it can provide a focus for cultural analysis of a very rewarding kind.

We all know the continuities that exist in the national culture. The eighteenth-century political framework remains; Puritanism and the frontier have left their residues; and slavery too has left its bitter legacy. Yet, if there are unifying strands running through American history, there is also a high degree of fracture and discontinuity and, paradoxically, it is one of those unifying strands which has been the effective agent of much of the discontinuity. For the early settlers brought not only Puritanism to the New World but capitalism (the New England Company was both a commercial, trading venture and a Puritan scheme) and there, after initial difficulties, it found a rich soil and a healthy climate. Untrammelled by feudal relations and restrictions and bolstered by the ideologies of individualism and Protestantism, capitalism

1

easily yoked America's development to its own dynamic. Obeying its imperative of accumulation, the settlers and their descendants, expanding ever westwards in pursuit of that major capital resource – land – transformed an untapped wilderness into both a massive agricultural producer and an industrial powerhouse.

From 1870 to 1950 in particular the United States underwent an extraordinarily dynamic economic development. In the last quarter of the nineteenth century the process of industrialisation and capital accumulation transformed a largely petty-bourgeois, handicraft and agrarian mode of production into one that was highly mechanised and centralised. The relatively homogeneous society that existed in the North before the Civil War became polarised into rich and poor, millionaire entrepreneurs on the one hand and impoverished immigrants on the other, and much of the working population become concentrated in the urban-industrial centres. Although the frontier was not officially closed until 1890, it was the densely populated manufacturing city with its factories and slums and not the open prairie with its farms and homesteads that increasingly represented the centre of gravity of American social life.

After half a century of rapid industrialisation America by the 1920s had achieved the highest standard of living any people had ever known. It was then that the features of consumerism we are familiar with today first came into prominence.[1] There was a marked growth in the marketing and distribution of personal goods and services, and the institutions of advertising and instalment credit came into being in order to increase demand for consumer goods such as automobiles, clothes, refrigerators, radios and phonographs. In order to man the expanded sectors of distribution and sales the white-collar middle class increased significantly in numbers and stamped its mark upon the American scene in its distinctive work-accommodation – tall office-blocks, and living accommodation – suburbia. How did the writers of imaginative literature respond to these complex social transformations?

Unfortunately, there has been a conspicuous lack of criticism which seeks to relate literary developments in America to economic and social change. The pre-war literary histories of Vernon Parrington and Granville Hicks now appear simplistic and unsystematic, and the dominant critical approach during the war and post-war years – the New Criticism – disengaged literature from its socio-historical context and emphasised its status as a self-contained aesthetic activity. The 'cultural' criticism practised by Lionel Trilling, Marius Bewley and others which drew on such broad notions as the 'American Dream', acknowledged that literature expressed deep issues in American culture, but that criticism suffers from a dissatisfying vagueness which has its origin in the inadequate attention paid to social reality. Such criticism, though it often purports to be about the writer and his society, displays a patrician aloofness in regard to social fact, resulting in a polished insensitivity to those sociological features of class and ideological conflict which make their appearance in the literature and even, from time to time, constitute its central concerns. Ignorance of a work's social milieu can lead us into two kinds of error: either we remain blind to the possibly oblique commentary the poem, play or novel is making on the contemporary world and concentrate entirely on form, or we ignore form altogether and read imaginative literature as if it were a transcript of actual social situations. We need to understand the economic, social and political developments to which a writer has responded and which he has helped to define before we can judge the degree to which he has exploited or distorted those developments for his own aesthetic or tendentious purposes. Fredric Jameson has written of the need for an historicist and sociological criticism which will restore literature to its concrete context.[2] This interdisciplinary study was written in response to that need and to remedy, partially at least, the lack alluded to above.

Its conceptual framework is supplied by that key element in Marxist cultural analysis – the proposition of a determining base and a determined superstructure: 'The economic structure of society always furnishes the real basis, starting from which we can alone work out the ultimate explanation of the whole superstructure of juridical and political institutions as well as of the religious, philosophical, and other ideas of a given historical period.' This was a restatement by Engels of Marx's view in his 1859 Preface to *A Contribution to the Critique of Political Economy* that: 'The mode of production of material life conditions the social, political and intellectual life process in general. It is not the consciousness of men that determines their being, but, on the contrary, their social being that determines their consciousness.'[3] The effect of material life upon cultural life may be delayed, attenuated or qualified, and there may be reciprocal modifying influences of the superstructure upon the base, but the main shaping thrust is from the realm of economic relations and processes to the realm of ideas and values and their expression.

The 'base' or economic relations of society formed the subject of *Capital* and in those volumes Marx made two important distinctions which are relevant to our purpose. First, he distinguished between two main sectors of the economy: Department I produces the means of production or capital goods such as machinery, factory buildings, energy and raw materials; Department II produces articles for individual consumption, either of a necessitous or luxurious nature. These two together carry out the total social production and the difference between them extends beyond the type of commodity they produce to the qualitative nature of the work they demand: 'Means of production and articles of consumption are wholly different kinds of commodities, products of entirely different bodily or use-forms, and, therefore, products of wholly different classes of concrete labour. The labour which employs machinery in the production of the means of subsistence [ie. Department II] is vastly different from the labour which makes machinery.'[4] Thus in Marx's view the general character of a society's production is determined by the balance maintained between these two sectors. A society in which Department I predominates will foster a distinctive type of work experience that will either generate its own, or reinforce, an inherited set of values and preconceptions. A society in which Department II predominates will tend to foster a contrasting value-system, one indeed that may come into conflict with that generated by Department I. The balance between these two sectors also possesses implications for the interests and attitudes of the capitalist class. The capitalists of the first sector manufacture capital goods which they sell to other members of the bourgeoisie, those involved either in their own or in the second sector. The capitalists in the latter sector, however, do not sell their products solely to other businessmen, although these in their private capacity as consumers do absorb some of the output of Department II. Instead, they sell mainly to the members of the other social classes which constitute the majority of the population. Any change, therefore, in the relative importance of the two sectors would have repercussions for the hegemonic role of the bourgeoisie and for the dominant social ideology.

Secondly, Marx identified two main phases in the cycle of

industrial capital: the productive phase, in which surplus-value in the form of profit is produced; and the circulating phase, in which surplus-value is not produced but in which it is realised. In its money form industrial capital enters the first phase with the purchase of raw materials, means of production and labour power. These are subsequently used to manufacture commodities, so completing the productive phase. Industrial capital (specifically that portion of it termed circulating capital) is now in its commodity form embodied in the products of the first phase. The second phase consists of the distribution of the goods and their sale, so effecting the conversion of the industrial capital back into its money form, in which form alone it can re-enter the cycle.[5]

The rate of profit, 'the incentive of capitalist production', is dependent, other things being equal, upon the rate of turnover of industrial capital.[6] The time of turnover or the duration of the cycle is comprised of the sum of the productive and circulating phases. Two separable sets of problems therefore present themselves to the manufacturer intent on raising his rate of profit: the length of the productive phase or the slowness of production due to the difficulty of the material and the lack of technique; and the length of the circulating phase or the slowness of distribution and selling due to poor communication and lack of consumer demand. The persistent endeavour to overcome the first knot of problems manifests itself in the constant development of technical skills and new instruments of production in order that more commodities can be produced in less time (the conveyor belt and the assembly line are the finest examples). The attempt to overcome the second set takes the form of improving the transport system and expanding the market in order that more can be sold in less time. This latter stage is less amenable to solution than the first since it is not under the manufacturer's complete control. The sale of the commodity presupposes a buyer who, as a free agent, is beyond the dictate of the individual capitalist (except in conditions of monopoly) though he may still be subject to the capitalist class as a whole. All the buyers operate abstractly together as 'the market' upon which the manufacturer depends for the sale of his goods, potentially the most crucial factor in the circulation of capital since only then is surplus-value realised as money in which form it can be employed as further capital.

The process of selling had from the first been at the heart of capitalism: 'Capitalist production makes the sale of products the main interest, at first apparently without affecting the mode of production itself.'[7] In the early stages of accumulation and in conditions of high demand the mode of production could be relatively autonomous and free from the effects of 'the main interest', but as the problems of production were progressively overcome, the imperative of selling was bound to permeate all the phases of industrial capital. As we shall see, there was a growing pervasiveness of this concern in the American economy. There was also a shift of relative importance from Department I to Department II, and their combined effect brought about a qualitative alteration in the character of capitalism, that is to say, a change in the base. I characterise this as a shift in the American economy from being *production-oriented* to being *consumption-oriented*. The primary producing industries continued to exist and indeed to grow but they ceased to be the leading sector of the economy as consumer-based industries came to the fore and the imperative of maintaining aggregate demand dominated business thinking. This process began in the early 1920s, was retarded by the severe recession of the 1930s, and reached full spate after the end of the Second World War.

In line with the base/superstructure formulation we would expect determinate shifts in the social and ideological realms to accompany this change of economic emphasis. It appears, for instance, that one section of the American bourgeoisie took on a hegemonic role in propagating a cluster of hedonistic values conducive to consumption, values which came into conflict with the conservative ideologies of the earlier agrarian and industrial periods. The social consciousness engendered by the consumption-oriented phase differed in significant respects from that engendered by the production-oriented phase and we would expect the literature as part expression, part moulder, of consciousness to embody that difference in various ways. This study, focusing on this shift in American capitalism, attempts in an innovatory way to read certain literary texts as articulations of that change and its attendant conflicts.

Since a comprehensive survey of the literature of the period is beyond the scope of this book, I have selected seven major authors – William Dean Howells, Frank Norris, Theodore Dreiser, F. Scott Fitzgerald, Sinclair Lewis, John Dos Passos and Arthur

Miller – chosen because of their assured place in the accepted canon, their generally acknowledged representative quality and their work's serious engagement with the character and texture of American social life. One of my aims is to show how these writers' concerns were shaped by industrialism and consumerism, and how family background, class and personal and national ideologies acted as mediations between their experience of society and their literary practice. In turning to the specific texts I situate them in their immediate socio-historical context and suggest how they embody, thematically and dramatically, the tensions set up within the American system of values by economic and social change. More broadly, I examine the degree to which literary form, in addition to content, may be regarded as historically conditioned. There was a persistence of certain literary modes beyond the conditions of their original inception, demonstrating their semi-autonomous character, but there was also a degree of formal innovation which represented a striving on the part of some writers to fashion literary techniques better able to express the new content of social experience.

This study is necessarily selective in its presentation of American economic, social and literary life, and certain limitations must be recognised from the beginning. The South has been ignored because of its rather separate economic and social development. The upheavals caused by involvement in two world wars are left in the background, and the Depression is largely passed over. Seven is a small number of writers to choose from the especially crowded fellowship of American letters. The social changes, ideological conflicts and literary developments dealt with in the following chapters, then, are far from being the only ones occurring in the United States between 1880 and 1950. They are, however, among the most central, betraying a secular trend in American society and culture of great importance. Tracing the themes of social change and ideological conflict in some of the major works of this period should not only enrich and render more specific our sense of their cultural representativeness but should also provide a useful 'breaking of ground' in the scarcely developed field of the sociology of American literature.

PART I
THE PRODUCTION-
ORIENTED PHASE

1 Hardware: the Economy, Society and Ideologies of Production

In the United States of the latter half of the nineteenth century the economy had not yet reached that stage of saturation by 'the main interest', the imperative of selling. The problems facing the capitalists were centred on the first phase, the phase of production. Until the Civil War America had seen little industrial development except in some northeastern towns and its economy was predominantly a rural and handicraft one. But the victory of the North in 1865 meant that the northern industrial and business interests, long held in check by a coalition of the agrarian South and Northwest, were free to develop the nation as they wished. With the compliance of a succession of federal governments sympathetic to the goal of economic expansion these interests began to exploit the resources of the American subcontinent and to take the economy through the process of rapid capital accumulation. Industrialisation took place on a massive scale.

All types of metal smelting – copper, lead, silver and gold – expanded enormously in the post-bellum period and there was a correspondingly great increase in the output of the ore-producing mines. Pig-iron production doubled between 1860 and 1870, and doubled again by 1880. By 1900 the USA was producing more than a third of the world's output. There was also a huge rise in the production of steel following the commercial application of two technical developments – the Bessemer conversion process and the use of coal instead of wood. Steel rails quickly replaced iron rails in the construction of the railways, and early in the twentieth century wide-flanged steel girders formed the framework for the multi-storey office-blocks being built in the cities.

Mineral sources of energy were increasingly exploited too, as the demand for power multiplied. Coal was used to supply heat

11

for all the steam-driven machinery as well as being the basis of coke in the steel industry. In 1866 only thirteen million tons of it were mined but by 1896 output had multiplied tenfold. Mineral oil used in the form of kerosene for lamps and burners replaced whale oil and became a main industry. In the 1880s electricity began to compete with these earlier means of power and by 1900 it was supplying about equal amounts of energy with steam. All machine manufacturing for both industrial and agricultural use developed tremendously. Several new inventions, such as McCormick's reaper, were in great demand owing to the expansion of the West and the settlement of new land. The mechanisation of farming further accelerated in the twentieth century with the manufacture and sale of diesel tractors and combine harvesters. As a result of this exploitation of natural resources the United States was transformed into a highly industrialised nation dominated by the industries of Department I. In 1859 the ten leading industries were mainly those producing food, clothing and other consumer goods, but by 1899 these had given way to capital goods industries such as iron and steel and forge manufacturing.[1] Manufacturing's share in the national income rose from 13.9 per cent in the decade 1869–78 to 18.4 per cent in the decade 1899–1908, while agriculture's share fell from 20.5 per cent to 16.7 per cent respectively. The industrialisation of the economy is also reflected in the changing employment pattern. In 1860 the number of workers in agriculture and allied occupations was much larger than the number employed in non-agricultural trades, but by 1880 the number engaged in non-agricultural work had exceeded those in agriculture for the first time.[2]

This rapid industrial growth, with its reliance on a continuous supply of raw materials and the efficient distribution of goods, soon outstripped the capacities of the earlier river and canal transport system. In line with Marx's observation that as the mass of commodities in transit grows so there is 'a simultaneous growth of that portion of social wealth which, instead of serving as direct means of production, is invested in means of transportation and communication', there was a massive capital investment in the railways and a corresponding increase in the amount of freight that they carried during the last quarter of the nineteenth century.[3] Railroad mileage grew from 35 000 in 1865 to 166 000 in 1890 and further to 403 000 in 1919 (*HS*, p. 429). The great railroad companies – the Great Northern, Union Pacific and

Central Pacific – came into prominence, transporting agricultural products from the North-Central states to the Eastern states
and manufactured products from these states back to the
expanding far-West. With the establishment of two transcon-
tinental lines the railways knitted the American economy together
and endowed it with a national unity, causing regional economies
to lose their autonomy and fall under the sway of the large industrial and financial centres of the East. The emergence of a fast,
efficient communications system was a natural outgrowth of
industrial capitalism's need to shorten the distance both between
the source of materials and the factory and between the factory
and the market in order to expedite the turnover of capital.

Supplied by the American continent on the one hand with
plentiful natural resources and by the European continent on the
other with cheap, docile labour, American businessmen were
able to expropriate surplus-value and accumulate capital at a
prodigious rate. During the three decades 1869 to 1899 as much
as 20 per cent of national output was devoted to capital formation, that is, investment in land, buildings and machinery.
Virtually all the capital growth took place in the industries of
Department I; over 80 per cent of net capital formation (gross
capital formation less depreciation) took place in the manufacturing industries, construction and railways between 1880 and
1900. The extent to which this capital growth was nationally
generated is indicated by Simon Kuznets's calculation that
foreign capital investment (to be more specific, the net balance of
foreign capital inflow) amounted to only 3 per cent of net capital
formation during this period.[4]

While capital accumulation is the product of the instruments
of production possessed by the bourgeoisie it is also a means of extending those instruments and so augmenting the production of
capital. Capital stock, that is, the number of factories and
number of machines, miles of railroad, size of mines and
steelworks, etc., increased much more rapidly than population
during the period 1869 to 1899 – by 322 per cent while
population grew only 87 per cent. Consequently, the capital stock
per capita doubled during these years. A worker who on average
had 3 520 dollars of means of production behind him in 1869,
had 6 660 dollars in 1899.[5] The over-all effect of this heavy capital
investment was a huge increase in national output; Gross
National Product increased fourfold from 1869 to 1900 and *per*

capita GNP more than doubled (*HS* p. 139).

Of course, the vast increase in national wealth represented by these figures was not shared equally by all those who helped to create it. As in Britain, so in America the members of the capitalist class appropriated the lion's share of it to themselves and the names of some of the entrepreneurs of this period have remained bywords for fabulous wealth well into the twentieth century. Andrew Carnegie, the Pennsylvania iron and steel magnate, left a personal fortune of 1000 million dollars; J. Pierpont Morgan, founder of the Federal Steel Company, left 100 million dollars; J. D. Rockefeller made 1500 million dollars out of his Standard Oil Company. Vanderbilt made a fortune of 105 million dollars out of steamships and railroads; William Randolph Hearst made 400 million dollars, more out of mining operations than newspapers; and the Guggenheims obtained their fortune of hundreds of millions of dollars from silver, lead and copper mining, while the Du Pont family wealth was derived from gunpowder and dynamite.[6] Most of these tycoons gained their enormous profits from a monopolistic position which they had managed to establish after ruthlessly ruining their rivals and then buying them out.

Another device they resorted to was the 'trust', by means of which key firms in a given industry maintained ostensible independence whilst in fact operating under the control of an over-arching board of directors. In the 1880s trusts were established in cotton seed oil, linseed oil, whisky, lead and sugar.[7] The Anaconda Mining Company was a trust established in this period between three or four erstwhile competitors to work the copper region of Montana. Standard Oil was built up by Rockefeller to be the biggest trust of these years, a leading position it did not relinquish until 1901 when Morgan formed the United States Steel Company by merging the Federal Steel Company with several other large steel firms, including Carnegie's. In addition, when several business giants reached a stalemate in the competitive struggle for domination of the market they frequently created a 'cartel' or price-ring which administered agreed, stable prices throughout that particular industry. In the railways in 1877 Vanderbilt, Jay Gould and Jim Fisk joined in a price-ring to raise rates and share revenues on operations in the area between New York and Chicago. In the 1880s the four big meat packers in Chicago, including the Armour Company, also formed a cartel.

The 1890s saw a further marked phase of combination between firms. Pure competition thus became a limited phenomenon in the closing years of the nineteenth century as major industries adopted these various devices to ameliorate, if not entirely abolish, price warfare. The formation of monopolies and trusts was part of the inevitable centralisation and consolidation of capital which accompanied and accelerated accumulation.

By the early 1900s capitalism's solution of many of the problems of the production phase and the massive accumulation of capital had brought into being vast new productive forces. These continued to multiply their level of output through the early decades of the twentieth century as indicated by the growth of GNP from 37 billion dollars in 1897 to 71 billion dollars in 1918 (constant 1929 dollars, *HS*, p. 139). Such a rise of manufacturing capacity, although testifying to the triumph of capital and technology over the resistant materials of nature, intensely exacerbated the lack of co-ordination between the productive phase and the circulation phase. Its ultimate effect was to bring to the fore those difficulties characteristic of the latter stage. Speed in the first stage had come to emphasise the slowness in the second; the hare of production chafed at the heels of the tortoise of sales and distribution. The American economy had reached a state of overproduction in which goods, far from being scarce, were surplus and could not be sold. The result was a tying up of capital in its commodity form with a reduction of profit rates and a compensating cessation of production, culminating in mild economic depressions in 1897 and 1920–1. The speeding up of selling by expanding the market increasingly became the main concern, and with the domestic market apparently saturated the successful establishment of foreign markets seemed vital for the future. The war with Spain over Cuba in 1898 and the subsequent annexation of the Philippines were motivated by the need for an international sphere of trading.[8]

This extended sphere was necessary not only to solve the problem of surplus products but also to provide an outlet for surplus capital. Ever increasing amounts of surplus-value were being accumulated but the potential investment field had narrowed markedly as accumulation had proceeded.[9] The industries of Department I simply could not offer as many opportunities for investment in 1919 as they had done forty years earlier. Railways, for instance, which had been particularly heavy absorbers of capital, ceased to grow significantly after 1919, and although new industries such as chemicals and electric power partly offset this loss, the general outlook was one of a contracting circle of business opportunities.[10]

In the domestic economy the giantism of the monopolistic concerns precluded competing ventures in their fields, and American investors consequently looked to overseas economies with more plentiful avenues for capital absorption for a solution to their problems. Many American business concerns made direct investments abroad. United States Steel bought iron mines in Cuba; International Harvester built plants in Russia, Germany and Canada; the Vanderbilts acquired Canadian railways; and oil companies bought wells in Mexico.[11] Over the period 1874 to 1914 the net balance of the inflow and outflow of capital was negative but this then became positive, that is, there developed an excess of the export of capital over its import. And by the 1920s the outflow of capital from the United States had reached enormous proportions.[12] But foreign palliatives for internal economic problems were insufficient. As we shall see when we return to the economy at the beginning of Part II, they had to be combined with new national developments if the American domestic economy was not to lapse into long-term stagnation brought on by an excess of capacity and a constriction of investment opportunities.

At the ideological level there was a persistence of residual elements from the previous phase and the emergence of new elements. Whilst the middle of the period 1870 to 1920 saw an ideology of capitalist competition peculiar to itself, many of the current beliefs and attitudes in the 1870s were a legacy of the agrarian period. Inherited from the seventeenth century was the Puritan tradition centred on the Protestant ethic, and inherited from the late eighteenth century was the democratic tradition based on the ideals of social equality and political freedom. Closely allied with these traditions and indeed derivative of them was the ideology of individualism. These three strands in the American culture of the last quarter of the nineteenth century did not remain static but were modified over the decades by the conditions and social relations enforced by large-scale industrial enterprise.

The Puritanism brought by the English settlers to the New

World was more than just a system of religious belief. It had political, economic and social manifestations as well, requiring of its adherents a number of convictions about the role of government, the nature of work and family relations. In particular it embodied a close coincidence of moral and business values suited to a production-oriented economy: 'The main economic dogma of the mercantilist had an affinity with the main ethical dogma of the Puritan. ... To the former, production, not consumption, was the pivot of the economic system. ... To the latter, the cardinal virtues are precisely those which find in the strenuous toils of industry and commerce their most natural expression'.[13] Max Weber postulated a more positive relationship than a vague affinity, claiming that it was Calvinism or the Protestant ethic which supplied the spirit of capitalism and helped to bring it into being. There is no space here to consider the controversy centred on his *Protestant Ethic and the Spirit of Capitalism* but we must take issue with his remark that 'in the country of Benjamin Franklin's birth (Massachusetts), the spirit of capitalism ... was present before the capitalistic order'.[14] This anti-materialist interpretation is historically unjustifiable. Just as the early settlers had been impelled across the Atlantic by a powerful combination of religious and material motives, so they brought with them to New England both Puritanism and capitalism. As a mode of ownership and exchange capitalism entered America fully formed since mercantile capitalism was there from the start in the form of the New England Company, which was both a commercial, trading venture and a Puritan scheme.[15] As a petty-bourgeois mode of production (and it seems to be in this sense that Weber uses 'capitalism'), it was also there from the start, since the colonies were organised on the basis of the private ownership of property and the private production of goods for profit. As a mode of production based on the expropriation of surplus-value from another's labour and the cash nexus it was, admittedly, in an embryonic form. Most people worked for themselves and those that worked for someone else were usually black slaves. The New England economy was based on the small independent farmer, artisan or merchant, and it was the value-system of this middling class of producers and businessmen that the Protestant ethic represented.

Although its roots were in theology, the Protestant ethic's effects were most pronounced in the world of business.[16] With production encouraged on the one hand by the moral duty of hard work, and consumption limited on the other by the Calvinist condemnation of luxury and extravagance, profits were increased and saved, providing surplus capital which could be reinvested in the business. Thus the Protestant ethic supplied an ideology appropriate to the period of primitive accumulation as well as a code of conduct which justified and ennobled the labour and hardships suffered by the settlers in mastering the hostile environment. It survived so long as a cluster of secularised values when its theological springs had run dry because the material and social conditions for which it provided ethical guidance – the necessity of hard work to overcome a wild nature and of gaining capital in order to rise in American society – remained essentially the same, especially with westward expansion, throughout the agrarian and early industrial periods of the production-oriented phase. For each generation until the early twentieth century it provided a ready-made rationale for the habits and activities demanded by the productive processes and social relations of the American economy.

Hector St John de Crèvecoeur frequently insisted on the value of industry and thrift to the small farmer and he advised his negro workers, 'Be sober, frugal, and industrious, and you need not fear earning a comfortable existence.' Benjamin Franklin, Max Weber's famous example, provided the classic creed of the petty-bourgeois mode of life in his extremely popular *Poor Richard's Almanack* and 'The Way to Wealth'. In his edition of *The Instructor or Young Man's Best Companion* he claimed categorically that the way to wealth 'depends chiefly on two Words, INDUSTRY and FRUGALITY'. These two virtues, together with a moral character, had to be much in evidence in order to secure the credit which was often the prerequisite to a capitalistic venture. 'The most Trifling Actions that affect a Man's Credit', Franklin warned, 'are to be regarded', and Crèvecoeur pointed out that a 'good name' secures credit. Thus an ulterior financial motive often attended the maintenance of a spotless character in this Protestant society of tight morality and tight money. By means of the interest rate, credit was linked to time. The quicker the principal was repaid, the less would be taken in interest, a consideration that demanded rational forward planning and a sustained sense of urgency. 'Remember that TIME is Money', Franklin instructed his Young Tradesman. It was a precept that applied equally well to the accumulation of capital, for the sooner a sum of money was saved the sooner it could be put to good use making more capital: 'Money is of a prolific generating Nature. Money can beget Money, and its Offspring can beget more, and so on. . . . The more there is of it, the more it produces every Turning, so that the Profits rise quicker and quicker.' The repeated injunctions to intense industry continued to be obeyed in the early nineteenth century, for in 1835 Alexis de Tocqueville observed that 'Not only is no dishonour associated with work, but . . . it is regarded as positively honourable; the prejudice is for, not against, it.'[17]

The Protestant ethic's close intermingling of material and moral values is nowhere more evident than in the religious sanction it extended to the possession of wealth. For the seventeenth-century Puritan concerned about his election, success in business was almost a sign of spiritual grace since it was proof that he had laboured faithfully in his calling and that Providence was on his side. Franklin testifies to the persistence of this notion through the eighteenth century: 'He that gets all he can honestly, and saves all he gets (necessary Expences excepted) will certainly become RICH: If that Being who governs the World, to whom all should look for a blessing on their honest Endeavors, doth not in his wise Providence otherwise determine.' Wealth, then, was regarded as a consequence of business practice *and* the approval of the Deity. It therefore took on the status of providential reward for the strict exercise of moral values. What better way could there be to fuse the religious and material concerns of the small businessman and to legitimate his profit-taking and capital accumulation than by endowing *practical* success with the badge of *ethical* superiority! Conversely, the Protestant, convinced that character was all, saw in the poverty of those who fell by the way not a misfortune to be pitied or relieved but a moral deficiency to be condemned. Within the Protestant scheme wealth was sinful only inasmuch as it presented temptations to idleness and the sensual enjoyment of life. As long as it did not corrupt the sober, ascetic mode of existence, it was regarded as honorific.[18]

The pursuit of wealth became the widely adopted specification of 'the pursuit of happiness', and the primacy of prosperity as a personal and social goal came to saturate American thinking. In the 1830s Tocqueville observed that Americans pursued pro-

sperity with 'feverish ardour' and that 'they are ever tormented by
the shadowy suspicion that they may not have chosen the shortest
route to get it'. And early in the twentieth century, according to
James Bryce, the worship of wealth was the fault most commonly
ascribed to Americans. The pursuit of wealth reached its most
extreme manifestations in the careers of the industrialists and
financiers of the Gilded Age, and the worldly asceticism of the
Protestant ethic played its part in the economic temper of that
period of rapid accumulation. The significant proportion of 30
per cent of national output during the period 1869 to 1899 was
devoted to capital formation and Simon Kuznets suggests that
such a high rate of savings represented a strong propensity to save
and was a major factor in accounting for the remarkable pace of
capital formation at that time.[19]

Max Weber's ideal type of entrepreneur was one 'who avoids
ostentation and unnecessary expenditure as well as conscious enjoyment of his power', and whose 'manner of life is distinguished
by a certain ascetic tendency'. And many of the nineteenth-
century entrepreneurs seemed to conform to this ideal type,
leading restricted, inconspicuous existences in deference to the
Protestant code. John Rockefeller Sr, though extremely rich, was
not ostentatious and he constantly cautioned associates against
any display of wealth. His qualities were those of the early Puritan
pioneer – piety, frugality and unremitting attention to business.
Marshall Field, who made 120 million dollars out of real estate
and railroads in Chicago, was also extremely frugal. More often
than not he walked from his home to his office and when he did
take a carriage he always had his coachman drop him off a few
blocks away. To drive up to his place of business with high-
stepping horses struck him as far too flagrant a show of wealth.
Whilst the majority led sober, restrained lives, there were
exceptions, of course, such as 'Diamond' Jim Brady who dressed
like a cardsharp and spent his fortune wildly, ordering cham-
pagne in hundred-case lots and giving gold-plated bicycles to
ladies of the stage.[20]

However, despite their ascetic lifestyle the nineteenth-century
millionaires like Rockefeller, Morgan and Carnegie did not owe
their large-scale capital accumulation to thrift. Whilst saving and
diligence may have been the prerequisites for a successful start in
life, the great fortunes were usually the result of high-risk/high-
return speculations, enormous capital gains, and the monopolis-

ation of markets or credit. Furthermore, although Horatio Alger, in his immensely popular improvement tales such as the *Ragged Dick* series (1867 on) and the *Tattered Tom* series (1871 on), always preached thrift and diligence, in the end he usually bowed to the demands of credulity and resorted to a gigantic inheritance to transport his boy-hero to the ranks of the rich.[21] Even in inspirational tales of this type it had to be admitted that by the late nineteenth century it was impossible to attain wealth simply by following the precepts of the Protestant ethic.

By this stage in the production-oriented phase of the economy this cluster of values derived from the Puritan tradition had become an ideology in the sense of a false consciousness. Whilst in the petty-bourgeois phase of production it had authentically reflected economic and social imperatives and had provided a suitable guide for meeting them, in the bourgeois-industrial phase of production it no longer did so. Hard work, thrift and moral piety continued to be promulgated as the necessary virtues for obtaining riches, but the entrepreneurial ruling class, whilst it continued to pay lip-service to the Protestant ethic, increasingly resorted to a newer, more aggressive ideology to sanction its position and business activities.

The democratic tradition stemmed, of course, from the American Revolution of 1776, which abolished the titled aristocratic hierarchy, including the monarch, and adopted the Enlightenment doctrine of 'natural rights', freedom and equality. America, Crèvecoeur claimed in celebratory tones, enjoyed 'new laws, a new mode of living, a new social system' and the American was 'a new man, who acts upon new principles'.[22] At the time of the Revolution the dominant class in the thirteen original states was the petty-bourgeoisie of small businessmen, farmers (like Crèvecoeur) and self-employed artisans, and this property-owning middle class initially fashioned the Bill of Rights and the Constitution (of 1787) to express its own economic and political interests, wrapped though these were in the appealing language of a universalising idealism.[23] 'Europe contains hardly any other distinctions but lords and tenants,' Crèvecoeur wrote, 'this fair country alone is settled by freeholders, the possessors of the soil they cultivate, members of the government they obey, and the framers of their own laws, by means of their representatives.'[24]

For Thomas Jefferson too the independent farmer was the basis upon which a healthy American democracy rested and he endowed the agricultural way of life with a heightened virtuousness, so contributing to that attractive image of an agrarian republic of free men which has played an important role in American cultural nostalgia: 'Those who labour in the earth are the chosen people of God, if ever he had a chosen people, whose breasts he has made his peculiar deposit for substantial and genuine virtue. ... Corruption of morals in the mass of cultivators is a phenomenon of which no age nor nation has furnished an example.' Whether or not the situation of the freeholder inculcated a moral superiority, it did indeed foster two principal elements of the national ideology. Since the freeholders' livelihoods were founded on the individual ownership of property and economic autonomy, the doctrine of individualism was a natural outgrowth of their social relations. Self-interest, the middle-class producer's experience taught him, was the dominant social force and the most effective motivation for hard work. An American's labour, Crèvecoeur remarked proudly, 'is founded on the basis of nature, *self-interest*; can it want a stronger allurement?'[25] Since the individual could best identify and best pursue his own interests, society, so the doctrine reasoned, should allow him to do so. That the individual's capacities for enterprise should be allowed full sway became a deep-seated social assumption, and *laissez-faire* individualism became the central creed of the small American producer and capitalist.[26] Protestantism reinforced individualism and self-reliance, since the essence of Puritan theology lay in a solitary communion between the individual and his Maker, and the Puritan was enjoined to be morally self-sufficient, self-disciplined and self-examining. This individualism in religion led to an individualistic morality and an individualistic morality to a disparagement of the social fabric as compared with personal character.[27]

Also, since ownership of the means of production, especially land, was widespread (though there was some social diversity with slave-holding planters in the South and bankers and merchants in the Northeast), equal economic status found expression in a political doctrine of equal rights (rights for a long time denied to those social groups such as women, negroes and native Americans, which did not enjoy equal economic status). Writing in 1835 Tocqueville was struck by the 'equality of conditions' operating in the United States and by the progressive, democratic nature of American society and its institutions. But with his well-ordered French society in mind he viewed individualism as a 'menace' which broke social bonds and threatened to atomise society.[28] As Émile Durkheim pointed out in *The Division of Labour in Society*, the maintenance of social cohesion is problematic for all societies, but in a community where there was little division of labour and where the prevailing economic conditions and avowed values encouraged a rampant individualism this problem was especially acute. For the early ideologues of American democracy, particularly Jefferson, the latent conflict between individual rights and society's collective needs was resolved by the belief in the innate sociability and morality of man.[29] An implanted moral disposition steeped in Christian ethics was relied upon to curb the possible excesses of *laissez-faire* individualism. In their schema of an open society, not governmental control but self-government was the key to reconciling individual liberty with the demands of social co-operation.[30]

Abraham Lincoln in his Gettysburg Address of 1863 drew on several important elements within the national tradition and fused them together into a powerful restatement of American democratic values:

> Four score and seven years ago our fathers brought forth on this continent, a new nation, conceived in Liberty, and dedicated to the proposition that all men are created equal.
>
> Now we are engaged in a great civil war, testing whether that nation, or any nation so conceived and so dedicated, can long endure. . . . It is for us to be here dedicated to the great task remaining before us . . . that this nation, under God, shall have a new birth of freedom – and that government of the people, by the people, for the people, shall not perish from the earth.[31]

Invoking the founding ideals of 1776, he identified national existence with democracy and then assimilated the cause of the Civil War to that of the Revolution in a call for the preservation of freedom and equality in American social and political life. Democratic values had been sustained in their original form through to the latter half of the nineteenth century, despite social change, by nationalism and also the frontier (as embodied indeed in the ex-Northwest-frontiersman President).

The Declaration of Independence had proclaimed not only the founding of democracy but also the founding of a new nation-state, and this coincidence of political and national revolution meant that from the beginning national, social and individual values were indivisibly fused. The abstract set of principles enunciated in the Bill of Rights and the Constitution represented a harmony of individual and national interests that was to have a powerfully cohesive effect on the country. For those who took part in the Revolution and the war against England a strong sense of national loyalty was a natural outcome of their experience, but for later generations, particularly immigrants, national loyalty could be fostered best through the influence of national ideology. The United States of the latter half of the nineteenth century lacked the ethnic, religious and cultural unity which a long common history provided for traditional societies. For those newly arrived on American shores national loyalty meant loyalty to the Constitution and citizenship was the only nexus which bound them to the American community.[32] Thus, while commitment to the State was secured by commitment to a set of liberating values expressed politically in that State, the historical continuity of the State reciprocally secured the continuity of the national ideology of democracy and individualism when the socio-economic phase which originally nurtured it had passed away.

The persistence of democratic and individualistic values was further secured by the persistence of the frontier. Until 1890, when it was declared officially closed, the frontier represented a repeated return to the primitive conditions of the eighteenth century as recurrent waves of settlers trekked West in pursuit of land and economic independence. Each man had to clear his own land, build his own house, grow his own food and cure his own illnesses. Such a self-reliant mode of life maintained the vitality and authenticity of individualism, while the equality of economic opportunity and absence of social rank ensured an egalitarian and democratic community. 'The frontier', Frederick Jackson Turner wrote, 'is productive of individualism, and frontier individualism has from the beginning promoted democracy.' James Bryce, recognising the continuity within the colonial, Revolutionary and frontier experiences, observed that 'the circumstances of colonial life, the process of settling the western wilderness, the feelings evoked by the struggle against George III, all went to intensify individualism, the love of enterprise, and the pride in personal freedom', and 'from that day to this, individualism, the love of enterprise, and the pride in personal freedom, have been deemed by Americans not only their choicest, but their peculiar and exclusive possessions'.[33]

By the latter part of the nineteenth century, however, Lincoln's restatement notwithstanding, economic and social changes were driving a widening rift between the ideology of democracy and the social political reality it was meant to express. After the 1840s in the East the independent farmer and artisan began to lose their hegemony as industrial production with its capital-intensive and collective operations grew in importance, and in the post-bellum period the relatively homogeneous society of independent producers gave way to one characterised by extremes of rich and poor. The transformation of the American economy of small, self-employed producers into a typical bourgeois-industrial economy with its polarities of workers and owners is reflected in the drop of the proportion of independent producers in the working population from 80 per cent early in the nineteenth century to 41 per cent by 1870 (and further to only 18 per cent by 1940).[34] The opportunities for rapid capital accumulation afforded by industrial development created a class of millionaire entrepreneurs, while the farmers and artisans consolidated themselves into a middle class, and those who gave up their independence sank into the swelling tide of people, mainly European immigrants, who owned no property and lived by selling their labour.

Between 1840 and 1910 a total of 27 000 000 immigrants from Europe entered the United States, arriving in four great waves – the Irish, the German, the Scandinavian, and the Central and Southern European. This seemingly endless supply of people served the needs both of frontier expansion, by providing settlers, and of industrialisation, by providing a docile, uprooted workforce. The Irish tended to settle in the Eastern cities where they constituted a pool of cheap labour, but the Germans and Scandinavians went West and set themselves to felling the woods and tilling the prairies in such areas as Ohio and Minnesota. As good farmers and businessmen, skilful artisans and stable citizens, they were easily assimilated into frontier society, so playing their part in sustaining the settler ideology of economic independence and self-reliance. The bulk of latecomers did not follow this pattern. Like the Greeks and Jews, they either flocked into the cities to set themselves up in service industries or, like the Poles and Italians, they found work in unskilled occupations such as mining or railroad construction. Few among the later Slavonic and Italian immigrants had either the knowledge of the country or the capital required to set up a farm, even though western land was still moderately cheap in 1890. They consequently constituted a high proportion of the labour-force required in increasing size by the large-scale development of the production-oriented economy. The characteristic occupations of the later immigrants therefore weakened the general applicability of the independent-producer based doctrines of individualism and equality. This huge influx of ethnically and religiously diverse groups into the once predominantly English Protestant society – by 1900 the foreign-born and their offspring constituted 48 per cent of the total population and much more than half of the population of the northern states, since the South took very few immigrants – was bound to undermine the Puritan and democratic traditions, and in the early twentieth century the immigrant population, especially the young, provided a fertile ground for newer, different values to take hold and grow.[35]

Industrial capitalism's formation of a massive proletariat on the one hand and a small, wealthy bourgeoisie on the other, meant that the inherited democratic doctrines came into contradiction with the social reality and had to undergo modification. Formal political equality still existed between the owners of the factories and the men who worked in them. Carnegie or Rockefeller, like the newly enfranchised immigrant on the shop floor, had only one vote to cast, but wealth was more than merely honorific; because of its unprecedented concentration it had become powerful, capable of exerting widespread political influence and bending the democratic processes. Also, the exercise of that influence could secure yet more wealth through land speculation, say, or through acting as banker to the government. As a result of such pressures, both local and national administrations in the United States of the Gilded Age became only a semblance of 'government of the people, by the people, for the people'.

The values of democracy were still strongly asserted, but in the last quarter of the nineteenth century they too came to constitute an ideology in the sense of false consciousness – a view of society kept alive by the ruling class of manufacturers and financiers because it mystified the real basis of power and the real processes of politics within the industrial republic. The big entrepreneurs bought senators and legislators, just as they bought newspapers, to promote their own business interests and keep any popular opposition at bay. They thus wielded an iron fist of autocratic power within the velvet glove of democracy, as graft, corruption, ballot-rigging, intimidation and violence became common features of the political scene, especially in the rapidly growing urban centres. 'There is no denying that the government of cities is the one conspicuous failure of the United States', James Bryce remarked, 'The faults of the State governments are insignificant compared with the extravagance, corruption, and mismanagement which have marked the administrations of most of the great cities.' Lincoln Steffens wrote a 'muckraking' exposure of city administration entitled *The Shame of the Cities* (1904). And if corruption from the top was eating away at the democratic framework in the cities, there was also apathy from below. Jane Addams, a social worker in Chicago, pointed out in 1892 that self-government (one of the key premises of Jeffersonian democracy) had broken down in her ward and that there was no initiative among the citizens, the sense of community was absent, and the countless poor had neither the leisure nor the energy for active participation in social life. It was only with the greatest difficulty that the old individualism based on the civic pride and economic self-sufficiency of the freeholder could survive in the alien environment of huge factories and sprawling slums, an environment that was ushering in the era of mass society.[36]

Social equality, the original basis of political equality, had never existed in the South, of course, but by the beginning of the twentieth century it had largely disappeared from the rest of the United States as well. Bryce observed in 1910 that though equality of conditions was 'almost universal in the eighteenth century' and still general in the nineteenth century, there was 'no equality now', a view supported by figures on the distribution of income. In 1910 the richest tenth of the population received almost 34 per cent of all personal income before taxes, a share which had increased to 39 per cent by 1929 and which was always greater than the share of the six lowest income tenths added together. One commentator estimated that in 1910, 17 per cent of American families lived on 'the pauper standard', 35 per cent on 'the minimum-of-subsistence standard', 44 per cent on 'the health and comfort standard' and 4 per cent on 'the luxury standard'. Thus the relatively egalitarian, democratic society that Tocqueville observed had been transformed into one characterised like European societies by stratification and great disparities of wealth.[37]

After 1870 then the traditional values inherited from the agrarian period increasingly became out of place in the new urban-industrial scene created by the production-oriented economy. Not only did social and political equality largely cease to exist, but the latent conflict within *laissez-faire* individualism between the unrestricted rights of the individual and the needs of society became acutely manifest. Tocqueville in his suspicion of individualism had demonstrated his prescience: 'Egoism', he had warned, 'sterilises the seeds of every virtue; individualism at first only dams the springs of public virtues, but in the long run it attacks and destroys all the others too and finally merges in egoism.'[38] During the phase of industrial production the sociability which had tempered settler individualism rapidly declined and the 'innate' morality and social disposition of men failed to check the powerful drives for survival or aggrandisement. Self-interest, no longer balanced by self-restraint, became the single, dominating force, and shorn of its humanising Christian morality, individualism was reduced to a hard egoism that prevailed among both ruling and working classes as civil society became the arena for fierce egotistical competition.

At the lower end of the social scale each person was pitched against another in a bitter struggle for a subsistence wage in a competitive labour market, and a competition for the lowest sustainable standard of living developed between the different immigrant groups. At the upper end of the scale individual was pitched against individual in a ruthless battle for the spoils of the richly developing economy. The unprecedented opportunities for wealth and power together with the absence of effective legal or governmental controls generated a shocking unscrupulousness in many entrepreneurs. Fraud and deception became normal business devices and even violence was resorted to in the furtherance of business interests. The 'Robber Barons' adopted an extreme form of *laissez-faire* individualism in order to excuse their social irresponsibility and justify their rapaciousness, and their ideology of capitalist competition found its most substantial articulation in Herbert Spencer's theories of Social Darwinism.

Herbert Spencer enjoyed a great vogue in the United States during the last quarter of the nineteenth century, his popularity attaining its peak in 1882 when he visited America and met prominent business and intellectual leaders. The basis of his appeal lay in his concept of individuality as the end of cosmic and social evolution; his ethic of competitive individualism based on a biological model; *laissez-faire* economics coupled with a suspicion of the State; and an optimistic theory of cosmic progress as culminating in a perfect adjustment between the individual and society.[39] Although some aspects of these doctrines were hostile to the tradition of equality and democracy they could easily be accommodated to the native individualism. Furthermore, the promise of an ultimate adjustment between the individual and society offered to resolve the tension which Jeffersonian individualism had recognised but whose optimistic moral solution had proved fragile in the rough conditions of the late nineteenth century. For the new élite of industrial capitalism Spencerian doctrines supplied a rationale that legitimised their unprincipled practices and glossed their economic activities with the prestige of science just as Protestantism had glossed those of the earlier petty-bourgeois producers with the prestige of religion.

The entrepreneurial class applied the popular catch-phrases of Darwinism, 'the struggle for existence' and 'the survival of the fittest', to current conditions in American society and used them to justify a situation in which the ruthless succeeded and the weak went to the wall. According to the theory, not only could nothing be done to ameliorate the social situation but nothing *should* be done. Rampant competition and its harmful effects were not to be deplored but rather to be applauded, since in society as in nature it led to the evolutionary advancement of mankind. 'While the law [of competition] may sometimes be hard for the individual,' Andrew Carnegie, steel king and friend of Spencer, wrote, 'it is best for the race, because it ensures the survival of the fittest in every department. We accept and welcome therefore as conditions to which we must accommodate ourselves, great inequality of environment, the concentration of business, industrial and commercial in the hands of a few, and the law of competition between these as being not only beneficial, but essential for the future progress of the race.' The poor had failed in the struggle for existence, and so were 'unfit'. It was natural and beneficial, therefore, that they be eliminated. Freedom and equality, once complementary elements in the national democratic tradition, were now brought by an ideological revision into opposition. William Graham Sumner, the most influential of the American Social Darwinists, wrote, 'Let it be understood that we cannot go outside of this alternative: liberty, inequality, survival of the fittest; not liberty, equality, survival of the unfittest. The former carries society forward and favors all its best members; the latter carries society downwards and favors all its worst members.' By means of such modifications individualism was reduced to an aggressive atomistic egoism which quickly destroyed any sense of community.[40]

The industrial oligarchy adopted and propagated an individualist interpretation of Darwinism at this time because it served to validate the processes of competitive capitalism. When in the 1890s and the early 1900s the merger movement and trustification displaced pure competition and the individualist basis of ownership, a 'tooth and claw' version of nature ceased to be a useful model for the business world and Spencer's philosophy lost its force to become a dead letter by 1918. 'The history of Darwinian individualism', Richard Hofstadter concludes in his survey of the intellectual movement, '. . . is a clear example of the principle that changes in the structure of social ideas wait on general changes in economic and political life.'[41]

Throughout childhood and adolescence a person is socialised by means of family, school, religion and the media into the behaviour to which he must conform and the socially acceptable goals after which he must strive. The system of values maintained by a society, therefore, has a profound effect upon the character of the individuals composing that society, since the economic system and the traditions out of which it has grown largely define the behaviour and goals which are approved. So having briefly sketched the main ideological elements in the production-oriented phase of the economy, we now turn to the social character, an anthropological concept favoured by neo-Freudian sociologists such as Erich Fromm and David Riesman which allows us to relate individual behaviour to the social structure by means of the socialising agencies named. Since fiction and drama (in this period at least) are pre-eminently concerned with the presentation of socially representative characters, the notion of social character, despite its tendency towards over-generalisation, may prove useful in considering certain personality types in novels and plays.

The Puritan mentality, implanted early in life by family and church, socialised the individual to observe inflexible, life-long moral principles. It was impressed upon him that he stood alone before his Maker and that the Puritan God did not ask for single good works but for a life of good works combined into a unified system, for the decision Chosen or Damned was based on performance in the never-ending struggle between good and evil. 'There is never an instant's truce between virtue and vice', Thoreau wrote, and Franklin conceived the project of achieving moral perfection by ordering his life according to thirteen virtues. Such a consciousness of the ever-present opportunities for evil led to a constant scrutiny of all actions for their ethical implications. Their impression upon others was relatively unimportant compared to the deep inner concern the Protestant felt for their possible status in the eyes of the Deity. All acts were meaningful because all acts were judged, and judged not by a shifting set of human criteria but by an eternal code with which there could be no argument. The postulate of an omniscient God underpinned the uncompromising moral absolutes which ordered the pious Protestant's behaviour. With the fading of Puritanism's influence the sternness of the moral temper softened, but the sense of life being held to fixed rules and of the central importance of self-communion continued. Emerson's dictum, 'Nothing can bring you peace but yourself. Nothing can bring you peace but the triumph of principles', could be taken as the credo of the social character generated by the Protestant tradition.[42]

Individualism also contributed greatly to the social character of the production phase through its emphasis on self-reliance and isolation. The two value-systems together can be regarded as producing an 'inner-directed' character-type, for in the influential typology of Riesman and his collaborators inner-direction means that *'the source of direction for the individual is ... implanted early in life by the elders and directed toward generalized but nonetheless inescapably destined goals'*. The value of the inner-directed type of social conformity was that it wedded flexible behaviour to fixed principles, a combination that was well adapted to the changing, mobile society of nineteenth-century America. During this period the inner-directed became the dominant character-type since it was particularly suited to a society 'characterized by increased personal mobility, by a rapid accumulation of capital (teamed with devastating technological shifts), and by an almost constant *expansion*: intensive expansion in the production of goods and people, and extensive expansion in exploration, colonization, and imperialism'. Such a claim for the dominance of a single character-type in the production-oriented phase is a gross generalisation, of course. Yet the concept of inner-direction, despite its vagueness, remains useful in summarising the effects of Protestantism and individualism upon character and seems apposite to a period dominated by manufacturing capitalism. Work for the inner-directed type was 'in terms of non-human objects, including an objectified social organization', and production was 'seen and experienced in terms of technological and intellectual processes rather than in terms of human cooperation'. For the inner-directed man 'the problem of marketing the product, perhaps even its meaning, receded into the psychological background before the *hardness of the material* – the obduracy of the technical tasks themselves'.[43]

Work for the small freeholder had meant a struggle with nature to produce agrarian commodities, and while industry changed the *form* of work by collecting hundreds of labourers together under one roof and using bigger machines, the essence of work still remained that of a simple process between man and nature: the former energetic and innovative, constantly evolving more elaborate means for manipulating material; the latter resistant and unaccommodating, bringing new physical problems to the fore just as soon as others were overcome. The main urgency in the production-oriented phase lay in working over the natural world in order to produce energy and commodities, and the ontological status of this material world was hardly questioned. It was hard, definite, undeniably there in all its concreteness, and men's relationship to it, as dictated both by their elementary needs and the drive to accumulate capital, was direct and exploitative.

2 The Literary Response (*i*)

The dominant mode of fiction before the Civil War had been romance. James Fenimore Cooper's 'Leatherstocking Tales' which include *The Last of the Mohicans* (1826) and *The Deerslayer* (1841) are romantic in conception and form and concern themselves with man and nature on the frontier, that is to say, on the periphery of normal social life. Herman Melville's *Moby Dick* (1851) is an epic romance whose heroes are those we would expect of mid-nineteenth-century America – the hunters, exploiters and economic adventurers (for Ahab is one of these too). As we would further expect, the relationship that is emphasised is the one between man and nature, an ambivalent relationship, violent and oppositional at one pole and mystical and unifying at the other. Also, since it is an epic in a democratic society, it celebrates equality through the fellowship of the different races aboard the *Pequod* and individualism through Ahab's self-reliance and single-mindedness of purpose.[1]

Nathaniel Hawthorne drew the distinction between romance and the novel in his Preface to *The House of the Seven Gables* (1851), stating that he preferred to call his book the former and not the latter because he wished to claim 'a certain latitude, both as to its fashion and material'. The novel, he remarked, did not offer such an accommodating looseness, since it aimed at verisimilitude, 'at a very minute fidelity, not merely to the possible, but to the probable and ordinary course of man's experience'. He emphasised that his book was not grounded in any real locality or based upon actual historical event; it was his object neither 'to describe local manners, nor in any way to meddle in the characteristics of a community', and he hoped his tale would be read 'strictly as a Romance, having a great deal more to do with the clouds overhead than with any portion of the actual soil of the County of Essex'. The romance then, for Hawthorne as well as for his contemporaries, Cooper and Melville, was not concerned with the accurate representation of actuality or with the spectacle of man in society. Complex social experience is characteristically absent from the main novels of the ante-bellum period.

Henry James, in his long essay on Hawthorne, criticised *The Scarlet Letter* (1850) 'for a want of reality and an abuse of the fanciful element', for being 'weak' in its 'historical colouring', and for lacking 'the modern realism of research'. Hawthorne, he pointed out, 'never attempted to render exactly or closely the actual facts of the society that surrounded him', and he attributed this to the thinness of social experience offered by ante-bellum America which lacked so many features, including traditions, cultural variety and upper-class institutions:

> No State, in the European sense of the word, and indeed barely a specific national name. No sovereign, no court, no personal loyalty, no aristocracy, no church, no clergy, no army, no diplomatic service, no country gentlemen, no palaces, no castles, nor manors, nor old country-houses, nor parsonages, no thatched cottages nor ivied ruins; no cathedrals, nor abbeys, nor little Norman churches; no great Universities nor public schools – no Oxford, nor Eton, nor Harrow; no literature, no novels, no museums, no pictures, no political society, no sporting class – no Epsom nor Ascot.

Since, he claimed, 'it needs a complex social machinery to set a writer in motion', the simple, egalitarian, homogeneous society of the 1840s did not provide an author with sufficient density or variety of experience for him to be a literary realist.[2] By the 1880s and 1900s, however, the relatively thin and even society of Hawthorne's day had given way as a result of capitalistic development to one characterised like European social structures by extreme stratification and the possession of most of those previously absent 'items of high civilisation', as James termed them.

The American State had begun to assert its international identity through the acquisition of Cuba and the Philippines and a sufficient length of time had passed for the native cultural inheritance of Puritanism, democracy and the frontier to take on the aspect of 'tradition'. And though there was no sovereign, nor even yet a First Family, there was an aristocracy in fact if not in name, as social critics claimed. The millionaire businessmen who had risen to power and wealth on the spoils of the Gilded Age had begun to consolidate themselves into a distinct social class with the foundation and endowment of exclusive boarding schools and private universities, the establishment of an exclusive lifestyle based on country clubs and fashionable resorts, and the founding of the *Social Register*, a *Who's Who* of the American élite.[3]

The central economic and social role of this élite elevated it to the status of a fit subject for fiction, indeed, even a compelling subject. The rich were significant. By virtue of their ownership of the Press and their influence through the political machines of both parties, they constituted a ruling class, able to foist its interests and ideologies upon the rest of the nation. Further, they provided sufficient drama and conflict to make studies of their rise to wealth or of the clash between the old-established echelons and the parvenus possible and interesting. Such studies required the representation of manners, of the actual social processes by which people gained wealth, of the strengths and weaknesses of the entrepreneurial character – required, in short, a close attention to, and detailed specification of, contemporary society. These demands were incompatible with romance, and those writers who wished to articulate and define the major developments and issues of the late nineteenth century found themselves forced to adopt from foreign sources and develop in relation to their native American material the assumptions, emphases and techniques of literary realism.

Realism became the dominant fictional mode of the production-oriented phase for reasons in addition to the rise of the rich. Ian Watt, in his discussion of the development of the English realist novel, makes the point that the novel's serious concern with the daily lives of ordinary people depends upon individualism and a sufficient variety of belief and action for a detailed account of others' lives to be interesting. It was Protestantism and industrial capitalism, he suggests, which brought the rise of individualism and the increase of economic specialisation that together produced the necessary diversity.[4] In America the strong Protestant and democratic traditions and capitalistic property relations had established a spirit of sturdy individualism early in the national history, but industrialism did not arise in any great measure until after the Civil War and did not reach full spate until the 1900s. It created a society which was much more heterogeneous in its composition both by the stratification and the economic specialisation it enforced. The extreme differentiation of function brought about by the division of labour produced a multiformity of new social types. The industrial mechanic, the office boy, the 'drummer', the locomotive driver, the typist, the engineer, the factory girl and many others combined with the entrepreneur, the middle-class farmer or professional, and the immigrant to bring a new richness of colour and density into social experience. Realism offered practical ways of rendering that experience and provided an aesthetic directly suited to the social consciousness generated by production-oriented capitalism. The lives and work of others became so different they became curious, fascinating even, and contrasts or conflicts of manners and types became evident everywhere, providing dramatic material for the aspiring novelist. To the writer who wished to portray contemporary America in fiction at the close of the nineteenth century the difficulty was less one of the paucity of subject-matter than of its overwhelming plethora.

The concreteness and immediacy of this social diversity were heightened by the city, which concentrated widely ranging class and ethnic types together and brought them into daily propinquity, if not interaction. Throughout the latter half of the nineteenth century urbanisation had accompanied industrialisation as the number and size of cities had steadily increased, and it is in portraying the industrial city and interpreting the problems of urban life that the realist writers came into their own. Some of them, such as Stephen Crane, Frank Norris and Theodore Dreiser, took their apprenticeship in the observation of city ways as newspaper journalists, and the development of factual reporting with its requirements of immediacy and verisimilitude certainly contributed its influence to the style and content of the new literature.[5] The metropolitan centre, New York or Chicago, constitutes the locale for much of the serious fiction of the period, and the main features of the urban complex – the streets, slums, factories and offices – provide the sensuous texture of the novels as well as the context for the narrative developments.[6] With some qualifying ambivalences these writers portray the urban conglomerations as a new, exciting phenomenon and tend to celebrate the concentration of energies they find there. William Dean Howells claims through Basil March in *A Hazard of New Fortunes* (1890) that the urban-industrial scene as instanced in the New York elevated railroad demands a new aesthetic and is a ripe subject for Art.[7] Theodore Dreiser uses the rapid growth of Philadelphia and Chicago to provide the narrative opportunities for, and much of the sense of dynamism of, Frank Cowperwood's entrepreneurial career in *The Financier* (1912) and *The Titan* (1914). Curtis Jadwin's rise and fall in Norris's *The Pit* (1903) are centred on Chicago and its Board of Trade. Later, John Dos Passos in *Manhattan Transfer* (1925), was to develop an impressionistic prose and a narrative structure which rendered the hectic rhythms and fleeting scenes of metropolitan life with especial force.

The expanding cities were the hubs of the expanding industrial economy and to the profit-seeking businessman interested in stock-market manipulation, manufacture, real-estate speculation or mass transport they represented golden opportunity. To the young rural labourer or immigrant nurtured on the American myth of success the cities also represented the promise of future prosperity. Thus to Jurgis and the other newly arrived Lithuanians in Upton Sinclair's *The Jungle* (1906), Packingtown, Chicago 'seemed a dream of wonder, with its tale of human energy, of things being done, of employment for thousands upon thousands of men, of opportunity and freedom, of life and love and joy'. But for the poor, whose condition also preoccupied novelists of this period, this vision of the city, though it began as an urban specification of 'the American Dream', soon betrayed itself as dream in the negative sense of illusion. They came to experience its lived reality not as liberation but as harsh necessity. Jurgis discovers that Chicago is no 'dream of wonder' but a nightmare of desperation in which 'he and all those who were dear to him might lie and perish of starvation and cold, and there would be no ear to hear their cry, no hand to help them'. This dual aspect of the industrial city, the close conjunction within it of promise and defeat, is neatly symbolised in *Sister Carrie* (1900) by Dreiser's use of Broadway and the Bowery: the one symbolic of Carrie's prosperity and fame, the other of Hurstwood's penury and suicidal despair. It was in the city too that the rapid pace of social change was most evident, and this brought society itself, as it responded to the transforming pressures of new economic concerns, to the fore as a complex, evolving phenomenon. The daily evidence of change instilled a strong historical sense in the realist authors, who frequently conceived of themselves as literary witnesses to a period of transition.

The felt need to record, the dense facticity of urban life, the positivistic assumptions of a production mentality, all drove novelists to adopt the techniques and emphases of realism, but since there was no one in the American literary tradition to whom emergent realists could turn they looked to the great European novelists for their models. Tolstoy, Balzac and Zola were particularly influential, affecting Howells, Dreiser and Norris respectively. In 1912, looking back over his career, Howells, the leading advocate and practitioner of realism in America in his day, said, 'I would fain have it remembered that it was with the French masters, the continental masters, we studied to imitate nature, and gave American fiction the bent which it still keeps wherever it is vital.'[8] The key phrase 'to imitate nature' indicates the primarily mimetic thrust of the new art. Truth of observation and of representation was set up as its high (if infrequently realised) ideal. 'Let fiction cease to lie about life,' Howells wrote as part of his realist's credo, 'let it portray men and women as they are, actuated by the motives and the passions in the measure we all know.'[9] Life in all its domestic ordinariness was to be the proper subject of the novel. The characters, settings, actions and speech were all to be taken from common everyday existence and rendered with illusory immediacy upon the written page. Howells was sufficiently affected by the positivistic assumptions of the period to take the possibility of an accurate perception of objective existence for granted. Like the literary naturalists who came after him, he was committed to the notion that the human eye could see 'real' life as it was in itself and that therefore language could represent it in fiction.

One of the main techniques by which this mimesis was to be achieved was the accumulation of realistic detail, providing descriptions with a specificity and a solidity reminiscent of the real objects or scenes. This attempt to recapture the materiality of existence in prose was expressive of the period's pre-eminent concern with property and possessions and the hard definiteness of *things*. Howells's novels possess their due amount of detail in order to render scene and character in some concreteness, but the Naturalists, Norris, Dreiser and Sinclair, went to extreme lengths in this respect. Their novels contain exhaustive descriptions of industrial and commercial processes in an attempt to convey an accurate similitude of American business life. Their characters are almost submerged in their social and environmental context as mountains of detail are heaped up around them, frequently bringing the flow of the narrative entirely to a halt. This piling up of facts was expressive both of a strong documentary impulse and of a philosophic determinism which had its origins (as we shall see below) in French Naturalism and American ideology and which regarded environment and circumstances as conditioning forces in a person's life.

Norris, Sinclair and Dreiser viewed themselves partly as social historians, recording a definite stage in the drama of industrial development. They visited the places they wrote about and read heavily in documentary sources, which they occasionally used verbatim in their fictions. *The Pit, The Octopus, The Financier, The Titan, An American Tragedy* and *The Jungle* were all researched novels. The fictive material in them was not only firmly grounded in historical reality but aspired also to the representativeness of an accurate social image. The materials furnished by contemporary industrial life – the millionaire's mansion, the tenement slum, the railroad, the business office, the factory and the crowded street – furnish their settings, just as the major issues of the day – strikes and the conflict between capital and labour, political corruption, the rise of the entrepreneurs, and the condition of the poor – furnish their narrative developments. As historians and sociologists they found the minutiae of everyday life worth recording as well as the industrial and commercial processes which shaped society.

In some cases it is the processes themselves which seem to have become the subject of the drama. Dreiser's Cowperwood trilogy, for instance, constitutes almost a textbook of finance capitalism with its detailed descriptions of commercial transactions and the manipulation of stock. The specificity of Cowperwood's business activities is in marked contrast to the vagueness with which Dickens enshrouds the activities and final bankruptcy of his financier, Merdle, in *Little Dorrit*. To the Naturalists the business affairs themselves were of vital novelistic interest, since, governed by their deterministic philosophy, they were intent upon putting men in the context of the large forces which ruled over their lives. It is in the service of this determinism that so much significance is attributed to the non-human in the novels. The sympathetic study of individual character still forms the basis of their fiction as the nineteenth-century form demanded, but looming behind the foregrounded characters are the huge structures and sweeping processes of the urban-industrial world in which they are enmeshed. The single telling detail, Flaubert's *bon mot*, was not for them; what their extravagance of information sought to convey was the extreme facticity of industrial life with its multiplicity of parts and activities that could, like items in a catalogue or job descriptions, all be precisely specified. The impression given is of a powerful world of the inanimate in which things rule over men and men themselves are frequently degraded to the status of things.

This diminishment of the individual wrought by industrialism was intensified by the growth of the city and mass society. The transition from small-scale independent production to large-scale industrial manufacture took the processes of production out of the human range, and the individual ceased to be the measure of his environment as extraordinary changes of scale took place in the size of buildings and the areas they covered. The result of this giantism, as these writers recorded it, was personal unease and bafflement. Dreiser's Carrie Meeber 'could have understood the meaning of the little stone-cutter's yard at Columbia City, carving little pieces of marble for individual use, but when the yards of some huge stone corporation came into view, filled with spur tracks and flat cars, transpierced by docks from the river, and traversed overhead by immense trundling cranes of wood and steel, it lost all significance in her little world'. This intimidating characteristic of the modern city was but one aspect of that alienation notoriously produced by the developing industrial order. For just as the industrial worker becomes alienated from the product of his labour because it has absorbed his creative energies and is owned by another, so the urbanite becomes alienated from the collective product of men's labour – the city in its constructed totality – because it contains men's collective energies in reified form and is owned by anonymous others. He has participated in building it and helps to maintain it; yet it stands against him, negating him, and refusing him the opportunity to be at home in it. The skyscrapers were symbols of the cooperative strength of men but to the individual below, whom they dwarfed and sent long shadows after, they suggested only his personal weakness. For could not they also be seen as the aggressive monuments of those vague, impersonal powers which seemed to rule his life?

A common response to this reification on a grand scale at the turn of the century was to consider the individual as drained of any significance and the swarming city as possessing a kind of autonomous life. Thus Carrie, on arriving in Chicago and looking for work, experiences 'a sense of helplessness amid so much evidence of power and force which she did not understand. These vast buildings, what were they? These strange energies and huge interests, for what purposes were they there?' This note of impotence and insecurity is also struck by Norris in his evocation in *The Pit* of Laura Dearborn's fear of 'the vast cruel machinery of the city's life' and her vision of Chicago as something which 'doesn't seem human' but 'like a great tidal wave' in which 'it's all very well for the individual just so long as he can keep afloat, but once fallen, how horribly quick it would crush him, annihilate him – how horribly quick, and with such horrible indifference!' This indifference attributed to the metropolis strongly echoes the vast indifference of nature that Norris emphasised in his previous novel, *The Octopus*, and it was part of the mystification embodied by the Naturalists in their writings that the historical and socially produced conditions of alienation and cruelty in the city should be regarded as *natural* ones. The explanation for man's state, so their thinking went, was to be sought in nature, not society, and in order to understand this displacement we must turn to the intellectual origins of that philosophic determinism which social conditions fostered.

The literary creed of Naturalism was first defined by Zola in his Preface to the second edition of *Thérèse Raquin* (1868) where he strikes the chord of determinism forcibly from the start: 'I have chosen people completely dominated by their nerves and blood, without free will, drawn into each action of their lives by the inexorable laws of their physical nature.' Not only is man subject to the inner compulsions of his animal nature but also to the external 'pressure of environments and circumstances'.[10] While *Thérèse Raquin* charts the triumph of the laws of physical nature, the later *Germinal* (1885), taking class conflict as its theme, demonstrates the crushing effect of inhuman conditions and circumstances upon the miners of Montsou. Norris in particular was influenced by Zola, and his *McTeague* (1899) was the first fully-fledged American Naturalist novel. Like his later *Vandover and the Brute* (posthumously published in 1914), it deals with the subject of 'the animal within' and the irresistible compulsion of inner physical drives. Men's lack of free will and their subjection to powerful animal desires is a recurrent motif in Naturalist novels. In *The Jungle* we are shown the 'wild beast' rising up within Jurgis, and in *An American Tragedy* Clyde Griffiths's fate is the result not only of outside pressures but also of 'a disposition easily and often intensely inflamed by the chemistry of sex and the formula of beauty'.

Socially, this biological determinism was engendered by the brutalising effects of heavy industry which treated men as so many 'hands' to be kept functioning by means of a subsistence wage. And just as dirty physical work and the filth of slum conditions seemed to justify the reduction of most men to the status of animals, so the increasing need for reliable timekeeping and factory discipline brought to the fore as obstacles to be overcome the anarchic, instinctual energies of men. Intellectually, it was derived from the late-nineteenth-century sciences such as physiology and from Darwinism, which, relentlessly materialistic, turned men into full members of the animal kingdom, the products like other members of a long, evolutionary, natural process and the unfree subjects of inescapable natural laws. For the American Naturalists there was, complementing this, a larger, abstract determinism derived from the cluster of doctrines put forward by Spencer, Sumner and others in the 1880s and 1890s. The ideology of Social Darwinism and its articulation in the work of the Naturalists provides a promising mediation between the socio-economic realm and the literature of the period, revealing how social relations conditioned a world-view which in turn conditioned the content and form of a certain type of fiction. The Naturalists accepted Spencer's plutocratic rationale of *laissez-faire* capitalism and their novels were frequently fashioned as tendentious demonstrations of its theses, though a humanitarian sympathy for the underdog often crept in too and led to a confused perspective.

As the examples already noted have suggested, the Naturalists' work was pervaded by imagery of man as an animal and of society as an arena of bitter Darwinian struggle. Norris's *The Octopus* is shot through and through with hunting images and comparisons with animals, as in the passage in which the Railroad makes known its extortionate terms to the farmers. Their response, we are told, was 'a cry of savage exasperation', representing 'the human animal hounded to its corner, exploited, harried to its last stand, at bay, ferocious, terrible, turning at last with bared teeth and upraised claws to meet the death grapple'. In *The Pit*, too, Norris portrays business life as battle and describes Jadwin at his moment of failure in the Corn Exchange as being 'assaulted by herd upon herd of wolves yelping for his destruction'. When Cowperwood in *The Titan* goes to the Illinois State legislature to fight for an extension of his franchises, Dreiser resorts to a histrionic train of images reminiscent of Norris: 'A jungle-like complexity was present, a dark, rank growth of horrific but avid life – life at the full, life knife in hand, life blazing with courage and dripping at the jaws with hunger.' The stock Darwinian metaphor of 'the jungle' is applied by Upton Sinclair to the whole of industrial society at that time and he describes his immigrants' lives in terms of a 'tooth and claw' struggle for existence. Jurgis learns quickly 'that it was a war of each against all', and Cowperwood at the other end of the social scale in *The Financier* justifies his actions by the Darwinian business credo: 'Life was war – particularly financial life.'

This Darwinian vision of society was a product of the extremely competitive individualism which *laissez-faire* encouraged at all levels. Howells, steeped in the earlier democratic values and Swedenborgian moralism of his father, insisted on the ethical accountability of the individual in the industrial age and was critical of the selfishness which such competitiveness inculcated.[11] But Spencerian Social Darwinism, as we have seen, applauded competition as being ultimately the best for the race, and the Naturalists conceived of and portrayed social competition as part of a natural order. For at the heart of this late-nineteenth-century ideology, as its characteristic imagery suggests, was a reduction of essentially social, historically specific processes to timeless, natural phenomena. While Spencer himself argued only for a parallelism between the organic world and the 'super-organic' world of human society, derivative writers conflated the parallelism into a complete identification.[12] As a part of nature men were under the sway of huge impersonal forces and inexorable laws, and consequently, so the argument went, men in general and businessmen in particular could not be held responsible for the ways of capitalism or the state of society. In *The Octopus* Shelgrim, the railroad king, expresses this viewpoint in an important speech. 'You are dealing with forces, young man,' he tells Presley, 'when you speak of wheat and the railroads, not with men', and he emphasises his point, 'The wheat is one force, the railroad another, and there is the law that governs them – supply and demand. Men have little to do in the whole business.' During the course of his argument the entrepreneur conflates the 'wheat' as growing plant with the 'wheat' as sector of the agricultural economy and then identifies it as belonging to the same order as the economic power of the railroad. Both wheat and railroad thus take on the abstract character of impersonal natural forces, operating according to scientific laws.

Dreiser was a more consistent determinist than Norris. In 'A Counsel to Perfection' he wrote, 'In so far as one may judge by chemistry and physics man appears to be in the grip of a blind force or process which cannot help itself and from which man can derive no power to help himself save by accident or peradventure.'[13] Illustrating this pessimistic view, he frequently portrays his characters, with the exception of the wheeling-dealing Cowperwood, as the passive victims of processes much larger than themselves. Lester Kane in *Jennie Gerhardt* (1911) sums up the personal experience of being determined and unfree: 'It isn't myself that's important in the transaction apparently. The individual doesn't count much in the situation. I don't know whether you see what I'm driving at but all of us are more or less pawns. We're moved about like chessmen by circumstances over which we have no control.'

The stature of the individual *was* much diminished in the context of urban mass society, and men *were* governed by circumstances over which they had no control and conceived of themselves as driven by large abstract forces, but these forces and circumstances were essentially economic and social, not natural. The Social Darwinists used a particular nineteenth-century conception of nature to mystify the laws and processes of capitalist development. 'Force' or 'Nature' became a kind of fetish for their collective economic activities, and their determinism mirrored their passive dependence on the forces of capitalist production. It is analogous to what Engels, in connection with another period, once wrote of Calvin: 'His predestination doctrine was the religious expression of the fact that in the commercial world of competition success or failure does not depend upon a man's activity or cleverness, but upon circumstances uncontrollable by him. It is not of him that willeth or of him that runneth, but of the mercy of unknown superior economic powers.'[14] Social Darwinism was a secularised, pseudo-scientific expression of much the same fact, and when trusts and mergers had put an end to much of the competition and demonstrated how much of the economy was in human control, it quickly lost its appeal.

The mystification of economic processes as natural ones meant that the city became something of a paradox in the Naturalists' world-view. The urban landscape, as the product of men, was a thoroughly de-natured and totally socialised environment. Yet the cities were the centres of the economy and it was in them that the 'forces' propelling men to sudden wealth or poverty had their keenest sway. They thus came to represent the concentration of vast *natural* forces, to become 'jungles' in which men were but insignificant things. 'It was true', Sinclair wrote in *The Jungle*, 'that here in this huge city, with its stores of heaped-up wealth, human creatures might be hunted down and destroyed by the wild-beast powers of nature, just as truly as ever they were in the days of the cavemen.'

The Social-Darwinian and Naturalist insistence on a mechano-materialist nature as a paradigm for society was part of a production mentality, reflecting the society's dependence upon the genuine forces of nature during the production-oriented phase for the harnessing of energy and the transformation of raw materials into commodities. This 'nature' was less the concrete, richly variegated nature that the early settlers experienced than an abstract, theoretical nature made up of scientific laws and forces. Since production was still essentially a simple process between man and nature, the physical sciences which were so successful in analysing and guiding that process became dominant in the world-view, and Naturalists sought to extend their models to other realms such as society and personal psychology.

Production may still have been a simple process but it was increasingly mediated by sophisticated technology. As in England, so in America industrialism meant the triumph of the machine, and the huge steam-engines of the day, the locomotives, drop-hammers and generators provided concrete symbols of those natural energies which were so much more powerful than individual men. Slightly later, Henry Adams was to regard the dynamo as the ruling symbol of the age, and Thorstein Veblen was to write on the domination of ordinary life by machine processes.[15]

The dual preoccupation of the production mentality with

nature and machinery is articulated in that incongruous combination of the mechanical and the organic which characterises Naturalist imagery. For, given the Naturalists' conviction of the importance of huge, impersonal forces, their problem as writers was to elaborate adequate images for them, and it was, after all, no easy task to give form and colour to these vast abstractions and fit them convincingly into a narrative. Zola, in *Germinal*, symbolised the economic forces that controlled men's lives by imaging capital as a fetish, as 'that crouching sated god, that monstrous idol hidden away in his secret tabernacle', but Norris in *The Octopus* chose the express locomotive as a fit symbol of both nature's and the railroad monopoly's power and indifference: 'the symbol of a vast power, huge, terrible . . . the leviathan with tentacles of steel clutching into the soil, the soulless force, the ironhearted power, the monster, the colossus, the octopus.' In *The Pit* Norris describes the impersonal market forces of the Corn Exchange and their widespread repercussions in terms of a Charybdis: 'Within then a great whirlpool, a pit of roaring waters, spun and thundered, sucking in the life-tides of the city . . . then vomiting them forth again, spewing them up and out . . . sending the swirl of its mighty central eddy far out through the city's channels.'

The immersion of the Naturalists in the popular ideology of the time undeniably influenced their writing for the worse. After the laconic lucidity of Hemingway or the well-orchestrated intensity of Faulkner the crudity of their symbolism, their tendentiousness and their heavy-handed extravagance of verbal effort now strike us uncomfortably and seem to be the high price they paid for seeking too earnestly to put across a certain vision of society. In extenuation of their literary defects we should remember that they boldly set themselves a difficult and ambitious task: to record and interpret a particularly dynamic phase of American history and to generate a literature commensurate to the largeness and complexity of the changing industrial republic. The possessor of the finest American literary imagination of that period, Henry James, had, after all, established his exile in Europe, and when he returned, the deep-seated conservatism of his mind and the fastidiousness of his taste led to that revulsion against urban-commercial America which we find in *The American Scene* (1907). Howells, his friend, stayed and wrote on what was happening in the burgeoning cities with style and humane concern, but his vision seemed too domestic and (owing to his sense of craftsmanship) his writing too tame to satisfy later authors such as Norris and Dreiser. These played down the significance of form and fashioned a coarse-grained prose that corresponded well with the rough, coarse-grained texture of their subjects. The Bossism of Chicago city-politics, the scheming of speculators, the crushing power of the big trusts, the bitter strikes and harsh conditions did not require the delicate nuances of Jamesian prose but a new rhetoric suitable to the thrusting crudity and angularity of industrial society. If their rhythms now read as too strident and some passages as too close to bombast we must remember that industrialism with its arrogance and inhumanity tended to provoke a certain high-pitched rhetoric, for it is a tone we meet in Carlyle and Marx as well as in Norris, Dreiser and Sinclair.

There is little doubt too that in their more ambitious works which attempted to fuse several diverse elements – economic history, documentary source material, fictive characters and events, and determinist philosophy – they overburdened a form of fiction governed by third-person narration and forced it to accommodate a great expansion of material with little innovation in technique. It was not until Dos Passos' *USA* trilogy (1930–7) with its fragmented, collage structure that the multifariousness of American economic and social experience found an adequate literary form.

Realism and Naturalism with their positivist emphasis on the primacy of fact and their preoccupation with new social formations articulated in a general way an historically specific capitalist mentality. We now turn to a detailed reading of individual texts, grouped according to two general themes, to examine how the ideological confusions and contradictions created by rapid social change were dramatised there.

3 The Rise of the Entrepreneur in the Work of Howells, Norris and Dreiser

During the late nineteenth century a novel social type, the millionaire manufacturer and financier, came to prominence on the American scene and provided writers with compelling literary subject-matter. The spectacle of the entrepreneurs' rise to wealth and power attracted William Dean Howells, whose *The Rise of Silas Lapham* (1885) was the first serious fictional study of this type, as well as Frank Norris and Theodore Dreiser. The ideological perspectives and literary preoccupations they brought to their subject were diverse, and realism of treatment was subjugated to the moralistic or tendentious interpretation of 'the captain of industry' that they each wished to present.

Howells's story of his big, bluff, kindhearted Yankee businessman promises initially to be a model tale of material success – of how by dint of hard work and saving (and some luck) a poor farmboy became an industrial entrepreneur, a man of wealth and position admitted into the highest circles of Boston society. At the height of his triumph, however, Lapham is suddenly threatened with financial ruin from which he can be saved by a straightforward deal over some mills. It is at this point that Howells foils our expectations. For Lapham is a man of rigid moral principles and in order to atone for his one transgression on his way up from farmboy to manufacturer he opts for a compensatory act of righteous self-sacrifice. He turns down the mills deal because it smacks of the unethical, goes bankrupt, loses his mansion and social position, and returns poor but honest to the Vermont farmstead from whence he came. It is evident that Howells has intended an irony in the title: Lapham's 'rise' is moral and not material.

There is thus an ethical progression in the novel from purity through sin and temptation to redemption and the re-establishment of purity. Accompanying this progression is a social cycle from agrarian simplicity through industrial and social attainment back to agrarian simplicity. The close association of these two movements with its equation of moral integrity with farmstead simplicity and moral ambivalence with wealthy sophistication suggests that Howells believed there was a fundamental incompatibility between material success and moral scruple in the late-nineteenth-century business world. It further suggests that while he was progressive as an author in broadening the range and relevance of the American novel by introducing new character-types, as a social critic he was backward looking, invoking Jeffersonian ideals of the virtuous agrarian life to set against the corrupt industrial present. Such a stance was an inevitable by-product of his own upbringing.

William Dean Howells was born in the frontier town of Martins Ferry, Ohio in 1837 and he grew up in the pre-industrial handicraft economy, even spending a year in a log cabin. From the agricultural society around him he absorbed the values of democracy and egalitarianism, and from his father, a Swedenborgian, he absorbed a strong moral absolutism. As a result of his father's influence he never lost the conviction that Christian principle and good works save and that self-concern and love of the world damn. 'Morality', he wrote in 1891, 'penetrates all things, it is the soul of all things.' Despite the commanding position he achieved in the Eastern literary establishment, he never lost his identification with the frontier and the West, but regarded himself all his life as a 'Buckeye', a boy from Ohio.[1] These two main strands in his make-up clearly determine many of the attitudes embodied in his fiction. *The Rise of Silas Lapham*, in particular, expresses Howells's nostalgic view of the ante-bellum agrarian era as a morally superior age, as well as his confidence in the power of its characteristic Protestant and democratic values to survive in the face of rapid economic change. Lapham's development from freeholder into industrial capitalist represents in microcosm both the transformation of the national economy and the persistence, alongside that transformation, of the older ideological patterns. Howells's hero is the embodiment of Jeffersonian individualism and the Protestant ethic, and the novel presents a commercial and social milieu in which these traditional codes of behaviour are tested and ultimately vindicated.

The Protestant ethic emphasised the spiritual duty to one's worldly calling, and Lapham shares with some of the real-life entrepreneurs of the time that attitude, identified by Weber and Tawney, of business as sacrament. His wife perceptively charges him with having made his paint his god, and, as an exchange with Tom Corey reveals, his faith in his product is quasi-religious in tone: ' "It's the best paint in God's universe," he said, with the solemnity of prayer. "It's the best in the market," said Corey.' As we have seen, this Protestant view of business arose out of and endorsed the behaviour demanded by a period of primitive accumulation. It exhorted an intense industry on the one hand and an ascetic compulsion to save on the other, two traits with which Howells fully endows his character. Lapham is extremely hardworking, arriving at his office in the morning before his employees and taking no summer holiday, and his lifestyle is very modest. Until he is tempted to social emulation he conforms closely to Weber's ideal type of entrepreneur who 'avoids ostentation and unnecessary expenditure as well as conscious enjoyment of his power' and whose manner of life is 'distinguished by a certain ascetic tendency'. Even after he and his wife have become wealthy and have moved to Boston, their lives are still characterised by a combination of asceticism and acquisitiveness. 'Their first years there', Howells informs us, 'were given to careful getting on Lapham's part, and careful saving on his wife's.' The result of such a combination is the accumulation of capital and the Laphams are eventually faced with an embarrassing growth of wealth: 'Suddenly the money began to come so abundantly that she need not save; and then they did not know what to do with it.' This new wealth could be absorbed either by reinvestment, but a general business depression proscribes that option, or by consumption, which is severely inhibited by the old habits of worldly asceticism.

One honorific way the millionaires evolved for absorbing their huge money surpluses was the adoption of an aristocratic lifestyle based on the hired services of butlers, footmen, chambermaids and so on, but Howells does not wish us to imagine the Laphams capable of such an abandonment of their erstwhile simplicity; they 'had not yet thought of spending their superfluity on servants who could be rung for'. Instead, he shows Lapham indulging in another form of conspicuous consumption and class awareness, namely the construction in the fashionable Back Bay area of Boston of a mansion which will serve to impress his pecuniary strength and social standing upon the community. The egalitarian Lapham has been oblivious of questions of status until he becomes acquainted with the Coreys, an aristocratic family who represent the traditional and well-entrenched Boston élite. Through the Coreys, Howells implies that the old Boston merchant class has lost economic leadership to the industrial manufacturer and now fears the loss of social leadership as well. 'The suddenly rich are on a level with any of us nowadays', Bromfield Corey observes regretfully. 'Money buys position at once.' 'Snobbery', Lionel Trilling wrote, 'is pride in status without pride in function', and Howells invidiously contrasts the pride in status of the functionless Coreys – Bromfield Corey is a dilettante artist – with the homely pride in function of Lapham.[2] If the Coreys and their class are guilty of a snobbish aloofness towards the parvenus, Lapham, Howells illustrates, also has all the arrogant faith of the bourgeois in the power of money to buy him whatever he wishes. His contact with the Coreys alerts him to the niceties of stratification in the Boston hierarchy and to the necessity of consolidating his financial success by establishing himself and his family in Society. The construction of the Beacon Street mansion is his first gesture in that direction.

Lapham is elated at the acceptance into the Boston élite which a dinner invitation from the Coreys implies, and the dinner itself provides Howells with the opportunity for a fine comedy of manners as we observe the gauche Laphams clumsily negotiating a path through all the unspoken proprieties of a Society occasion. Tom Corey, having been exposed to the more egalitarian West, has a more open and democratic outlook than his family. He recognises Lapham's essentially fine nature, courts his daughters, and goes to work for him, so restoring that active participation in economic life which his 'India Merchant' grandfather had enjoyed but which his father had lost. It was necessary, Howells implies, for the Boston Brahmins to revivify their class by allying themselves with the new business forces in America. For Lapham, however, his association with the Coreys and his financial pride tempt him towards the abandonment of two major elements of traditional agrarian ideology.

First, he attempts a transition from the Protestant scheme of modest living to a tentatively asserted scheme of conspicuous consumption, and secondly, he deserts his erstwhile egalitarianism by identifying himself with the rigid and snobbish hierarchy of the Boston Brahmins. 'He had always said that he did not care what a man's family was, but the presence of young Corey as an applicant to him for employment, as his guest, as the possible suitor to his daughter, was one of the sweetest flavors that he had yet tasted in his success.' The 'moral' of the novel as summarised by Howells at the end refers not only to the main developments of the business plot but also to these ideological desertions: 'Adversity had so far been his friend that it had taken from him all hope of the social success for which people crawl and truckle, and restored him, through failure and doubt and heartache, the manhood which prosperity had so nearly stolen from him.' Lapham, impelled by the Coreys' regard, had begun to 'crawl and truckle' for social success and was beginning to prejudice his 'manhood' by moving away from a modest lifestyle and democratic frontier outlook. After he has lost his mansion, so symbolic of his success, and becomes bankrupt, he no longer takes a snobbish pride in the Corey connection: 'Neither he nor his wife thought now that their daughter was marrying a Corey; they thought only that she was giving herself to the man who loved her.' Their reversal of fortune thus leads not only to a resumption of a frugal, agrarian way of life but also to the reassertion of egalitarian, humane values.

Other ideological issues also play their part in the thematic structure of the novel but these are more closely integrated with the central ethical dilemma of the business plot. In his characterisation of Silas Lapham Howells fused his own moral absolutism with the moral integrity demanded by the two dominant value-systems of the early nineteenth century – Jeffersonian individualism with its premise of self-restraint, and Protestantism with its emphasis on the scrutiny of all actions for their ethical implications. Yankee Silas Lapham is steeped in Christian ethics (but not religion) and is endowed with an acutely moral conscience. One of the purposes of the romantic sub-plot in which the Laphams agonise over the correct course to adopt in regard to Tom's proposal to Penelope is to emphasise the centrality of moral decision in the Laphams' lives. Existence for Silas Lapham, as for Howells, we are made aware, is inescapably moral. He is an inner-directed man, independent in his judgement, self-reliant in his actions, and guided in his life by his 'underlying principles'. In this respect he is representative of the dominant social character found in the production-oriented phase. There is, however, a flaw in his otherwise spotless record, one ethically dubious act, a sin, to which he later attributes his downfall.

Once, he allowed self-interest to overcome his scruples and forced his former partner, Milton K. Rogers, out of the business so that he could reap all the profits himself. His conscience is only slightly uneasy over this manoeuvre which he regards as common business practice, but his wife sensitises him to its moral dubiousness and in an effort to rectify his previous selfishness he makes some large loans to Rogers. Then various developments characteristic of the late-nineteenth-century commercial world force Lapham – and here we clearly see Howells's realist strategy of grounding his fictional developments in the processes and complexities of contemporary society – to the point of yielding to amoral self-interest once again. The business plot of the novel can be read, therefore, as a dramatisation of the difficulty of maintaining a proper equilibrium between self-interest and moral scruple, a balance central to Jeffersonian individualism, against the corrupting pressures of the Gilded Age.

The stock market, a significant factor in post-bellum finance capitalism, tempts Lapham to speculate in stocks and shares and he finds himself caught up in the dynamic of the accumulation of capital. 'Seems as if the more money he got, the more he wanted to get', his wife bemusedly remarks. When other matters are already pressing him he begins to make heavy losses which aggravate his financial position and cause him to revert to his earlier moral stance on speculation: 'I always felt the way I said about it – that it wan't any better than gambling, and I say so now. It's like betting on the turn of a card.'

Further, Lapham is shown caught in a crisis of overproduction. American industry grew so rapidly in the 1870s and 1880s that its productive capacity repeatedly outstripped the demand from markets, resulting in the periodic closure of factories and economic slumps. 'The market's overstocked. It's glutted. There wan't anything to do but shut *down*', he tells his wife after reluctantly closing his paint factory. An expansion into foreign markets was undertaken by American businessmen in order to raise demand, a development represented in the novel by Lapham's hiring of Tom Corey in preparation for the Latin American market. But with the current downturn in business Lapham is caught with a great deal of his capital tied up in its commodity form in his unsold stocks of paint. Much of his capital is also tied up in his new Beacon Street mansion and when it burns down (a heavily contrived development on Howells's part that too obviously plays its role in the theme of retribution and the return to simplicity), he is unable to realise a fraction of his investment, so that his urge to self-aggrandisement also contributes to his downfall.

Howells further places Lapham's career in the context of contemporary commercial developments by depicting his attempt to form a combination, as many firms were doing in the 1880s, in order to avoid price competition. To form his trust with some West Virginia manufacturers, however, he requires a large amount of ready capital, something he does not currently possess owing to the stock market, the slump and his new house. When he tries to raise it from bankers and associates he discovers that in the late-nineteenth-century business world moral scrupulosity and fairness are not reciprocated. A good name is no longer sufficient to secure credit. Instead, there is a merciless spirit of Social Darwinism abroad: 'He had not found other men so very liberal or faithful with him; a good many of them appeared to have combined to hunt him down.' Howells does not provide a detailed account of Lapham's commercial transactions during his financial collapse, as Dreiser does of Cowperwood's in *The Financier*, for his purpose is not to focus on the processes of economic failure themselves but on the moral quandary into which his entrepreneur is driven by the threat of failure.

Lapham could sell some mills he owns out West but he knows them to be worthless and is righteously indignant when Rogers suggests he unload them on to some supposedly naive English buyers: 'And do you think that I am going to steal these men's money to help you plunder somebody in a new scheme?' But financial pressures bear more and more heavily upon him, bringing him face to face with ruin and causing him to waver in his resolution. The individualistic urge of economic self-interest, the intensely competitive milieu, and the desire to preserve his social success all war with his refusal to act unethically and bring on an acute crisis of moral decision, a crisis that is intensified by the connivance of the English agents in the deal and Rogers's offer to take responsibility for the transaction upon himself. Having skilfully sketched in the cumulative pressures, Howells now brings his protagonist to a moment of great trial: 'He walked out into the

night air, every pulse throbbing with the strong temptation. . . .
It was for him alone to commit this rascality – if it was a rascality
– or not.' Howells has also been at pains to emphasise Lapham's
isolation at this crucial time. Alienated from the members of his
own class by their pursuit of unrestrained self-interest, from the
Boston Brahmins by their snobbish aloofness, and from his wife
by her unjust suspicions of his infidelity, he is thrown back on his
inner-direction, on his self-communion and the strength of his
'underlying principles'.

Refusing this time to yield to the lure of self-interest and
material gain, he keeps steadfast to those principles and retains
his moral integrity. He turns down the deal so precipitating his
bankruptcy and, a poor but purified man, he returns to the
Vermont farmstead, where, improbably, not even the stigma of
debt is allowed to follow him. There is a strong note of cultural
nostalgia in Howells's image of the Laphams' return to 'the day of
small things' as Persis describes their reversal of fortune. There,
on the farm far away from the complex moral pressures associated with industrial capitalism, the simple lifestyle and values of the
agrarian era live on and are validated by Lapham's prescriptive
example. For Mr Sewell he provides a 'moral spectacle' and
though the loss of his social success has been a kind of death for
him, the entrepreneur, Howells assures us, is now restored to that
'manhood which his prosperity had so nearly stolen from him'.
Material success and moral integrity, Howells suggests, were
unable to coexist in the 1870s and 1880s and the only *right* way to
act in business was to obey the traditional dictates of the
Protestant ethic and Jeffersonian individualism.

Howells was unequivocal about the didactic purpose of writing.
'No conscientious man', he wrote, 'can now set about painting an
image of life without perpetual question of the verity of his work,
and without feeling bound to distinguish so clearly that no reader
of his may be misled between what is right and what is wrong,
what is noble and what is base, what is health and what is
perdition, in the actions and the characters he portrays.' *The Rise
of Silas Lapham* is thus a kind of morality tale for the Gilded Age,
demonstrating the triumph of sound moral principle over
business expediency and holding up the Yankee paint manufacturer as an *exemplum* of the good and noble, of how indeed all
entrepreneurs ought to behave. Fortunately, Howells was not only
a moralist but also a realist in his fiction, and his quality of light

irony, his humane sympathy, and his fine capacity for realising scene and character based on a sharp observation of everyday detail and a scrupulous attention to the individual idiom of personal speech mean that the novel rises far above the drily schematic. Yet, though Howells emphasised the importance of realism in the novel, he failed to consider the degree to which his didactic intention might compromise or even contradict realism's demand for accurate representation. The first question we ought to ask of a book, he said, is 'Is it true? − true to the motives, the impulses, the principles that shape the life of actual men and women?'³ So, is *The Rise of Silas Lapham* 'true' as an image of business life? Is it true to the motives and principles of actual entrepreneurs in the late nineteenth century?

On the basis of broad historical evidence the answer can only be in the negative. This was, after all, the era of the graphically termed 'Robber Barons' who grabbed so much of the new land's wealth and established themselves in unassailable monopolistic positions by the most ruthless means. Business 'morality' was kept distinctly separate from personal morality, and such a dilemma as Lapham agonised over never disturbed for a moment even the more scrupulous of the entrepreneurs. The climactic decisions of their lives were not moral but material and practical, related to concrete problems of manufacture, transport, expansion and finance. The harsh realities of competitive business life exist only in the wings in *Silas Lapham* and Howells's ethical and domestic focus succeeds in softening and humanising, and so mystifying, the rampant industrial capitalism which demanded a more realistic presentation than the pioneer of American realism could bring himself to provide.

As a product of frontier society and its ideologies, Howells tended to analyse social situations at this point in his life in warmly optimistic and individualistic terms. 'Our novelists,' he observed approvingly, 'therefore, concern themselves with the more smiling aspects of life, which are the more American, and seek the universal in the individual rather than the social interests.'⁴ This attitude lies behind the relative absence in the novel of any sense of Lapham's belonging to a class composed of similarly situated people with common interests and under common threat from the growing labour militancy of the day. The one or two hints Howells provides about the manufacturer's relationship with his workers imply that he is a paternalistic employer, and Lapham's visit to Zerilla's dingy home offers only the briefest glimpse of life 'on the other side of the tracks'. Howells was later to demonstrate a greater awareness of both the class nature of society and the condition of the poor, but in *Silas Lapham* the image he conveys of American capitalism is naive, indicating that he did not understand the impersonal economic forces which held sway within it. He sought to reassert the viability of the democratic and Protestant traditions in the face of the social and economic developments that marked the industrial-production phase, but these schemes of values became an increasingly inadequate source of critical perspective as industrialism progressed. They could not continue to supply either a ready comprehension or a relevant critique of contemporary American reality when that reality diverged more and more markedly from the ante-bellum conditions out of which those values arose. At the time of *The Rise of Silas Lapham* Howells's criticism of *laissez-faire* capitalism was still a moral and not a social one, a perspective that enabled him to make the issues in the book clear within his own terms but which prevented him from correlating those issues more closely with the central social and business conflicts of his day.

He did, however, modify his viewpoint to accommodate historical change, his own observation of industrial conditions, and his growing sense of social injustice. He later adopted a socialist and collectivist stance and by his next important novel, *A Hazard of New Fortunes* (1890), his criticism had broadened to include a social as well as a moral dimension. This enlargement of perspective is evident in his treatment of the entrepreneur figure, Jacob Dryfoos. Dryfoos, like Lapham, begins economic life as an independent farmer with all the traditional virtues, including 'hard-headed, practical commonsense', 'intense individualism', and the 'conservative good citizenship, which had been his chief moral experience'. Industrial change suddenly intrudes upon the stable agrarian pattern in the form of natural gas found beneath his land, and against his better judgement Dryfoos sells his farm for the huge sum offered. Initially, his loss of occupation and the meaning it gave his life leaves him disconsolate, but then he discovers speculation and with seemingly inexhaustible luck rapidly turns his thousands into millions.

Uprooting themselves from Indiana, he and his family vainly try to adapt themselves to the lifestyle of the *nouveaux riches* in

New York, a significant choice of novelistic locale by Howells, reflecting his awareness of New York's growing status as a metropolitan economic centre. The Dryfoos' mansion and the artefacts within it, 'whose costliness was too evident', testify to their tasteless conspicuous consumption. Dryfoos, it is indicated, may drive a hard bargain but he never swindles or doublecrosses, and once again Howells paints his fictional representative of the nineteenth-century millionaire as essentially a virtuous man. The transformation from Midwest farmer to Wall Street speculator has, however, had its costs, and here as in *The Rise of Silas Lapham* Howells implicity equates farmstead simplicity with moral integrity and urban wealth and sophistication with moral decay. 'He must have undergone a moral deterioration, an atrophy of the generous instincts', Basil March remarks of old Dryfoos, 'and I don't see why it shouldn't have reached his mental make-up. He has sharpened, but he has narrowed; his sagacity has turned into suspicion, his caution to meanness, his courage to ferocity. . . . I am not very proud when I realise that such a man and his experience are the ideal and ambition of most Americans.' In the figure of the speculator, Howells, addressing an audience which took the entrepreneur for its model and hero, attempts to define critically that spiritual impoverishment, that cultural barrenness, which results from the loss of productive function and the monomaniacal pursuit of money.

By the time of *Hazard* Howells had come to appreciate some of the importance of social forces. Through Basil March, the liberal centre of consciousness, he expresses the proviso that character is partly to blame for the faults of *laissez-faire* capitalism but also acknowledges that 'conditions *make* character' and that 'people are greedy and foolish, and wish to have and to shine, because having and shining are held up to them by civilisation as the chief good of life'. The moral judgement on Dryfoos is therefore softened by the consideration that he is more the passive victim of industrial and social change than its dynamic hero. Far from it being he who has made the money, it is the money which has made him, and Howells's portraiture inclines us to pity rather than personal condemnation. Dryfoos becomes conscious of the loss which his sudden riches brought in their train but unlike Lapham – and here we see Howells's sterner, less retrospective vision at work – he cannot, any more than American society at large, return to the old agrarian way: '"We *can't* go back!"

shouted the old man fiercely. "There's no farm any more to go back to. The fields is full of gas wells and oil wells and hell holes generally; the house is tore down, and the barn's goin'." ' It sounds like the agonised cry of a whole culture that has just awoken to the relentless irreversibility of the industrial changes it has embraced and to the irrecoverable loss of the homestead republic with its democratic and moral virtues. In his earlier portrait of the entrepreneur Howells was concerned to demonstrate the continuing relevance of the traditional moral and democratic values to the age of big business, but in *A Hazard of New Fortunes* his confidence in the durability and adequacy of the middle-class agrarian ideology is considerably qualified and he succeeds in communicating (in spite of himself perhaps) a sense of its insufficiency in a society of plutocrat and proletarian.

The younger generation of Naturalist writers, whom Howells befriended and helped, did not share either his frontier upbringing or his cultural nostalgia. More attuned to the era of large-scale production, they felt compelled to adopt a different ideological stance and literary mode in order to comprehend and then portray in fictional terms the changes and conflicts they saw around them. If Howells was the first to bring the industrial entrepreneur on to the literary stage, Frank Norris in *The Pit* (1903) and Theodore Dreiser in *The Financier* (1912) and *The Titan* (1914), were to advance beyond his treatment and present the tycoon in a less morally structured, more aggressively realistic light.

Frank Norris had introduced the figure of the entrepreneur into *The Octopus* in the character of Shelgrim, the railroad magnate, but *The Pit*, like *The Rise of Silas Lapham*, is wholly centred on the rise and fall of an entrepreneur, reflecting the importance this new social type had come to enjoy in late-nineteenth-century America. From its opening pages it is evident that the novel is going to be set almost entirely in the milieu of wealthy businessmen. Although our glimpse of the Chicago poor 'shivering in rags and tattered comforters' outside the Opera House reminds us briefly of the existence of that other class, it is the 'prolonged defile of millionaires' entering the Opera House which the novel takes up and follows. Norris, the son of a successful Chicago jeweller who provided six fine horses, monogrammed carriages and a large mansion on Michigan Avenue for his family, was the child of that milieu, and he drew upon his upbringing not only for the documentation of the lifestyle of the Chicago rich but also for the originals of his two main characters. The hero, Curtis Jadwin, is based in his appearance, mannerisms and tastes upon Norris's father, and Laura Dearborn with her physical charm, forceful personality and love of the dramatic is a faithful portrayal of his mother.[5] Unlike Howells's Silas Lapham, Norris's Jadwin is not placed in the manufacturing class, but is presented first as a rentier and then as a speculator.

Both *The Octopus* and *The Pit* were part of Norris's projected 'Epic of the Wheat', the first dealing with production in the San Joaquin Valley in California, the second with distribution and the activities of the Chicago Wheat Pit, and a never-to-be-written third with the consumption of the wheat in Europe. Like *The Octopus, The Pit* was based upon an historical event, Joseph Leiter's spectacular 'corner' in wheat in 1897 when he achieved a monopoly of the wheat market by buying up all the available supply. Eventually, the market broke and the price plummeted, bringing about his ruin.[6] Norris modelled Jadwin's career on Leiter's, for the speculator's triumph offered drama and his demise exactly suited the epic's overarching theme of the insignificance of men before the force of the wheat. As in the preparation of his earlier wheat novel, Norris closely researched his documentary material, studying the operation of the Wheat Pit at the Chicago Board of Trade with the help of George Gibbs, and seeking the advice of the young broker, George Moulson, during the writing of the narrative.[7] As a result, *The Pit* is firmly grounded in the business and social world of turn-of-the-century Chicago, the main commercial centre for the Mid-West, and Norris's command of realistic detail, particularly of the financial transactions, is evident throughout. Norris, however, had no coherent view of life with which to organise his materials. The duality of perspective and lack of cohesion that mar *The Octopus* persist, albeit less markedly, into *The Pit*, as at times he interprets his story according to a philosophy of free will and at others according to a Spencerian determinism.

In *The Rise of Silas Lapham*, as we have seen, Howells assumed the primacy of individual free will and moral responsibility and organised the novel on a cycle of poverty–purity/ riches–corruption/poverty–purity in order to endow it with the structure of a cautionary tale. Such a cycle in attenuated form, moderate wealth–purity/speculation–corruption/poverty–

purity, underlies *The Pit* and similarly invites a didactic interpretation of the novel. Jadwin is credited with social origins very
similar to Lapham's. He 'had begun life without a sou in his
pockets' and 'his people were farmers, nothing more nor less than
hardy honest fellows'. Thus is the agrarian background rather
distantly sketched in, together with his self-advancement from
farmboy to rentier. The story then documents his steady abandonment of normal business activities and his increasing
absorption in wheat speculation. It was one of Norris's tenets that
the business barons were driven by the excitement of making a
fortune rather than by the acquisitive desire for money.[8] And this
interpretation of entrepreneurial activities informs his portrayal
of Jadwin who, he makes plain, speculates not out of the rapa-
cious greed usually associated with his kind but out of the 'fun' of
playing a 'rich man's game'.

Jadwin's blasé approach to the operations of the Wheat Pit
bespeaks the lack of that moral consciousness which Howells
made so central in his characterisation of Silas Lapham, but
while Norris, realistically, does not image the entrepreneur as an
ethically alert character, he does bring Jadwin's complacency into
relief. This is principally achieved through the retired speculator,
Cressler, in whose mouth Norris places a cogent criticism of the
moral and social consequences of wheat speculation. First,
Cressler condemns speculation morally as a species of gambling,
just as Lapham had condemned his own gambling in stocks, and
then in a passage of fine polemic he indicts the social instability
and injustice that inevitably arises out of the wheat's status as a
commodity in a free market:

> Those fellows in the Pit don't own the wheat; never even see it;
> wouldn't know what to do with it if they had it. They don't
> care in the least about the grain. But there are thousands upon
> thousands of farmers out here in Iowa and Kansas or Dakota
> who do, and hundreds of thousands of poor devils in Europe
> who care even more than the farmer. I mean the fellows who
> raise the grain, and the other fellows who eat it. It's life or
> death for either of them. And right between the two comes the
> Chicago speculator, who raises or lowers the price out of all
> reason, for the benefit of his pocket.

Finally, Cressler returns to speculation's moral aspect, emphasising its personal corrosiveness and instancing the promising young

men who have been 'wrecked and ruined' and who have lost 'the taste, the very capacity for legitimate business'. In these passages Norris explicitly sets forth a critique of wheat speculation which, though it tends to become submerged beneath the drama of the gambling itself, is endorsed and amplified by the story of Jadwin's rise and fall.

Jadwin swings a 'corner' in May wheat which, illustrative of the widespread repercussions of speculation, has international ramifications, as Norris emphasises. To the farmers of the Mid-West Jadwin's monopoly and his 'booming up' of the price bring unprecedented prosperity: 'Mortgages were being paid off, new and improved farming implements were being bought, new areas seeded, new livestock acquired.' But to the European consumer his 'corner' brings only high bread prices and hunger: 'We know of your compatriot, then, here in Italy – this Jadwin of Chicago who has bought all the wheat. We have no more bread. The loaf is small as the fist and costly. We cannot buy it; we have no money.' In this way Norris demonstrates the human chain of producer, distributor and consumer which underlies the abstract processes of market economics, and highlights his speculator-protagonist as a man possessed of power without responsibility.

Norris also uses Jadwin's career in the Wheat Pit to illustrate the personally corrosive effects of speculation. After an energetic pursuit on his part Jadwin has married Laura Dearborn, but the growing excitement of his gambling at the Board of Trade, well communicated by Norris, leads him to neglect his new wife more and more and she drifts towards a liaison with her former lover, Corthell. Jadwin is shown becoming increasingly monomaniacal in regard to his wheat dealings and, losing all financial judgement, he rashly decides to swing his 'corner' into July wheat as well. So unchecked is his ambition that he seems prepared to combat nature itself in order to fulfil his aim. His broker warns him that because he has sent the price up so high more wheat is being planted than ever before. 'Great Scott, J., you're fighting against the earth itself', he tells him. 'Well, we'll fight it then', Jadwin replies impetuously. 'I'll stop those hay-seeds.' Norris thus attributes a rather Promethean grandeur to what is essentially a purely egotistical and socially ruinous business greed.

In *The Octopus*, an epic tale of the fight between the farmers of the San Joaquin Valley, California and the Pacific and South-western Railroad, Norris had employed the Spencerian notion of the primacy of large, impersonal forces in natural and economic life and the insignificance of men before them. Since that novel ends with an affirmation of the wheat as a mighty world force, readers coming from it to *The Pit* would be aware of the dramatic irony which Norris extracts from Jadwin's bravado. His proposal to 'fight the earth' is a gross act of *hubris*, and in conformity with the classical pattern retribution from the mighty powers he has provoked is certain to fall upon him: 'Why, the Wheat had grown itself; demand and supply, these were the two great laws the Wheat obeyed. Almost blasphemous in his effrontery, he had tampered with these laws, and had roused a Titan.' With the supply of grain vastly increased Jadwin is unable to hold the market; the price drops catastrophically and he loses his entire fortune. Norris, intent on driving home his theme of the wheat as a mighty force, makes it plain that it is the wheat and not his human opponents that effects Jadwin's nemesis.

Thus Jadwin is punished for his speculation and the novel's aspect of cautionary tale is reinforced by Cressler's ruin and subsequent suicide after he has re-entered the market against his better judgement. In the wake of his financial, and physical, collapse, Jadwin and his reconciled wife prepare for a life of poverty and simplicity. 'What do "things", servants, money and all amount to now?' Laura declares defiantly, if unconvincingly for a lady of expensive and cultured tastes, as she and the penitent speculator move on to make a new start in the symbolic West.

Norris uses Laura in a similar way to Presley in *The Octopus*. Like his, her arrival and departure from the scene of economic conflict frame the story and, like his naivety, her ignorance of the ways of commerce provides the occasion for her 'education' into its dubious methods, its glamour and its overarching rationale. It is she who listens to Cressler's strictures on speculation, and as she and Jadwin are leaving Chicago at the end, it is she who questions the rightness of the free market system: 'This huge, resistless Nourisher of Nations – why was it that it could not reach the People, could not fulfil its destiny, unmarred by all this suffering, unattended by all this misery?' The strong thread of social criticism that runs through *The Pit* and culminates in Laura's question indicates that Norris intended it, partly at least, to be an anti-speculation novel in the same way that *The Octopus* in one of its aspects is anti-trust. But any critical perspective present is overlaid by his Spencerian determinism and his view of business as romance, attitudes which are also mainly conveyed through the vehicle of Laura.

In *The Responsibilities of the Novelist* Norris made a plea for 'romance', by which he seemed to mean an odd combination of Scott and Zola rather than Hawthorne, against Howells's type of tame realism, and claimed that romance was as inherent in the modern milieu as in the historical settings of its traditional forms.[9] Rather pointedly, it is while Laura is enjoying the romantic excess of the Italian opera that she first becomes aware of 'that other drama' of the workaday business world which was 'equally picturesque, equally romantic, equally passionate'. Howells had gently alluded to the 'romantic' aspects of Lapham's activities and despite his different standpoint, Norris shared with Howells the impulse to bring together a modified notion of romance and modern commerce. We can perhaps explain their attitude in the following way. Both were bringing new content into fiction and developing first realism and then Naturalism as literary modes for communicating that content, which was drawn heavily from contemporary society. However, they could not escape the legacy of outmoded literary attitudes entirely nor the prevailing literary vocabulary. Although they both recognised that 'romance' as it was conventionally conceived was irrelevant to any serious encounter with urban-industrial America, they sought at the same time both to revivify the jaded mode with their new content and to legitimate that content as proper literary material by appropriating to it a tone and form that had a long traditional sanction. The main thrust of their literary practice was progressive, therefore, but it carried along with it some residual responses and concepts.

The real adventure of modern times, Norris indicates in *The Pit*, is to be found in business and the entrepreneur is the true descendant of the heroic man of action of the past. He repeatedly describes the money-grabbing activities of the Wheat Pit in terms of valiant struggle and warfare, and the haughty and cultured Laura is significantly overawed by this martial economic dynamism. Her choice of the unpolished but energetic and commanding Jadwin in preference to the ineffectual aesthete, Corthell, like her migration from Massachusetts to Chicago, represents Norris's affirmation of the raw. bustling Mid-West and his rejection of New England and its genteel tradition.[10]

Through Laura several Social Darwinian themes are introduced into the novel. As an outsider she is acutely aware of the 'vast cruel machinery of the city's life' and of the callous indifference of the metropolis to the fate of the individual, an indifference which recalls that of nature in *The Octopus*. Her Spencerian evolutionary optimism, which she expresses during the course of a conversation with Corthell – 'the individual may deteriorate, but the type always grows better' – echoes Presley's conviction in the earlier novel that 'the individual suffers but the race goes on'. And in her role of vehicle for the Spencerian viewpoint she attempts to exculpate Jadwin from the consequences of his speculation, just as Presley exculpates the Railroad from responsibility for its actions in the San Joaquin Valley, by appealing to those large, deterministic forces that sweep through economic affairs.

According to the moral perspective adopted by Cressler, Jadwin is responsible for the widespread recession that followed the collapse of his corner, since his egomania disturbed the proper harmony of supply and demand. But Laura 'would not admit her husband was in any way to blame', and in order to convince herself, as well as to reiterate the theme of determinism, she recalls the apologetic defence of his actions that Jadwin had made at the time of his successfully engineered 'corner': 'I corner the wheat! Great heavens, it is the wheat that has cornered me! The corner made itself. I happened to stand between two sets of circumstances, and they made me do what I've done.' Norris has established Laura as someone who is naive where finance is concerned and so her credulousness in the face of Jadwin's explanation is entirely in character, but we can hardly be expected to take seriously his posturing as the passive victim of converging forces. Only two pages previously Norris tells us Jadwin 'had discovered that there were in him powers, capabilities, and a breadth of grasp hitherto unsuspected', and that his estimation of himself has risen: 'He could control the Chicago wheat market; and the man who could do that might well call himself "great" without presumption.' Here the uncertainty arising out of Norris's confused perspectives is made manifest. While it is of a piece with his Spencerian determinism that Jadwin should appear a mere atom before the mighty Wheat, it is also necessary, in the service of that impulse to lionise the entrepreneur which is more pronounced in Dreiser but is also present in Norris, that he should attain an heroic stature as a giant among men. Norris could have achieved some telling dramatic irony by encouraging *us* to view Jadwin as merely a pivot in the market mechanism while he conceived of himself as the master of the Wheat, but to attribute to the bluff speculator a consciousness both of power and of passivity is evidence of a contradictory conception of his character.

As a literary representative of the American entrepreneur, Curtis Jadwin makes a small advance upon Silas Lapham. There is more realism of motive and character; the acutely moral consciousness has been shed, though Jadwin is endowed with some business ethics; and the more prevalent egomania of the businessman has been acknowledged and presented. The various stages of Jadwin's career, his intricate manoeuvrings, his clash with the Crookes gang, his gradual exhaustion and final ruin are related with gripping naturalness, and the theme of the impersonal force of the Wheat arises credibly from the main plot development. But Norris's attempt to raise his speculator to the status of an Ahab of the Wheat is unsuccessful; Jadwin remains too human a figure. With his good nature, his childish fondness for his fishing and his steam yacht, and his lack of intellectual or spiritual largeness, he is too ordinary and fallible a man, too domestically realistic a character ever to bear the weight of any grandiose conception.

It is in the general treatment of business that *The Pit* gains most ground over *The Rise of Silas Lapham*. Norris, born of a later generation that Howells, did not share his cultural nostalgia and drew upon contemporary rather than agrarian ideologies for the perspectives that informed his fiction. He accepted, even rejoiced in, modern commercial America, and his enthusiasm, partly critical as it was, enabled him to portray some of the processes of American capitalism with greater specificity. For Howells, the main focus in the story of Lapham lay in the ethics of business, but for Norris business provided interesting material not for the questions it raised about proper moral conduct but for its intrinsic drama and sweep. This led, inevitably, to a focus on business *itself*, for it was out of the conflict of material interests and the deviousness of the methods that the drama and the plot arose. In order to convey those interests and methods Norris had to establish a documentary framework of complex financial operations. This new territory for fiction was to be exploited more fully by Dreiser in his Cowperwood novels.

Dreiser's trilogy, *The Financier* (1912), *The Titan* (1914) and *The Stoic* (1947), is the most substantial representation of the nineteenth-century entrepreneur in American fiction in this period and his portrayal of Frank Algernon Cowperwood marks considerable advances over Howells's Silas Lapham and Norris's Curtis Jadwin. In particular, he strips the entrepreneur of any residual Christian morality and redeeming human warmth to present him as nakedly competitive and manipulative. Dreiser rightly saw that the rise of the entrepreneur and *laissez-faire* industrial capitalism had rendered traditional American values irrelevant. He also saw that people were slow to recognise this uncomfortable fact because they continued to structure the social experience of the present according to received models from the past. In his essay 'The American Financier' he wrote:

> The trouble in America is that when the financial mind appeared it came rather speedily and roughly into contact with the pen-written notion or ideal embodied in our American Declaration that all men are born free and equal, and that they are possessed of certain inalienable rights, among which of course are those of life, liberty, and the pursuit of happiness. And these latter were not supposed to be interfered with by the financiers or organisers seeking power. Yet, the race has always been, and will so remain, of course, to the swift, the battle to the strong; chemical and physical laws not being easily upset by fiats of government.[11]

Dreiser, his journalistic eye keenly observant of the social realities, recognised that the petty-bourgeois ideology of natural rights was demonstrably out of date in the era of the Robber Barons and, responsive to the intellectual climate in the first decade of the century, he adopted the plutocratic rationale of Social Darwinism and propagated it in his trilogy as the only valid explanation of man and society. Partly then, these novels demystify the exploiter and the processes of exploitation and corruption by stripping them of the hollow pieties in which they were usually clothed. But the Social Darwinian perspective also implies an affirmation of business and its methods. By the traditional standards asserted by Howells and other critics the tactics of the captains of industry were indefensible, but in the Social Darwinian view the tycoons were merely obeying the natural law of competition. Dreiser's study of the entrepreneur, therefore, can be read as both an exposé and a celebration of the world of finance capitalism.

Dreiser grounded his trilogy thoroughly in the economic and social life of the late nineteenth century by basing it closely upon the life of Charles T. Yerkes, the traction magnate. Although he was very rich and powerful, Yerkes did not belong to the élite of the Gilded Age financiers composed of the Vanderbilts, Rockefellers and others. Yet Dreiser especially selected him as the model on which to base Cowperwood. He told Masters that he 'had looked into the careers of twenty American capitalists and that Yerkes was the most interesting of them', and he seems to have seen in this particular magnate a figure of almost mythic proportions. In an interview given just before the publication of *The Titan* he said:

> Certain I am of one thing, the age that produced at once the mechanical perfection of the world and its most colossal fortunes is classic. From that period certainly some Croesus, Lepidus or Maecenas is sure to show forth in fable, song, or story. In my limited search and with my selective tendencies none seemed of so great import, socially, sociologically, financially, philosophically as the individual whom I have selected. A rebellious Lucifer this, glorious in his somber conception of the value of power. A night-black pool his world will seem to some, played over by fulgurous gleams of his own individualistic and truly titanic mind.[12]

Dreiser's high regard for his subject obviously precluded any undercutting irony or debunking over-inflation in his treatment. The result is a sycophantic portrait which has a myth-making function in that it attempts to endow the entrepreneur with epic dimensions – to make him, in fact, a colossus of the age. Dreiser's irony is directed instead at the hypocrisy, as he saw it, of the public and private moral codes. It was Yerkes's lack of such hypocrisy, his unabashed practice of dishonesty, which appealed so strongly to Dreiser, providing him with a foil against which to set the hollow sentiments which were supposed to govern American business life. Furthermore, Yerkes had a strong interest in art, as well as a taste for attractive young women, two pursuits which Dreiser adapted and idealised as aspects of Cowperwood's quest for pure beauty.

Dreiser thoroughly researched his material, concentrating on American economic history from the early 1860s, the social and political history of Philadelphia, Chicago and London, and Yerkes's career, including details of his private life. The account of Yerkes's public life in the trilogy is for the most part literally correct, and Cowperwood's financial dealings closely follow those of his original: ruin in Philadelphia at the time of the Chicago fire of 1871; recovery in 1873 during the collapse of Jay Cooke's empire; the formation of a gas trust in Chicago followed by increasing control of the street railways; a victory in the American Match trust battle; failure in 1897 to control the State legislature and the Chicago City Council in the crucial matter of extending his street railway franchises; and finally, the premature conclusion of his London plans with his death. It is Dreiser's portrait of the financier's personal life that is largely imaginative.[13] Since the documentary content of the business plot is so high, we shall pay scant attention to developments there in order to concentrate upon the ideological and imaginative reshapings which the material underwent at Dreiser's hands.

In the main, the trilogy constitutes one long *Tendenzroman* in which Dreiser sets out to demonstrate the tenets of Social Darwinism and the insufficiency of moral codes. In the opening pages of *The Financier* the young Cowperwood, a boy of ten, watches a struggle to the death between a lobster and a squid in a fish-tank. So impatient is Dreiser to establish the dominant perspective that he has Cowperwood, with improbable precocity, draw a Darwinian generalisation from the incident: 'Things lived on each other – that was it . . . men lived on men.' This imposed vision of a fiercely competitive society sustains the financier throughout his career. 'Life was war – particularly financial life', he reassures himself during his trial at Philadelphia, and his general conviction that 'the race is to the swift . . . the battle is to the strong', is reiterated through the three novels. Early in the novel we also learn that he is a 'dynamic, self-sufficient, sterling youth', and that his most powerful motive is the 'desire for wealth, prestige, dominance'. The unchecked individualism which is to be the keynote of his character is expressed early in his motto, 'I satisfy myself', and later hardens in *The Titan* into the determination that 'he could, should, and would rule alone. . . .

By the right of financial intellect and courage he was first, and would so prove it.' Ruthless, egotistic and admitting bonds with no one, Cowperwood represents Emerson's doctrine of self-reliance taken to its inevitable and harsh extreme.

In constructing his myth of financial success Dreiser includes one or two elements from the older Franklinesque myth of self-improvement. Cowperwood, for instance, devotes his life to a strong work ethic and continues to do so even when he has a massive fortune to enjoy. While work and business are hardly sacramental in character to him, they do all the same become ends in themselves. The domination of his life by work becomes an occasion of regret for him in *The Stoic*, but because of the 'current American contempt of leisure' it enables him to compare favourably with the emergent American leisure class in the figure of Polk Lynde and with the English aristocracy in the figure of Lord Stane who, although he 'knew how to play', could not match Cowperwood for 'vigour, resourcefulness, naturalness'. The great entrepreneur-hero must obviously not appear deficient in any respect!

Although Cowperwood may be bound to the work ethic, Dreiser is sufficiently alive to the trends of his time to equip his protagonist with a mentality suitable not to an age of early accumulation but to an age of high finance. Contrary to Franklin's admonition, not thrift but credit and risk are necessary in these conditions to amass capital on any scale. 'It was not his idea that he could get rich by saving', we learn in *The Financier*. 'From the first he had the notion that liberal spending was better.' He early recognises that the way to wealth in the late nineteenth century lies not so much through manufacture as through the manipulation of stocks and the capital gains accruing therefrom. The stock market was the central institution of the finance capitalism which emerged in the United States after the Civil War, and Dreiser's depiction of its role in the centralisation of capital and his identification of it as, in Engels's words, 'the hearth of extreme corruption' and the medium for 'the annihilation of all orthodox moral concepts' reveal a deep insight into its economic and social effects.[14]

It is a concomitant of Cowperwood's involvement in the competitive milieu of finance, as well as a consequence of his Darwinian view of society, that he should be totally amoral. We learn in *The Financier* that he 'was an opportunist' and that 'his financial morality had become special and local in its character', for morality 'varied, in his mind at least, with conditions if not climates'. In stark contrast with Howells's Silas Lapham, there is none of the steadfastness of the morally principled man here. Dreiser expunged any trace of vestigial Protestantism from his characterisation; Cowperwood utterly lacks a conscience and has no 'consciousness of what is currently known as sin'.

It was in order to exemplify the healthy honesty of Cowperwood's rejection of the current conventions governing private and public life that Dreiser invented the Butler family. The adulterous affair between Cowperwood and the daughter, Aileen Butler, is presented by Dreiser as conspicuously lacking in that guilt and remorse which the Puritan moral code asserted was both inevitable and proper. Butler himself, though as corrupt and ruthless in practice as the opportunist financier, still pays lip-service to the ethics which were supposed to rule in business and political life. While his public morality may be hypocritical, however, his family morality is sincerely conservative, and he is genuinely outraged at the affair between his daughter and Cowperwood. As Donald Pizer points out, the discrepancy between Butler's business and family values is cleverly and economically employed by Dreiser as the pivot on which to turn both the public and private plots of *The Financier*.[15] Butler's moral outrage against Cowperwood on family grounds is the real motivation for his determination to ruin the financier and bring him to trial for the embezzlement of Philadelphia City Council funds.

Similarly in *The Titan*, Dreiser develops two features of Yerkes's experience in Chicago – his failure to gain a place in Society and his many affairs with young women – into major aspects of Cowperwood's personal life in order to highlight the hypocrisy of the Chicago élite. The millionaire businessmen and financiers cloak their economic opposition to Cowperwood by invoking a moral code which looks askance at his history of adultery, divorce and imprisonment, and at his continuing infidelities. In the struggle for control of the Chicago street railways which takes up much of the latter half of the novel both Cowperwood and his opponents, Arneel, Schryhart, Merrill and Hand, wish to satisfy themselves, but this group hides its material motives behind a veil of seeming concern for the public. As Dreiser makes plain during his documentation of the corruption of city politics, these financiers also engage in the bribery and purchase of politicians and the manipulation of the democratic process in order to further their nefarious ends. Yet they use their control of the Press to have Cowperwood branded as the real threat to the city. When the public agitation they have whipped up begins to embrace socialistic demands for the public ownership of *all* street railways (as municipal reformers were pressing for at the turn of the century), then the capitalists, mindful of their own interests, close ranks and withdraw their opposition to Cowperwood's monopoly.

Egotism and the lust for power are hardly sympathetic traits, and to render them acceptable in his financier Dreiser subsumes them as part of a larger, questing temperament. It is frequently impressed upon us that Cowperwood is no ordinary mortal but more a kind of 'superman', and repeatedly we are meant to recognise in him a Renaissance vitality and hunger for the sensuous riches of life. 'To live richly, joyously, fully – his whole nature craved that', we are told in *The Financier*. But the two activities in which Dreiser seeks to convey, as opposed to merely insisting upon, the financier's spiritual largeness – his collection of art and pursuit of women – are weak and unconvincing. Both seem rather mechanical extensions of his obsessive acquisitiveness and we never see Cowperwood making anything other than wooden responses to either life or art.

It is also impressed upon us that finance itself is no ordinary, money-grubbing activity. 'Finance is an art', we are informed in *The Financier*, and we are meant to view Cowperwood admiringly in the manner of one of his lovers in *The Titan*, as 'a very great artist in his realm rather than as a businessman'. When Dreiser attempts to illustrate or define this special artistic quality of Cowperwood's mind, however, the results are only large and vague gestures. His difficulty in successfully realising the attribute he so vehemently insists upon is an index of the imaginative invention required, for the documentary facts militated against this aspect of his conception of the entrepreneur.

Most of the financiers of the Gilded Age were noted for the cultural barrenness of their lives and for their incapacity to sustain interest in, or conversation on, any topic not directly related to the making of money. Yerkes's own maxims – 'It's the straphanger who pays the dividends', and 'The secret of success in my business is to buy old junk, fix it up a little and unload it upon other fellows' – may reveal a hard, practical grasp of business but they certainly do not indicate a promising foundation on which Dreiser could erect the philosophic grandeur of a Cowperwood.[16] So concerned is Dreiser to image the financier as the dynamic multifaceted hero of a phase of capitalism which was already passing that he turns a blind eye to the impoverishment a monomaniacal pursuit of money and power could inflict upon the whole personality.

In this trilogy Dreiser dramatised an account of the main drift of American economic development from the Civil War until the early 1900s, and his passion for documentary frequently leads him to lose Cowperwood in his surroundings. So much historical and economic information has to be provided, and so much is done by others to whom attention is shifted for whole chapters at a time, that we never really gain a clear sense of Cowperwood, the arch-manipulator, sitting at the centre of his financial empire and pulling the strings. Norris was able both to keep his entrepreneur in sharp focus and convey some of the excitement of business by concentrating on Jadwin's own activities in the hurly-burly of the Exchange, but in Dreiser's trilogy the events tend to be too vast and abstract (with the possible exception of the bankruptcy) for one ever to feel the drama and sweep of high finance. Dreiser also failed to integrate his adopted ideology of Social Darwinism unobtrusively into his narrative, so that it remains at the level of imposed authorial rhetoric. However, he did see correctly that the financier was a social type of consequence who deserved extended literary treatment, and his trilogy can be read as an education in the methods and corruptions of the Gilded Age, closely documenting the distortion of city politics carried out by the urban plutocracy.

4 The Condition of the Poor in the Work of Howells, Dreiser and Sinclair

Those economic and social developments of the latter half of the nineteenth century which constituted the American Industrial Revolution were not, of course, unique to the United States. They paralleled in direction and effect those which had taken place in England some fifty years earlier. Both historical movements were marked by the supersession of small-scale production by large-scale manufacture, the rapid decline of the independent producer, the centralisation of capital, and the concentration of the population in the industrial towns and cities. *Laissez-faire* capitalism was international in its features, and its typical spirit of vicious competition and social inequality triumphed in the New World just as it had in the Old. American society had become polarised into rich and poor and Engels's characterisation of the industrial city, based on his observation of Manchester, Leeds and London in the 1830s and 1840s – 'everywhere barbarous indifference, hard egotism on the one hand, and nameless misery on the other, everywhere social warfare, every man's house in a state of siege, everywhere reciprocal plundering under the protection of the law' – applied equally accurately to Chicago, Pittsburgh and New York in the 1880s and 1890s.[1]

Conditions in these mushrooming cities were appalling, for in them were concentrated the poor and the newly arrived immigrants. For those fortunate to have regular work the average wage throughout the United States in 1886 was one dollar fifteen cents a day, a sum quite insufficient to keep a family, and while some occupations such as mining paid as much as two dollars a day there were others that paid as little as fifty cents. All the endemic diseases of poverty were rife, and the problems of infant mortality, malnutrition and premature death were aggravated by the intense overcrowding in slum tenements which often lacked sanitation or civilised amenities of any kind. In 1883 there were 25 000 tenement houses in New York with one million inhabitants. Often six or seven people shared one room and there were an estimated 19 000 tenements which accommodated fifty people each.[2] By the 1880s any intelligent observer could see that the urban-industrial centres presented a spectacle of such gross immiseration as to call into serious question native American optimism about the prevalence of prosperity and the fulfilment of guarantees of life, liberty and happiness for many inhabitants of the United States. Yet imaginative literature which focused on the condition of the poor was slow to emerge.

'Where are the American writers of fiction?' Edward and Eleanor Marx Aveling asked in 1891. 'With a subject, and such a subject lying ready to their very hands, clamouring at their very doors, not one of them touches it. ... There are no studies of factory hands and of dwellers in tenement houses; no pictures of those sunk in the innermost depths of the modern *Inferno*. Yet these types will be, must be dealt with; and one of these days the Uncle Tom's Cabin of Capitalism will be written.'[3] Although there had been a few studies before the 1890s, it was not really until that decade that fiction dealing with the effects of industrial capitalism and protesting against its human cost began to appear in any quantity and quality.

The aspect of the American working class most apparent to those writers who turned their attention to its condition was its unrelieved misery, and those who, like Howells, wrote out of humanitarian sympathy, portrayed it as a suffering class, as 'the poor'. But many workers did more than suffer their oppression; they also fought it. Many labour unions were formed in the 1860s and 1870s; the Knights of Labor held its first General Assembly in 1878; the American Federation of Labor was formed in 1886; and wave after wave of strikes proclaimed that there was a determined war on between capital and labour. In 1905 Eugene Debs, 'Big Bill' Haywood and other labour leaders founded the Industrial Workers of the World, 'one great industrial union embracing all industries ... founded on the class struggle', which was most successful in organising unskilled workers in the western mining and lumber camps.[4] Industrial strife features significantly in some novels of this period, such as I.K. Friedman's *By Bread Alone* (1900), which deals with a steel strike, Howells's *A Hazard of New*

Fortunes (1890) and Dreiser's *Sister Carrie* (1900). Against this background of labour militancy Upton Sinclair in *The Jungle* (1906) and Jack London in *The Iron Heel* (1907) moved beyond responses of indignation and sympathy to portray the workers as a potentially revolutionary class, as a proletariat.

William Dean Howells had, until the writing of *The Rise of Silas Lapham*, been confident that the American social system was fundamentally right and that it bestowed a general benefaction upon all its citizens. However, while he was writing that novel in his new Beacon Street home in Boston, he became increasingly aware of the disparities of wealth which gave the lie to that egalitarianism upon which his confidence was based. Simply to be alone in the relative comfort of his huge empty house on the water's edge in the heat of August made him feel guilty. 'How unequally things are divided in this world', he wrote to his father. 'While these beautiful airy wholesome houses are uninhabited, thousands upon thousands of poor creatures are stifling in wretched barracks in the city here, whole families in one room. I wonder that men are so patient with society as they are.'[5] His social conscience was further sensitised first by what he regarded as a disturbing miscarriage of justice – the trial and execution in an atmosphere of hate and hysteria and on the basis of spurious evidence of some anarchists for their alleged part in the Haymarket Riot of 1886 in Chicago, and secondly, by his first-hand acquaintance with industrial conditions when in February 1887 he visited factories in Lowell, Massachusetts. He was shocked by what he saw there and used the experience in *Annie Kilburn* (1888), in which he condemned labouring conditions and false, middle-class philanthropy.[6]

Howells was familiar with the ideas of the American social critic, Henry George, who in *Progress and Poverty* (1879) had questioned traditional American confidence in the virtues of American society, and he also knew the ideas of Marx as predigested for the American public by Laurence Gronlund, author of *The Co-operative Commonwealth* (1884). Tolstoy, too, became a spiritual, as well as a literary, influence. Increasingly, his intimate correspondence became loaded with the problem of contemporary American society and expressive of a critical attitude. 'I should hardly like to trust pen and ink with all the audacity of my social ideas', he announced to Henry James, 'but after fifty years of optimistic content with "civilisation" and its ability to come out all right in the end, I now abhor it, and feel that it is coming out all wrong in the end, unless it bases itself anew on a real equality. Meantime, I wear a fur-lined overcoat and live in all the luxury my money can buy.'[7] He thus found himself caught in the contradictions of the humane liberal who, though he might feel sympathy for the poor, could never express solidarity with them since his own financial and class position by no means coincided with theirs. Howells was both Ohio democrat and dean of American letters and the egalitarian thrust of his social thought coexisted uneasily with the income and social success that he enjoyed. So hand in hand with his moral indignation at poverty there walked a guilty acknowledgement of his egotistic indulgence. These ambivalences of social life, these contradictions which contemporary circumstances forced upon the humane, middle-class liberal and the weak compromises that usually resulted, are dramatised and explored in *A Hazard of New Fortunes*.

In 1888 Howells moved from Boston to New York and he begins the novel with a similar migration on the part of the Marches. They leave the comparatively protected milieu of the older cultural centre for the teeming heterogeneity of the economic capital and through their reactions of bewilderment and disillusion Howells was able to present his own sense of social change and class conflict. New York better represented the new social and ethical context created by industrialisation and urbanisation, and Howells, both fascinated and repelled by the city, could draw upon his own fresh experience for striking realistic detail and perceptive psychological response. The Marches' middle-class sentiments, then, provide the novel's controlling perspective, but they are brought into relief, redefined and measured, against several other ideological standpoints embodied in appropriately conceived characters.

Jacob Dryfoos, whom we have already discussed, totally accepts the 'dog eat dog' basis of *laissez-faire* economics and has nothing but contempt for the poor. Fulkerson is a more humane but nevertheless complacent apologist for the status quo. 'One of those Americans', Howells tells us, jibing at the shallow optimism which he had found inadequate, 'whose habitual conception of life is unalloyed prosperity.' Ranged as a battery of representative critical viewpoints upon the condition of the working class are the

Christian Socialism of Conrad Dryfoos, who prefers the rigours of charity work amongst the poor to the luxurious entertainments of his class; the patriarchalism of Colonel Woodburn, who compares the cash-nexus callousness of the industrialised North unfavourably with the feudal relations of a romanticised ante-bellum South; and the materialistic socialism of the old German, Lindau, who in the most cogent critique presented in the novel points to capitalism and big business as the real cause of mass poverty and the corruption of the ideals contained in the Declaration of Independence: 'Dere *iss* no Ameriga any more: You start here free and brafe, and you glaim for efery man de righdt to life, liperty, and de bursuit of habbiness. And where haf you entedt? No man that vorks vith his handts among you hass the liperty to bursue his habbiness. He iss the slafe of some richer man, some gompany, some gorporation, dat crindts him down to the least he can lif on, and that rops him of the marchin of his earnings that he might pe habby on'. The republic, he says, is 'bought oap by monobolies, and ron by drusts and gompanies, and railroadts andt oil gompanies'.

Edwin H. Cady interprets the old German as a fanatic and idealist committed to an 'irrational philosophy of violence', but such a view, heavily ideological in itself, distorts Howells's presentation.[8] Nowhere in the novel, through either direct or reported speech, does Howells show Lindau advocating the destruction of life or property or calling for violent revolution. It is only the *tone* of his arguments which is violent, not their content. The sentiments put into his mouth were shared, after all, in part by that gentlemanly Anglophile, Henry James, whose views, though more measured in their expression, still directed their critical thrust at the same objects. 'You are as constantly reminded, no doubt,' he remarks in *The American Scene* (1907), 'that these rises in enjoyed value shrink and dwindle under the icy breath of Trusts and the weight of the new remorseless monopolies that operate as no madnesses of ancient personal power thrilling us on the historic page ever operated. ... There is such a thing, in the United States, it is hence to be inferred, as freedom to grow up to be blighted, and it may be the only freedom in store for the smaller fry of future generations.'[9]

Howells's solitary stand in defence of the Chicago anarchists had taught him that the conservative prejudices of a large section of the American public, including his friends, required undermining and not reinforcement. In the light of the Haymarket affair any characterisation of a left-wing opponent of *laissez-faire* capitalism as a bomb-throwing hothead would have seemed reprehensible to Howells since it was upon such vicious caricature that a conscienceless repression had based itself. Consequently, Howells takes pains to portray Lindau as a highly cultured, patriotic (he is an injured veteran of the American Civil War), compassionate and justly embittered man. However, he was also aware of the limitations of his audience, and he knew that such socialistic views could not be put forward in the novel unless they were at least formally, if not polemically, countered. The process of emasculating Lindau's subversive critique is accomplished first by the careful rendering of the German accent, which emphasises his foreignness, and secondly, by the Marches' evasion or complacent rejection of his arguments.

The Marches represent the liberal centre, half-way between the callous Social Darwinism of Dryfoos senior and the uncompromising socialism of Lindau. Basil March, humane, observant, critical, is, in the Jamesian phrase, 'the centre of revelation' of the novel, and the story charts his deepening unease as his traditional ideology of Jeffersonian individualism and egalitarianism is forced to come to terms with the brute realities and inequalities of urban-industrial America. On his arrival, New York seems a personal, hospitable place. The familiar hotels and restaurants welcome him and his wife and reception clerks and waiters remember their names. Their initial image of the city is thus inevitably coloured by their financial and class security, and they do not suffer the dispiriting anonymity which is often the fate of the newcomer to the metropolis. Although the city is teeming with thousands of immigrants, these do not threaten the Bostonian Marches with 'dispossession' of their Americanness as they would with Henry James.[10] Rather, the Marches take pleasure in the impression that Southern Europe has been transported across the Atlantic and, like tourists in their own city, they relish the sights and sounds of the ethnically diverse neighbourhoods. To them the immigrants are so 'picturesque' and 'gay', an exclusively aesthetic appreciation that denies the human reality of poverty. 'I don't find so much misery in New York', Basil announces complacently to his wife. Gradually, Howells displaces this bland view of the city as colourful spectacle by showing how a growing acquaintance with the suffering of the poor deepens and humanises the Marches' response.

To appreciate fully the mild, and probably self-deprecatory, irony with which Howells depicts the Marches' accommodation to an uncomfortable social awareness we must recall a telling sociological detail. Howells informs us several times over that the Marches receive an unearned income of 2000 dollars from stocks together with an unspecified rent from their house in Boston. As we have noted, the average working wage at this time was one dollar fifteen cents a day, or about 400 dollars annually, assuming a full year's work. Howells, therefore, means us to recognise that the Marches are comparatively well-off and that they belong in a moderate way to the propertied class. As sensitive, humane people they may come to have sympathy for the poor, but they could never, as Lindau does, express solidarity with them since to do so would clash with their own class and material interests. This tension between altruism and egoism in which the Marches are caught and the shifts they adopt in order to resolve or evade its contradictions provide the novel's central ideological issues.

The Marches, as relatively prosperous citizens of the republic, are convinced of the essential rightness of the American social system and, as members of the petty bourgeoisie, they cling to its ideology of individualism and egalitarianism. Lindau tries to expose that ideology to them as false consciousness in the light of contemporary conditions, but they resist his criticisms, preferring the security of their reassuring middle-class values. It alarmed Mrs March 'to hear American democracy denounced as a shuffling evasion' and to be told that 'there was not equality of opportunity in America', and Basil dismisses Lindau's ideas as 'false' even though he himself recognises the loss of the old egalitarian society and the rise of an aristocracy in fact if not in name. It is part of Howells's irony that despite March's growing perception of the arrogance of the *nouveaux riches* and the undeserved suffering of the urban poor, he does not shift his ideological stance until his own material prospects and middle-class lifestyle are threatened by the collapse of the journal. The sudden possibility of having to struggle himself in a hostile social world inclines him to a much more cynical view of American civilisation: 'Some one always has you by the throat, unless you have some one else in *your* grip.' He has arrived at Jacob Dryfoos's conception of society as Darwinian struggle, but unlike Dryfoos he finds such a state of affairs reprehensible for the individual corruption it entails: 'So we go on, pushing and pulling, climbing and crawling, thrusting aside and trampling underfoot; lying, cheating, stealing; and when we get to the end, covered with blood and dirt and sin and shame, and look back over the way we've come ... I don't think the retrospect can be pleasing.'

March, Howells's liberal representative, tends to think of society largely in moral categories and sees capitalists and entrepreneurs naively in individual, ethical terms as men of ill will or good will. He criticises Jacob Dryfoos for his moral decay but not for his social parasitism as a speculator on Wall Street, and he seems unable to see (as Howells seems unable) that membership of the property-owning class inevitably involved the selfishness of living off the work of others. Yet in the compromises of viewpoint Basil is forced into, Howells does present a half-hearted adoption of social determinism.

In the moralist-individualist perspective derived from Protestantism the blame for conditions lies not with the social structure but with personal character. Mrs March propounds this view, but her husband, while partly agreeing, also significantly qualifies it: 'We can't put it all on the conditions; we must put some of the blame on character. But conditions *make* character; and people are greedy and foolish, and wish to have and to shine, because having and shining are held up to them by civilisation as the chief good of life.' This mild determinism with its insight into the conditioning to which individual values and behaviour are subject represents the farthest point of the Marches' education into the nature of the new socio-economic order. Towards the close of the novel there is a retreat from the understanding gained and the book's conclusion is marked by a conservative reassertion of the continuing reality of American democracy and egalitarianism as Lindau's views are finally dismissed as 'wrong'. *A Hazard of New Fortunes* then, like *The Rise of Silas Lapham*, represents the testing of a traditional ideology against a complex contemporary situation and the eventual validation of that ideology. Unconvincingly, Christian moralism and middle-class values (and middle-class income!) are left secure at the end so that the novel's departing note is one of comfort and reassurance. It is to the climactic strike scene that we have to look for any audacity in Howells's presentation of social conflict.

In the year he moved to New York Howells came face to face

with the war between capital and labour when a serious traction strike was called. The dispute lasted for months and erupted into violence when the company brought in strike-breakers and every car had to be guarded by police. Howells uses this strike to bring his plot to a dramatic head and to provide a focal event around which the contrasting social perspectives of the main characters are brought into relief. Basil March, petty-bourgeois intellectual, decides to stand on the side-lines and be a 'philosophical observer' of the struggle between the workers and owners; Jacob Dryfoos, millionaire speculator, is not so detached, regarding the strikers as a 'pack of dirty, worthless whelps' who deserve to be shot; and Conrad, his Christian Socialist son, believes they have 'a righteous cause, though they go the wrong way to help themselves'. Even this gentle assertion of support is too much for the speculator embittered at his son's class betrayal and he hits him, causing a wound on the temple. Subsequently, Conrad comes upon a violent scene in which strikers are being attacked by the police and there sees Lindau taunting the lawmen and about to be clubbed to the ground. As he moves to the old man's rescue he is shot through the heart, and Basil March (by one of those strained coincidences Howells occasionally resorts to in the novel) finds the two bodies of Conrad and Lindau lying together on the pavement. It is an intense and emotive passage of social drama and a close reading reveals how Howells uses certain details to manipulate our feelings against the police and, by implication, in favour of Lindau and the strikers.

He emphasises the brutality of the police; when they attack the strikers, 'Conrad could see how they struck them under the rims of their hats; the blows on their skulls sounded as if they had fallen on stone.' He reminds us of Lindau's age and patriarchal dignity just before the old German becomes a target, and of his infirmity and self-sacrifice during the Civil War when he throws up his arm to protect himself and Conrad sees 'the empty sleeve dangle in the air, over the stump of his wrist'. Conrad, it seems, is shot by a policeman. This is left unclear, but since the bullet came from the tramcar which had police guards it is a plausible deduction. The specific and general culpability of the police is further indicated by Conrad's perception on immediately being shot of the policeman who is clubbing Lindau. His face 'was not bad, nor cruel; it was like the face of a statue, fixed, perdurable; a mere image of irresponsible and involuntary authority'. In one remarkable moment of insight Howells succinctly conveys the petrifaction of the human responses and the abdication of moral responsibility – the pejorative tone of that 'irresponsible' is forceful – the dehumanisation in short that the policeman has undergone during his metamorphosis from individual to 'authority'.

Howells thus makes it plain that Conrad and Lindau are both victims of police repression, a repression that is associated in two ways with the ruling class.[11] Before being clubbed into silence, the indomitable old socialist accuses the police of being the partisan agents of the bosses and physical violence as an aspect of authority is embodied directly before the strike passage in Jacob Dryfoos, arrogant millionaire. Why does Howells have Dryfoos hit his son? It seems unlikely that a writer of his mature artistry would have engineered the incident solely to exploit some coffin-side sentimentality later. The wounding is surely intended to prefigure the mortal wounding by the police and the blow of the authoritarian father against the son's opposition is the dramatic equivalent of the violence of the ruling class against those who, however slightly, threatened its domination. That Dryfoos is himself an indirect victim of that violence is, of course, an irony calculated to enforce the pacifist point that those who advocate the use of brute force against others may themselves come to suffer by it. 'I should hardly like to trust pen and ink with all the audacity of my social ideas', Howells wrote, and he seems to be conveying dramatically here what he dare not have made explicit. Interpreted in this way, *A Hazard of New Fortunes* reveals more tensions in its attitudes than are superficially apparent, and it shows how bravely, if finally inadequately, Howells came to grips in literary terms with the problems posed for traditional American values by society's polarisation into rich and poor.

As we have seen in the previous chapter, Dreiser possessed a widely differing view from Howells both of American life and the fiction required to express it. Dreiser's interpretation of current society was heavily influenced by his own social experience, an experience that impressed upon him the poles of poverty and success which governed the metropolitan world. He had known at first hand what poverty was like and how rigidly society was gradated when as a boy he had followed his large family from one Midwestern town to another as his father, an economic failure, sought work. His upbringing provided that haunting fear of penury which forms a bass undertone to both *Sister Carrie* and *Jennie Gerhardt*, and he was able to draw on his family for some of the details of both their plots.[12] His work as a city newspaperman also brought him into contact with many of the sordid aspects of urban life and highlighted the fatuity of the traditional ethical codes.[13]

Like Norris, Dreiser found Howells's novels too tame, and the aesthetic qualities of style and craftsmanship which render *The Rise of Silas Lapham* and *A Hazard of New Fortunes* a continuing pleasure mattered little to the Naturalists. To them the mere recording of the changes occurring during their particularly dynamic phase of American history was a far too urgent, and indeed mammoth, task for much consideration to be spared for the refinement of narrative art. Looking back on *Sister Carrie*, Dreiser said, 'It is not intended as a piece of literary craftsmanship, but as a picture of conditions done as simply and effectively as the English language will permit.'[14] The pictorial analogy reveals the positivistic assumptions, characteristic of the production-oriented phase, that Dreiser held about the relation of art to reality, assumptions that had their basis in a crudely empirical model of perception, as the beginning of Chapter 29 indicates: 'Things new are too important to be neglected, and mind, which is a mere reflection of sensory impressions, succumbs to the flood of objects.' *Sister Carrie* is, of course, far more a created fiction than Dreiser's conception of it as transparent *reportage* would have us believe. Yet, despite the imaginative reshaping of family material which forms the kernel of the novel and despite the stylistic lapses into the language of sentimental fiction, the novel displays Dreiser's documentary aim well to the fore in many sections.[15]

From the opening pages describing Carrie Meeber's journey to, and arrival in, Chicago, it is apparent that Dreiser conceives of himself as adding to the historical record of American life. Of Drouet, the salesman whom Carrie meets on the train, he writes: 'Lest this order of individual should permanently pass, let me put down some of the most striking characteristics of his most successful manner and method.' And there follows a description which concentrates not on his personally unique qualities but on the typical attributes of the 'drummer' that he embodies. Dreiser was explicit on the social positions of his three protagonists for he wished to indicate that part of their significance lay in their being representative sociological types of the era. If Drouet was 'a type of the travelling canvasser', Carrie was 'a fair example of the middle American class', and Hurstwood 'was altogether a very acceptable individual of our great American upper class – the first grade below the luxuriously rich'.

Sister Carrie can best be viewed as an arc with two varieties of urban poverty at its poles. The ascendant is formed by Carrie's rise out of the 'lean and narrow life' of the working-class Hansons to eventual Broadway success, and the descendant is composed of Hurstwood's decline from upper-middle-class security to the hunger and despair of the Bowery. This upward and downward movement is expressive of Dreiser's sensitivity to social mobility and to the indices of class and status which measure that mobility. In the competitive, atomistic society he paints everyone is both above and below someone else, and it is impossible for people to meet as genuine equals. Carrie's impression on meeting Drouet is 'of an inequality', and she feels superior to her sister workers in the factory. The salesman in turn admires Hurstwood, the manager of Fitzgerald and Moy's, to which resort he is attracted 'by his desire to shine among his betters'. The most common index of social position in anonymous urban society is, of course, dress, and it was clothes which Thorstein Veblen was currently identifying in his *The Theory of the Leisure Class* (1899) as a particular means of pecuniary display. Carrie's sense of inequality with Drouet stems mainly from her impression of those symbols of prosperity, 'the purse, the shiny tan shoes, the smart new suit', which the salesman flaunts, and Hurstwood's status is revealed in his 'excellent tailored suits of imported goods, a solitaire ring, a fine blue diamond in his tie, a striking vest of some new pattern, and a watch-chain of solid gold'. The department store, another expression of Veblen's 'pecuniary culture' and its emergent consumerism, encourages her desire for fine clothes and the status they provide, and her observation of the rich as they parade on Broadway keenly exacerbates that desire later.

In *Sister Carrie* Dreiser offers no social explanation of either poverty or riches. Despite his references to 'large forces' and his Spencerian determinism, the fact of mobility in a stratified society inclines him to an individualist interpretation. His 'forces' seem to refer more to the impulses and weaknesses embodied in character than to social conditioning and, consequently, it is still personal attributes which ultimately make and unmake men and women. Carrie's great quality, Dreiser insists but really fails to demonstrate, is her imagination and capacity for growth, and she is superior in this respect both to Drouet and later to Hurstwood.

It is not until New York, over half-way through the novel, that the limiting aspects of Hurstwood's personality are brought to the surface and the main dramatic contrast between Carrie's rise and his decline is set in motion. In Chicago Hurstwood had enjoyed a certain social lustre as the manager of a 'way-up, swell place', but the new, hostile environment dwarfs what previous stature he enjoyed by its metropolitan massiveness and anonymity. 'Whatever a man like Hurstwood could be in Chicago,' Dreiser comments, 'it is very evident that he would be but an inconspicuous drop in an ocean like New York', and with cruel finality he is dismissed as 'nothing'. Shorn of his familiar middle-class role and comfortable surroundings he is revealed as lacking in any real personal core, any ineffaceable source of strength and integrity, a deficiency hinted at in the early description of him as a 'starched and conventional poser among men'. The social basis of Hurstwood's identity, based on an occupation in the service trades where an easy manner and the ability to make a good impression are prerequisites, means that he has no groundrock of principle, no inner direction, with which to guide his life.

In his presentation of Hurstwood, Carrie and Drouet, Dreiser displays his realistic sense of the decline of the Puritan tradition and its clear moral guide-lines. Hurstwood at first appears to be a respectable bourgeois, but his lack of principle is made evident during his indecision about stealing from the open safe when he seems blind to the moral aspects of the act: 'The true ethics of the situation never once occurred to him, and never would have, under any circumstances.' Drouet, as a salesman, is also occupied in a trade which requires an ease of manner and which finds a sharp moral sense a hindrance. With his 'insatiable love of variable pleasure', his women friends, and his mind 'free of any consideration of the problems or forces of the world' he seems devoid of any ethical notions at all. Carrie, we are told, 'had no excellent home principles fixed upon her', and so she too is without the inner direction which an early and strict training from elders might have provided. Later, Dreiser rather redundantly makes explicit what he has already successfully dramatised, namely, that Carrie's behaviour is dictated not by principle but by convention. Hers is not the stern, value-laden conscience of the Protestant; hers 'was only an average little conscience, a thing which represented the world, her past environment, habit, convention, in a confused way'. And for such a conscience popular opinion has replaced the omniscient Deity as the final arbiter: 'With it, the voice of the people was truly the voice of God.' She allows herself to become Drouet's mistress, and then when Hurstwood takes her from Chicago on false pretences she allows 'the drift of things' to make her his as well.

In New York financial failure and unemployment uncover the debilitating weakness in Hurstwood's character and in a last desperate effort to prove his independence and regain his self-respect he takes a job as a strike-breaker during a streetcar stoppage. The 'Strike' chapter is a powerful episode of industrial violence informed by Dreiser's memory of a streetcar strike he covered as a reporter in Toledo in 1894 and his researches into the hard-fought Brooklyn streetcar dispute of 1895.[16] During it and until Hurstwood's suicide the condition of the city's poor becomes one of the binary themes of this last section of the novel. Dreiser, however, despite his judgement of Howells as too tame, uses the strike to present far fewer issues than did the older writer in *A Hazard of New Fortunes*. It is not class conflict or social injustice that the strike serves to present and explore but another stage in Hurstwood's decline. Initially, the ex-manager feels superior and patronising towards the other strike-breakers, and then in a fine moment Dreiser shows Hurstwood being offered the opportunity to shake off the atomising, competitive individualism which can provide no way out of his predicament. One of the striking drivers who have forcibly stopped his streetcar asks him, 'Come down, pardner, and be a man. Don't fight the poor. Leave that to the corporations.' Dreiser could have been tempted to make an easy didactic point here and have Hurstwood join the strikers in their collective action as the only effective solution to his problems, but he sticks to the unerring realism of his presentation instead, by having Hurstwood fail to identify with that class to which he now objectively belongs and so turn down the appeal to human solidarity. In lucid, restrained prose Dreiser then portrays the typical hunger and hopelessness of the New York unemployed as experienced by Hurstwood until he kills himself in a Bowery rooming house.

The other, contrasting theme in this part of the book is Carrie's rise to success in the Broadway world of the stage. From the beginning her main drive has been directed to escaping the cramping drabness of poverty and she uses her lovers, Drouet and Hurstwood, as means to that end. But her ambition, we are meant to believe, has not been purely materialistic, for once her financial needs are fulfilled by well-paid theatre-work, her 'imagination', Dreiser stresses unconvincingly, her sense of the possibilities of life, still leaves her vaguely dissatisfied with the present. This aspect of Carrie as the questing soul comes into contradiction with the determinist viewpoint which underlies most of the novel. Although Carrie possesses little strength of will, her haunting sense of the possible and hence of the inadequacy of the actual carries her above determinacy to indeterminacy. Thus, while Hurstwood discovers the city as the harsh realm of necessity, Carrie discovers it as the bright realm of freedom, a complex dual vision which successfully renders the dialectic of metropolitan social life.

Dreiser's presentation of American society at the turn of the century, then, emphasises the contrasts of success and failure, riches and penury, thrown up by that society. It also indicates the ways in which the traditional value-systems, Puritanism and Jeffersonian individualism, had lost much of their force in a metropolitan environment which was creating new social types and bringing new pressures to bear on personal character. Dreiser could never devote a whole novel to the condition of the poor since the irresistible allure of success was also one of his persistent themes, but Upton Sinclair, who was much more concerned with producing a 'literature of exposure' than was Dreiser, could and did. [17]

In *The Jungle* Sinclair brings the foreign immigrants who are only in the wings of *A Hazard of New Fortunes* on to full centre-stage and he depicts the immigrants' inhuman lot not from a middle-class observer's viewpoint but from the perspective of a Lithuanian worker. Having read Sinclair's earlier novel, *Manassas* (1904), based on the Civil War, the editor of the socialist weekly *Appeal to Reason* had written to him suggesting that since he had described the struggle against chattel slavery he should now do the same for wage slavery. Accordingly, Sinclair spent seven weeks in the autumn of 1904 in the Packingtown district of

Chicago where the meat-packing workers had just lost a bitter strike, collecting oral documentary material. The living and working conditions he found there were appalling and in transcribing these directly into his novel he produced a powerful portrait of 'those sunk in the innermost depths of the modern *Inferno*'.[18]

The rapidly developing industrial economy drew upon the dispossessed of all the countries of Europe for a supply of cheap labour, and net immigration between 1881 and 1910 amounted to 12.5 million people, or one third of the total increase in population in the United States. The overwhelming majority of the newcomers were crowded into the tenement areas of the big cities, and the problems of urbanisation were compounded by the different languages and religious affiliations of the Slavic and Latin races of Central and Southern Europe who dominated this wave of immigration.[19] These immigrants represented the condition of the American working class *in extremis*, since in addition to insecurity and exploitation they had to bear with being strangers in a strange land. To survive, and to rise, they had to break the ties with home and shed their own languages and customs. This process of deracination, whilst it was liberating in some respects, inevitably involved a large element of loss. The culture of their European origin provided them with a social code, rituals to mark the important events of life, a language and a social identity. To lose this culture and its folklore – and many immigrant groups strenuously resisted such a loss – was to be denuded of much of one's humanity and, in the absence of any compensatory acculturation, to be degraded to the level of animals or machines. In order to demonstrate this degradation and dramatise it by contrast, Sinclair opens *The Jungle* not with the story's chronological starting point but with the focal occasion of the wedding feast.

Jurgis's marriage to Ona and the subsequent celebration are carried out 'in due form, and after the best home traditions', for the feast or *veselija* is a vestige of Lithuanian folkways to which the immigrants have clung tenaciously. Through his lively and finely realised description Sinclair intimates the richly human and densely communal texture of the peasant society they have left behind. Here is animation, joy, trust, fellowship, music, dancing, intensely felt life. It is all in telling contrast to the atomistic individualism which *laissez-faire* capitalism is enforcing in the streets outside. 'It was one of the laws of the *veselija* that no one goes hungry', and the impecunious hosts do their best to meet the obligations of traditional hospitality, but their efforts are poignantly out of place. The social system they have brought with them from the forests of Lithuania and temporarily resurrected in the Chicago stockyards is based upon human reciprocity, upon the tacit acquiescence of all in the give and take of ritual customs: 'The *veselija* is a compact, a compact not expressed, but therefore only the more binding upon all. Everyone's share was different – and yet everyone knew perfectly well what his share was, and strove to give a little more.' Such accepted responsibilities, Sinclair shows, were rapidly being eroded by the egoism fostered by the competitive economic climate. Many of the young men do not honour the compact but brazenly avoid paying their share towards the cost of the wedding feast.

Other customs too are quickly dying in the inhospitable air of Packingtown. 'The older people have dances from home' and wear 'clothing reminiscent in some detail of home', but all 'these things are carefully avoided by the young, most of whom have learned to speak English and to affect the latest style of clothing'. It was characteristic of immigrant youth that they were eager to slough off the vestiges of Europe and assimilate themselves to the American way of life.[20] By the backward-looking glimpse it provides of a fast vanishing tradition the dramatic presentation of the *veselija* heightens our impression of the spiritual impoverishment and cultural insecurity of the immigrants. This retrospective orientation is reinforced by Sinclair's shift of focus from the wedding feast to an account of life in Lithuania and then the coming of Jurgis and the others to America.

In 'The Physiognomy of "The Poor"' Howells drew attention to an extra dimension he thought poverty in the United States held for the immigrant. 'The physiognomy of the poor', he wrote, 'varies from land to land and from age to age. It expresses patience, and despair, or oblivion everywhere, but in our country there is conjecturable also a certain surprise, the bewilderment of people who have been taught to expect better things of life, and who have fallen to the ground through the breaking of a promise. Was this, their faces ask, really the meaning of the glad new world?'[21] Jurgis and his family come to America expecting prosperity and freedom and are full of pitiful illusions. Packingtown to them 'seemed a dream of wonder, with its tale of human energy, of things being done, of employment for thousands upon thousands of men, of opportunity and freedom, of life and love and joy'. This is Sinclair's savagely ironical articulation of the 'promise' of life in America. At first, Jurgis, optimistic about his own future and confident of the rightness of the American system, does not believe the disturbing stories he hears of men being broken down and of the trickery of big business. Then step by step Sinclair charts his loss of naivety and his disillusionment as the promise of prosperity turns out to be a sham and he is gradually broken down until he comes to the awful realisation that he too has become one of 'the worn-out parts of the great merciless packing machine'. The other members of his family are similarly broken down and forced by the brutally competitive existence to descend ever lower into the social pit.

As the title of the novel indicates, American society in Sinclair's Social Darwinian view is an arena in which a ferocious tooth and claw struggle for existence takes place. Jurgis soon learns that people get on only through others' misfortunes and comes to the conclusion that 'it was a war of each against all, and the devil take the hindmost'. The intense competition between individuals is compounded for the immigrant, Sinclair points out, by the competition between different national groups. 'The competition of races', James Bryce noted, 'is the competition of standards of living. . . . The race with the lowest necessities displaces others.'[22] Jurgis and his family, having once benefited by this competition, eventually find themselves undermined by it as new, less demanding arrivals drive wages down: 'The Poles, who had come by tens of thousands, had been driven to the wall by the Lithuanians, and now the Lithuanians were giving way to the Slovaks. Who were poorer and more miserable than the Slovaks, Grandmother Majauszkiene had no idea, but the packers would find them, never fear.'

During the course of *The Jungle* Sinclair exposes many of the major oppressions and injustices suffered by the American working class under industrial capitalism as it then operated. First of all there is the detailed specification of the work in the packing factories, a specification which substantiates Sinclair's passionate indictment of the alienating, dehumanising character of much industrial labour: 'It was stupefying, brutalizing work; it left her no time to think, no strength for anything. She was part of the machine she tended, and every faculty that was not needed for the machine was doomed to be crushed out of existence.' Then there is the long catalogue of the subsistence level of the wages, the economic insecurity caused by repeated lay-offs, the horrific working conditions, and the shame of child labour. He also brings into the public eye those endemic diseases of the poor – tuberculosis, pneumonia, rheumatism, infant mortality, and premature ageing and death. He demonstrates that Jurgis and his family's descent into the social pit cannot be explained in ethical terms as being due to the immorality and shiftlessness of individuals (as Howells's Marches tend to think), but only in social terms as the result of *laissez-faire* capitalism and the callous greed of big business.

Sinclair's dramatisation of the workers' plight never lapses into sentimentality but is shot through with a compassionate humanity, and the indignation which gives the prose much of its power occasionally breaks through the mask of fiction to address the reader directly. 'This is no fairy story and no joke', Sinclair bursts out at one of those moments when he seems to lose patience with the novel form and tries to impress upon the reader that the barbarity being described is no imaginative creation but a hideous social reality. He shared the documentary methods of Norris and Dreiser, but as a polemical writer he was concerned not simply with recording conditions but also with changing them.

This activist stance is represented in his portrayal of the poor as not only a suffering class but also as a rebellious and potentially revolutionary class. When Jurgis joins the union he discovers a solidarity with his fellow workers which the divisive individualism of a competitive society has denied him; he found he had 'brothers in affliction, and allies', and realised 'their one chance for life was in union'. But the fight for survival later drives him to work against the union during the big Beef Strike and to take part in violent attacks upon the strikers. Then, one evening after he has experienced the sham democracy of the political bosses, he wanders, homeless and friendless, into a Socialist Party meeting. There he discovers socialism in terms reminiscent of religious conversion: 'It was a miracle that had been wrought in him . . . a new man had been born.' Jurgis's adoption of socialism is, of course, a dramatic expression of Sinclair's own political viewpoint and a logical extension of his critique of capitalism. Despite the suddenness and the obvious tendentiousness of this development it is prepared for within the narrative scheme. Sinclair has taken his representative immigrant through all the alternative responses to his condition – optimism, disillusionment, escape as a hobo, individual rebellion, conscientious work, crime, election racketeering – and demonstrated that no way out exists for him within 'the system'. Socialism alone, he proclaims, could offer the harried workman hope for the future.

Contemporary developments lent weight to this claim. In the Chicago election of 1904 the Socialist Party made some astonishing gains and in the heady days before the First World War was increasing its membership by leaps and bounds. The socialist weekly *Appeal to Reason* had a circulation of half a million in 1904 and in the presidential election of 1912 Eugene Debs, the Socialist Party candidate, was to poll nearly a million votes.[23] It was not unnatural then for Sinclair to feel optimistic that the victory of socialism through the ballot box was near at hand, and he accordingly converts Jurgis and concludes the novel with the exultant expectation of a socialist takeover in Chicago. These final socialist chapters are, however, the least satisfactory artistically. First, as Walter B. Rideout points out, Jurgis as socialist is a far less realised character than Jurgis as suffering worker.[24] This is due partly to the loss of that animus which energised Sinclair's indictment of class oppression but mainly it is due to his failure to integrate the intellectual arguments for a socialist society put forward in the last pages of the book into the specific texture of Jurgis's thought and character. Secondly, the socialist perspective, with its emphasis on men's rational control of their own production, is difficult to reconcile with the Social Darwinian perspective which mystified social processes into natural processes, as Sinclair's own language demonstrates: 'Of these [tramps] there was an army, the huge surplus labour army of society; called into being under the stern system of Nature to do the casual work of the world.' How was socialism expected to change 'the stern system of Nature'? Here again we meet that inconsistency of viewpoint so prevalent among the Naturalists.

The Jungle, despite its faults, remains one of the classic American texts on the condition of the poor and shows Sinclair reaching beyond the aims of *exposé* to bring bourgeois society back into the continuing processes of history. For the novel opens with the dying embers of a peasant past, documents the industrial-capitalist present, and ends with the roseate dawn of a socialist and collectivist future.

PART II
THE CONSUMPTION-
ORIENTED PHASE

5 Software: the Economy, Society and Ideologies of Consumption

As we saw in the Introduction, capitalists of Department I of the economy, that is, manufacturers of heavy industrial goods and suppliers of energy and raw materials, sell their products largely to the capitalists of Department II, manufacturers of personal goods and suppliers of services. In Chapter 1 we noted how the production-oriented economy by the early twentieth century was faced with an excess of capacity and a constriction of investment opportunities. An expansion of the second sector, then, could provide both the extra market and the widening investment field required to counteract these factors for economic stagnation. Owing to the qualitatively different nature of the two sectors, a shift of emphasis from one department to the other would constitute a structural change in the economic base, and such a change would be registered by a marked upswing in personal consumption as the consumer industries of Department II rapidly developed. This is, in fact, what seems to have taken place round about 1920.

Using data drawn from a large number of sources, Louis J. Paradiso made the important observation that the average propensity to consume over the period 1900 to 1920 did not continue into the 1920s and 1930s but took an abrupt upward turn. Consumer expenditures for the same amount of disposable income were generally about five billion dollars higher in the years after 1920 than before. He also found that the ratio of the savings of individuals to their disposable income declined from an annual average of 16 per cent in the period 1910 to 1920 to an annual average of 9 per cent in the period 1921 to 1940. Also, H. T. Oshima has shown that in the American economy of the post-First World War period producer or fixed-asset production ceased to dominate the total production of durables and structures, and was replaced as the leading characteristic of the economy by the formation of consumer assets, that is, the purchase of dwellings and durables by households corresponding respectively to the purchase of factories and machinery by business. In his conclusion he propounded the view that this development of the consumer sector was 'a natural outcome of the maturation of the business sector of the capitalist economy' and did indeed mark a new phase of capitalism. Walter Rostow is another exponent of the view that a structural change occurred in the American economy. He sees a shift from the phase of 'the drive to maturity' to the phase of 'high mass consumption' as having happened round about 1920, and regards the cheap mass automobile as the decisive element.[1]

The motor car industry, with its demands for capital goods such as steel and heavy machinery and its rich possibilities for capital absorption, provided the model solution to the problems of excess capacity and surplus capital that had arisen in Department I. The turning point in its development was Henry Ford's moving assembly line of 1914, a far-reaching technical innovation which enabled automobile manufacturing to become the fastest growing industry of the period. By the mid-1920s it was providing employment for 7 per cent of the total work-force and consuming 15 per cent of total steel output.[2] Ford's Model T was the first cheap, mass-produced car and, as such, the first significant consumer durable. Ford, then, was one of the initiators of the consumer phase of the American economy and in his attitudes as a businessman he heralded a whole new approach. 'Industry must manage to keep wages high and prices low', he told the Press, 'otherwise, it will limit the number of its customers. One's own employees should be one's own best customers.'[3] He cut the factory day from nine to eight hours and raised the daily wage to five dollars (twice the highest common labour wage) in 1914, a policy that was in marked contrast to the traditional attitude of employers, who paid as little as possible and kept their employees near to subsistence level. Employers in the past viewed the workman solely as a producer, but Ford viewed him also as a consumer and he realised from the start that industrial as his enterprise was, it was a different kind of industry, one that sold its commodities not to other capitalists but to the ordinary public; in other words, an industry of Department II.

Ford's attempt to provide his workers with purchasing power was based not upon any altruistic desire to improve their lot but upon an intuitive grasp of the new consumer economics, in which the crucial factor became the speed with which the product could be sold. As we have seen, the rate of profit is dependent upon the rate of turnover which in turn is dependent upon the lengths of the productive and circulation phases, and while the moving assembly line enabled Ford markedly to reduce the time of production, he could secure a cut in the time of circulation only by rapid sales. Mass production demanded, and, by keeping prices low and creating high wages, brought into being, the mass market. Through the efforts of Ford and his main rival, General Motors, the mass ownership of cars became one of the distinctive features of the 1920s. Factory sales rose from a mere 4000 in 1900 to nearly a million in 1918, doubled in the next two years, and climbed steadily through the decade to reach a peak of four and a half million in 1929, a sales record for automobiles that was not equalled again until 1946.[4]

It was during the 1920s (particularly after the recession of 1920–1) that the industries of Department II came to dominate the American economy. Not only cars but every other type of consumer durable came to be produced and sold on a mass scale during these years. Sales of radios and electrical equipment, for instance, rose from 28 million dollars to over 388 million dollars between 1922 and 1929.[5] According to Rostow, 'that decade is ... to be understood as the first protracted period in which a society absorbed the fruits and consequences of the age of durable consumers' goods and services', and in the view of Peter d'A. Jones much that is typical of the American consumer economy came into being in the 1920s.[6] Of course, the heavy industries of Department I were still very active and their output increased every year, but they had ceased to represent the growing points of the economy. They were rapidly being overlayered as the dominant characteristic of the economic base by the developing consumer goods sector.

Closely allied with this development was a shift of focus from the difficulties of the production phase to those of the circulation phase. The 1920s saw massive increases in both productive capacity (GNP rose 40 per cent from 1919 to 1929) and worker productivity (output per man hour in manufacturing rose from 42 in 1919 to 72 in 1929, taking productivity in 1947 as an index of 100).[7] There seemed to be no limit to how much the nation could produce. As the distinguished group of social scientists who composed the Committee on Recent Social Changes commented in their report *Recent Economic Changes* (1929), 'never before has the human race made such progress in solving the problem of production'.[8] The result of such advances, however, for consumer industries as well as for capital goods industries, was to raise the spectre of chronic overproduction. The Brookings Institute report, *America's Capacity to Produce and America's Capacity to Consume* (1933), revealed that available plant worked at only 80 per cent capacity from 1925 to 1929, and its contributors observed that 'if each industry would run to its full capacity huge surpluses of some goods would no doubt soon pile up'.[9] The problem facing the 1920s was to create new techniques of mass consumption to meet the new techniques of mass production. A far-reaching alteration in the character of capitalism had taken place. While the phase of industrial capitalism had faced the challenge of production, of how to make enough of life's essentials, the phase of consumer capitalism faced the new challenge of maintaining aggregate demand,[10] and whereas the traditional problems of economics had been related to scarcity, those facing the age of 'high mass consumption' were related to abundance. But how was aggregate demand to be maintained? How were hardheaded, thrifty Americans to be induced to spend money on goods they did not really need? The problem facing production-oriented capitalism had been the 'hardness of the material', the physical problems of manufacture itself, but the major problem in the consumption-oriented phase was the resistance of the consumer. The need to maintain or increase market demand led to a heavy focus on *selling*, and the closely related need to overcome consumer resistance led to the adoption of three main strategies – ceaseless product innovation, consumer credit and intensive advertising.

The automobile industry set the pattern for all the other consumer durable industries by pioneering these strategies. In 1928 Ford brought out his Model A in order to counter the drop in sales of his Model T, but whereas the first model had remained in production for fifteen years, the Model A lasted only five. Ford's competitors, General Motors and Chrysler, made it obsolete, not in performance but in appearance.[11] They modified and elaborated the style and visual appeal of their models, while Ford, with a farm-mechanic's functional view of machinery, found it difficult to adapt to the rise of fashion in the world of car manufacture. Unnecessary product innovation or planned obsolescence was early adopted by the big car makers (including Ford later) to maintain demand, as each year new models, bearing no significant functional improvement, appeared in the showrooms and rendered the previous models out-of-date. Owning the newest type of car became one of the main ways in which people could trumpet their business and financial success. Other consumer industries, in despair at the durability of their products which simply would not wear out as fast as they were made, adopted the same methods.[12] Radios and electrical goods were soon to sport style-features, the sole purpose of which was to emphasise the age and unattractiveness of the earlier models.

Consumer credit, or hire purchase, also made its appearance in the 1920s through the efforts of the automobile industry. In 1925 General Motors financed an academic study, *The Economics of Instalment Selling*, to test the soundness of consumer credit, and on the basis of its findings set up a credit agency to facilitate the purchase of its products.[13] This was so successful it was adopted by other consumer industries such as electrical goods, and it constituted a major factor in making mass consumerism possible. In 1929, it has been estimated, instalment sales approximated to some 7 billion dollars.[14] A related development that also encouraged consumer habits was the growth of the chain department store, the number of which rose from 29 000 in 1918 to 160 000 in 1929.[15]

A further important factor in maintaining aggregate demand that was quickly exploited by the automobile industry was advertising. Money spent on periodical advertising by the car manufacturers rose from 5 million dollars in 1915 to 23 million dollars in 1929. Other consumer industries soon followed suit and mounted their own intensive advertising campaigns, bringing about a growth in the total volume of expenditure on advertising from nearly 1500 million dollars in 1918 to nearly 3500 million dollars in 1929.[16] Advertising had been common in American newspapers since they began, but it had been largely of a straightforward, informative character with little irrational impact, since pictorial display was either prohibited or discouraged.[17] But a marked qualitative change accompanied the huge quantitative increase of advertising in the 1920s. Advertisers increasingly resorted to irrational appeals and drew upon J. B. Watson's behavioural psychology to manipulate the subconscious needs of the consumer. Watson himself left Johns Hopkins University to become vice-president of an advertising agency.[18]

Closely associated with advertising, public relations also rose to prominence in the 1920s. Many of the men who set themselves up as public relations counsellors received their training in ideological manipulation in George Creel's Committee on Public Information, which was responsible for the anti-German propaganda aimed at Americans during the First World War.[19] Companies aware of the importance of their 'image' began to hire these counsellors, as the Rockefellers hired Ivy Lee, to improve the impression that the general public had of them. Standard devices used were favourable news releases, articles planted in ostensibly independent magazines, and advertisements which did not sell a product so much as promote a particular quality such as size or progressiveness that the company wished to project. Such expensive efforts to influence public opinion were a far cry from the 'public-be-damned' attitude of William Vanderbilt and the other aggressive, individualistic entrepreneurs of the nineteenth century, but in a consumer economy companies depended upon customer approval for the sale of their products as well as for forestalling any hostile legislation which might otherwise be enacted.

The structural change in the economy, augmented by these selling strategies, led to a massive growth in personal consumption comparable only to the 1950s and 1960s. As well as the spectacular increase in cars, telephones increased from 13 million to 20 million between 1920 and 1929; the number of families with a radio rose from 60000 in 1922 to 10 million in 1929; annual sales of vacuum cleaners amounted to 40 million dollars in 1925, of electric cookers to 20 million dollars in 1927, and of refrigeration equipment to 167 million dollars in 1929. Estimated expenditure on recreation also doubled in the decade 1919 to 1929 with mass entertainment such as movies and records showing a great increase.[20] In the 1920s a revolution in the texture of everyday personal and social life was taking place as American society truly became consumption-oriented.

By the 1920s too, the age of 'the captains of industry' was virtually at a close, brought to an end by the massive centralisation of capital which took place in the 1890s, 1900s and 1920s. In

1900, 31 per cent of top executives had been entrepreneurs but in 1925 only 20 per cent had been so.[21] Mergers took place in all fields of business —public utilities, iron and steel, food, textiles, chemicals and films. Between 1919 and 1930 some 8000 businesses disappeared as a result of the merger movement. In 1919 there were 80 bank mergers while in 1927 there were 259. Chrysler took over Dodge Brothers in 1928 and Palmolive merged with Colgate.[22] Berle and Means noted in their study *The Modern Corporation and Private Property* (1932) that whereas in 1909 the 200 largest non-financial companies held about one third of all corporate wealth, by 1929 they held nearly half of all corporate assets and over one fifth of the entire wealth of the nation. They also noted that as a result of this consolidation of commercial power 'the principles of duopoly have become more important than those of free competition'.[23] The giant semi-monopolistic corporation had, therefore, become a significant feature of the American economy, and it contributed in two main ways to that complex social transformation I have characterised as a shift from production to consumption.

The first lay in the necessity of employing a large bureaucracy of trained personnel to run the corporation. This was partly a function of the separation of ownership and control which Berle and Means also commented upon, ownership being exercised through the stock market and possession of stock while control was exercised by a salaried manager who commonly replaced the owner-director of the nineteenth-century firm. The corporation had become too large and too diverse to be administered by only a few men without any formal training. At his disposal the executive manager now had a whole pyramidal structure of ranked authority and specialised expertise to aid him in his business decisions. The expansion of the company bureaucracies, together with the much heavier emphasis on distribution and selling, resulted in a considerable growth in the number of white-collar workers. In 1900 their number had been half that of manual workers but by 1930 their number together with that of service workers equalled the number of manual workers and by 1940 they easily constituted the dominant proportion of the work-force. During the decade 1920 to 1930 the number of sales workers rose by 50 per cent, of service workers by 45 per cent and of clerical workers by 29 per cent. Another index of the growing importance of white-collar groups in the labour-force is the ratio of their salaries to the wages of production workers; this rose from 19 per cent in 1899 to 29 per cent in 1919 and to 37 per cent in 1929. This decline in the ratio of productive workers' wages is indicative of the decreasing importance of production as American capitalism moved into its new phase.[24]

The second contribution this change in the character of business made was geographical and architectural. The white-collar personnel required offices to work in and the corporations located these in the centres of the large metropolitan cities where, because of high land values, they were extended vertically rather than horizontally. The 1920s were the great years of skyscraper building, with almost 400 of them being built, including the Empire State building, completed in 1930.[25] These tall buildings significantly altered the social environment of the big cities, and the workers they attracted contributed to the continuing process of urbanisation. By 1920 the urban population equalled the rural population for the first time and continued to rise faster than over-all population growth through the decade.[26] The distribution of this rise between the towns and the cities points to the influence of the new forms of business. Towns grew at a slower rate in the 1920s than in any previous decade but the giant metropolitan centres grew dramatically. New York increased by almost one and a half million to seven million; Chicago grew to three and a half million; Detroit doubled to one and a half million; and Los Angeles also doubled in size to one and quarter million.[27] It was the commercial cities then, rather than the manufacturing towns, that experienced the most marked increases during these years. 'The civic force which brought about the concentration of the population in the cities', Lewis Mumford observed, 'was the centralization of the organs of administration in the great capitals, and the growing dependence of every type of enterprise, political, educational, economic, upon the process of administration itself.'[28] Accompanying the rise in the white-collar workforce was a growth of residential suburbs on the outskirts of the big cities. The middle class lived in suburbia and commuted daily to office work in the city centres. This concentration of non-productive workers in the metropolitan centres fostered the emergence of a new urban and suburban lifestyle which was thoroughly assimilated to the new consumer capitalism.

The shift into a consumption-oriented economy manifested in the 1920s was largely arrested during the Depression and war years but resumed with greater intensity in the post-Second-World-War consumer boom.[29] During the war average incomes rose considerably but there were few consumer durables on which they could be spent since most industries had been converted to the production of war *matériel*. As a result, savings reached the record level of one hundred billion dollars during the three years 1942–4 and it was widely expected that this pent-up spending power would boost consumerism when the economy reverted to normal. 'The end of the war will inaugurate the most gigantic sales promotion program in all of our history', a contributor to a symposium on consumption economics prophesied in 1945. 'There is reason to believe', another contributor confidently remarked, 'that high-level consumption may well become the permanent characteristic of our economy.'[30]

As predicted, the sales of consumer durables expanded at an enormous rate during the period 1946 to 1956. In 1946, 69 per cent of houses wired for electricity possessed electric refrigerators while ten years later the proportion had risen to 96 per cent, and the increase was similar for other electrical goods. Television, for instance, was installed in 86 per cent of homes by 1956. In 1946 the annual sale of new cars reached the 1929 level, and the proportion of families owning their own car rose from 54 per cent in 1948 to 73 per cent in 1958.[31] In the five-year period 1953–7 the purchase of major consumer durables amounted to 150 billion dollars and residential construction to 88 billion dollars, a total of 238 billion dollars. This was 120 per cent of the total purchase of equipment and construction by business (197 billion dollars) during this period. Consumer asset formation, which had shown a marked rise during the 1920s, had thus come to exceed capital asset formation by a substantial margin in the 1950s.[32] In the post-war era, then, Department II of the economy became well established as the dominant sector.

Once the war-time savings were spent, the still rapidly increasing consumption was financed more and more by consumer credit. In the earlier post-war period from 1947 to 1950 annual instalment credit extended to consumers amounted to 69 per cent of all consumer goods purchased, but for the later period of 1960–3 this proportion had risen to 88 per cent.[33] The consumer economy, it became evident, was increasingly financed by debt.

'Down through the ages in most places the dominant economic problem has been production', Dexter M. Keezer remarks, but 'in an economy of abundance such as that which has been created in the United States successful selling is a key ingredient of successful performance.'[34] To help them sell successfully manufacturers resorted more and more to advertising to bolster aggregate demand, causing the amount spent on it to multiply three-fold during this period from over three billion dollars in 1946 to over ten billion dollars in 1957. Not only was there a quantitative increase but also a qualitative change as depth psychology was extensively employed to manipulate people's responses to consumer goods.[35] Advertising also penetrated the home a great deal more through the sponsoring of radio and television programmes and the use of 'commercial breaks' between programmes. Together with sales promotion there were many other non-productive costs, such as maintaining sales forces, showrooms, prestige office-blocks, public relations and market research, which spiralled during these years. Baran and Sweezy estimate that this whole phase of circulation rose from 5 billion to 29 billion dollars between 1929 and 1963.[36]

The circulation phase, the phase of distribution and selling, had emerged as dominant over the productive phase, its particular demands ramifying back through the organisation to affect the character of the entire mode of production:

A major change in thinking is now making itself felt. Today, the orientation of manufacturing companies is increasingly toward the market and away from production. In fact, this change has gone so far in some cases that the General Electric Company, as one striking example, now conceives itself to be essentially a marketing rather than a production organization. This thinking flows back through the structure of the company, to the point that marketing needs reach back and dictate the arrangement and grouping of production facilities.

The classic pattern of industrial organisation, in which production was the key, had given way to a pattern in which the imperative of selling was saturating every aspect of the industrial process. '*The* business problem shifts from being one of production to being one of marketing, distributing and selling.'[37]

Largely as a result of this shift of emphasis, the white-collar occupational groups – clerks, administrators, accountants, salesmen, managers – grew much faster than the blue-collar groups and came to dominate the labour-force. By 1950 white-collar workers together with service workers outnumbered manual workers by three and a half million, so that production workers in manufacturing became of diminished importance in the over-all pattern of employment.[38] There was a rise in average wages created by an expanding middle class of office workers and management, and this rise in middle income contributed to the consumer boom.[39] These middle-income groups tended to live in suburbia, thus continuing the pre-war trend, and created an increase in the suburban population of 44 per cent between 1950 and 1958, while the urban population proper rose only 4 per cent.[40]

One final index of the economy's emphasis on consumption is the decline in the proportion of capital investment. Total investment in fixed-capital producers' durable equipment and non-residential construction dropped from 10.3 per cent of GNP over the years 1947 to 1957 to 8.6 per cent over the years 1958 to 1964. Of this investment a swelling share was directed into office-blocks, shopping centres, banks and so on, rather than into productive equipment for manufacturing commodities. In 1957, 28 per cent of total expenditures for plant and equipment went into commercial enterprises as distinguished from mining, manufacturing, transport and public utilities, but by 1964 this proportion had risen to 34 per cent.[41] The long-term trend of capital formation over the whole period covered in this brief analysis of the American economy was markedly downward. For the years 1869 to 1888 the ratio of capital formation to GNP was 22 per cent, but in the post-war period 1946 to 1955 it had dropped to 17 per cent.[42] This decline indicates both an increased pressure upon individuals to consume rather than to save and a constricted field of domestic investment as every market became saturated.

According to our adopted conceptual framework – the Marxist formulation of a determining base and a determined super-structure – a change in the American economy from being production-oriented to being consumption-oriented should have effected a corresponding shift in American ideology. Influential commentators on American culture agree that such a shift, originating in the 1920s and continuing in the post-Second World War period, has occurred. David Riesman and his collaborators claim that there was a revolution taking place in the United States, 'a whole range of social developments associated with a shift from an age of production to an age of consumption', and William H. Whyte sees a major change of values in the decline of the Protestant ethic and the rise of 'the Social Ethic'. David M. Potter regards American society as having been reoriented from a producers' into a consumers' culture, and Daniel Bell argues that in the 1920s 'a consumption society was emerging, with its emphasis on spending and material possessions, and it was undermining the traditional value system with its emphasis on thrift, frugality, self-control, and impulse renunciation'. Bell points out that although there was an intellectual attack on traditional values, it was capitalism itself which sent them into decline by means of advertising, the instalment plan and the credit card. Mass consumption, in his view, led to the eclipse of Puritanism and the Protestant ethic and the rise of a consumer hedonism which propagated the idea of pleasure and gratification as a way of life.[43]

There is, inevitably, a time-lag before the ideological realm responds fully to the transforming pressures of economic change, and the ideology of the production phase did not disappear overnight but persisted as an increasingly residual set of values. The success of the Anti-Saloon League in securing nationwide Prohibition through the Eighteenth Amendment in 1920 illustrated the continuing vitality of Puritan moral values. And in 1935, for instance, the Lynds found that there was still a strong emphasis on the Protestant ethic and *laissez-faire* individualism in the Midwestern city of Muncie, Indiana that formed the subject of their famous study.[44] It was not until the 1950s that the hedonistic values of consumerism became dominant, and during the transition period of the 1920s the two ideologies uneasily coexisted in the national culture, a state of affairs summed up in 1933 by the President's Research Committee on Social Trends:

The lingering Puritan tradition of abstinence which makes play, idleness and free spending sin; and the increased secularization of spending and the growing pleasure basis of living.
    The tradition that rigorous saving and paying cash are the marks of sound family economy and personal self-respect; and the new gospel which encourages liberal spending to make the wheels of industry turn as a duty of the citizen.

The deep-rooted philosophy of hardship viewing this stern discipline as the inevitable lot of men; the new attitude toward hardship as a thing to be avoided by living in the here and now, utilizing instalment credit and other devices to telescope the future into the present.[45]

These contradictions within American ideology produced by the emergence of the consumption-oriented economy also lay within the character and aims of business itself: 'On the one hand, the business corporation wants an individual to work hard, pursue a career, accept delayed gratification – to be, in the crude sense, an organization man. And yet, in its products and its advertisements, the corporation promotes pleasure, instant joy, relaxing and letting go.'[46] Such opposing guides to behaviour and the tensions between them could produce considerable confusion on both a social and a personal scale.

While advertising helped undermine the Puritan abstinence which inhibited consumer demand and propagated values and a lifestyle based on consumption, it did not create those values or that lifestyle. Their origin in a society dominated by the production-oriented values of work and thrift and a scarcity psychology can be traced to the rise and influence of a new hegemonic group, the leisure class, whose historic function it was to educate America in the meaning of abundance and make acceptable hedonism, personal consumption and status rivalry.

After the rapid industrialisation and capital accumulation of the late nineteenth century American society had become characterised, like traditional European societies, by great disparities of wealth and income. As we saw in Chapter 1, the rich were a very small minority of the population who enjoyed enormous economic advantages and who had consolidated themselves into a class by the foundation of exclusive boarding schools and country clubs and the establishment of the *Social Register*. Wealth and social position were increasingly transmitted through family connections, and second and third generation descendants of successful entrepreneurs and financiers lost active contact with commercial and manufacturing processes and lived entirely on their share income. As a result, they developed a new complex of attitudes which carried far-reaching implications in the American context. The inheritance of money, the regarding of wealth and its attendant privileges as natural-born rights rather than as justly acquired deserts for success in the business struggle, induced an *aristocratic*, as distinct from a *bourgeois*, spirit. This spirit manifested itself in a lifestyle that was blatantly imitative of the Old World aristocracy, as polo ponies, huge mansions, footmen, English butlers and long sojourns in Europe all became *de rigueur*. The leisure class was born, its emergence in early twentieth-century America belying the image of the republic as a fluid, democratic society.

Thorstein Veblen described and analysed the distinctive features and developing lifestyle of the *nouveaux riches* and their descendants with sardonic detachment and pinpointed the great significance of what was really a status group within the class proper of the bourgeoisie. The leisure class, according to him, set the standards followed by every level of society and, indeed, largely instigated the whole system of stratification based on status. It 'stands at the head of the social structure in point of reputability; and its manner of life and its standards of .worth therefore afford the norm of reputability for the community'. Consequently, 'its example and precept carries the force of pre-scription for all classes below it'.[47] As the son of an artisan-farmer, Veblen had imbibed all the production-oriented virtues of thrift, self-reliance and industry and hence was especially alert to the leisure class's establishment of values antithetical to the Protestant ethic.

First, its members rejected the practice of thrift and industry, for 'the substantial canons of the leisure-class scheme of life' were 'a conspicuous waste of time and substance and a withdrawal from the industrial process'. Secondly, they rejected the sober, restrained lifestyle of the typical nineteenth-century entre-preneur. 'The duty of the man of Wealth', Carnegie, the steel king, had written, was 'to set an example of modest unostent-atious living, shunning display or extravagance', for 'whatever makes one conspicuous offends the canons [of good taste]'. But the American rich shifted from a code of inconspicuousness to one of ostentatious display or 'conspicuous consumption' because 'in order to gain or hold the esteem of men it is not sufficient merely to possess wealth or power'; they 'must be put in evidence, for esteem is awarded only on evidence'. Wealth, previously regarded as the just reward for abstinence and struggle, had become respectable in itself and 'by a further refinement, wealth acquired passively by transmission from ancestors or other antecedents presently becomes more honorific than wealth acquired by the possessor's own effort'. Hand in hand with this exaltation of inherited wealth went a corresponding denigration of work and occupation. The life of conspicuous leisure, far from being a subject for moral condemnation, became elevated to high status since 'conspicuous abstention from labor' became 'the conventional mark of superior pecuniary achievement'. The example of the leisure class thus severely undermined production-oriented values and generated attitudes towards leisure and luxury which came to constitute a consumption-oriented ideology. Also, by inaugurating the system of status and 'pecuniary emulation' the leisure class enabled manufacturers to exploit the desire to emulate and the need for approbation by marketing their consumer products as indicators of social position, as 'status symbols'.[48]

Of course, many members of the capitalist class in the early decades of this century still engaged in manufacturing and commerce and led a life of sobriety and industry as the Protestant values taught them. The emergence of the leisure class took several decades and the validity of Veblen's observations gained with time. Evidence of a leisure class was available in the East as early as the mid-1890s as confirmed by James Bryce, but in the Midwestern city of Muncie, Indiana such a group within the bourgeoisie did not form until the 1930s. Until then the few wealthy families of the city had avoided ostentation and had merged themselves into the general business class, but the second-generation wealthy had begun to mark themselves off as a distinct social stratum through the exhibition of conspicuously expensive leisure pursuits involving horses and private aircraft.[49]

Accompanying the development of localised leisure-class groups such as that at Muncie, was the formation during the 1920s and 1930s of a national leisure class. This was composed not only of the hereditary rich but also of the new rich such as millionaires created by the boom in manufactures during the First World War, stock market and property speculators, and Hollywood film stars. These social developments greatly disturbed national values as a large section of the ruling class publicly abandoned the production-oriented ideology and generated in its place a consumer hedonism that was propagated throughout society. This change was felt all the more acutely in the 1920s because the First World War acted as a watershed between the old and the new and the economic boom of the 1920s brought the leisure class into great social prominence. Its tastes and lifestyle were impressed upon the public through the newspapers, glossy magazines and the movies. The activities of the rich, particularly the young rich, made good copy, and the impression to be gained from their typical behaviour as retailed in the popular media was of wealth acquired without effort and used without responsibility. The display of wealth on such a lavish scale without moral restraint and the threat to traditional values that it posed led some commentators to view the institution of the leisure class as a problematic phenomenon.

Some contemporary discussion of the social role of the leisure class and of the implications of leisure in general took place. Herbert L. Stewart, in 'The Ethics of Luxury and Leisure' (1918), quoted defences of the English aristocracy and gave qualified approval to the view that the rich acted as reservoirs of culture and taste. He thus echoed in part James Russell Lowell, one of the Boston Brahmins, who in 1884 in his 'Democracy' address had defended hereditary wealth as an institution which would preserve culture in a democracy. This positive value assigned to the rich was being attacked by the early 1930s by C. D. Burns who argued that the most significant change in the social system was 'the displacement of the leisured class as the preservers and promoters of culture'. And for Stewart any beneficial effect of the American wealthy was offset, first, by their lifestyle of conspicuous consumption which he castigated with a Puritan fervour, and secondly, by their conspicuous idleness which he condemned by appealing to the Protestant work ethic: 'The legitimacy of the leisured and luxurious life can never be admitted in any sense which would conceal the eternal principle that some form of useful, strenuous, even exhausting work is both the duty and privilege of every man and woman in good physical and mental health.' If Stewart's response can be regarded as representative, it is evident that the rise of the leisure class called forth dual feelings of approbation and condemnation from the middle class. This reflected the tension they felt between their traditional production-oriented ideology and the consumption-oriented ideology of hedonism which the leisure class represented.[50]

American capitalism in its consumption-oriented phase required contrasting behaviour to that demanded by the production-oriented phase. People were now required not to save, but to spend and get into debt; not to deny themselves possessions and comforts, but to gorge themselves on consumer items; not to work long and hard, but to enjoy themselves in marketed leisure-time activities. The worldly asceticism of the earlier phase was to be replaced by a worldly hedonism in which pleasure and gratification formed the basis of living. Social values help condition social character and, as Riesman and his collaborators observed, Veblen's emphasis on leisure and consumption is an index of social changes pointing the way for characterological ones. W.E. Leuchtenberg also believes that facets of American character which had developed under the nineteenth-century regime of scarcity were undermined by the prosperity of the 1920s and new facets allied to an economy of abundance took their place. In particular the leisure class's instigation of a status system of pecuniary emulation, coupled with other social changes in occupational and residential patterns, eroded the self-reliant individualism and principled basis of behaviour characteristic of the inner-directed producer.[51]

Individualism, the other main complex of production-oriented values, continued to survive, but it hardened into a conservative dogma as the consumer phase brought with it new social and working conditions for which it had less and less relevance. It retained its political expression in the democratic forms of government but it had lost much of its original liberating meaning even there with the Democratic and Republican Party machines dominating the political process, and the sheer expense of political campaigning severely circumscribing any independent individual's aspirations to election at either state or national level. The high cost of electioneering and of maintaining an efficient political organisation meant that the two main parties were heavily dependent on large interest groups for financial backing, and since the large corporations had massive resources of business wealth and influence to call upon, big business exerted its muscle in the political arena to secure favourable legislation as the tycoons had done in the late nineteeth century. It was the critical view of socialists and radicals that the power of the huge monopolies threatened the traditional democratic freedoms and this received reinforcement in 1920 when the Supreme Court did not dissolve the United States Steel Corporation despite its being the biggest industrial corporation and hence in contravention of the anti-trust policy of the 1914 Clayton Act. The decision left the way clear for the merger movement to continue in the 1920s, so leading to a greater concentration of capital and financial power.[52]

It was large changes within the heart of business itself which rendered individualism as it had been inherited increasingly incongruent with everyday reality. The nineteenth-century entrepreneur had been an individualist *par excellence*, often a self-made man, who had achieved material success by reliance on his own cunning and skills and by cultivating a complete indifference to the impact of his self-advancing activities upon other people. But the separation of ownership and control that Berle and Means had noted, the merger movement, and the growth of joint-stock companies meant that American business by the 1920s had ceased to be characterised by the aggressive tycoon and was characterised instead, as we have already remarked, by large staffs of managers and other white-collar personnel.

While the entrepreneur had been his own man, as the free-holder before him, the salaried manager was an 'organisation man', dedicating his energies and skills to the corporation and subjugating his personal autonomy to its bureaucratic procedures and commercial aims. In the hierarchical structure of the business firm decisions were arrived at not on the basis of the judgement or the whim of one man but according to consultative reports and committee discussion. Collective action and collective responsibility increasingly became the keynote of modern commercial practice. And just as the individualist was squeezed out of the smoothly operating, formal pattern of the organisation's bureaucracy, so in the economy as a whole the giant corporation squeezed the small independent producer out of his small sphere of profitable operation. With the largest 200 corporations owning half of all business assets, school-leavers after the Second World War saw their careers not in terms of the traditional Protestant aim of securing economic independence by setting up business on one's own, but in terms of the hierarchy of the modern corporation, their ambition being to rise as high as possible in as large an organisation as possible.[53]

The skills required to achieve such an ambition were of a different order from those required in the earlier agrarian and industrial periods. The freeholder and, later, the industrialist depended for their prosperity on an understanding and manipulation of the physical materials and natural forces, but the salaried manager had little or no contact with the raw materials of manufacture and worked in an environment – typically a city-centre office-block – that was a thoroughly human and social construction. Unlike the worker of the production phase, the white-collar worker did not make things at all but rather spent his time organising and co-ordinating the decreasing proportion of the work-force that did actually manufacture commodities. The characteristic skills demanded of him were, therefore, not those concerned with the handling of materials but with the handling of people. Even for the technically specialised man in middle management the abilities required of him became less and less to do with material techniques and more and more with the administration of personnel.[54]

The shift from a technique-oriented to a people-oriented management practice is well illustrated by the change in emphasis between two major works of the period on management theory. Frederick Taylor's *The Principles of Scientific Management* (1911 and 1925) paid attention only to the mechanical techniques such as speeding up processes, time and motion studies, and so on, for increasing output, but Elton Mayo's *The Social Problems of an Industrial Civilization* (1933) pointed to the harmonious adjustment of the individual to the group as the prime aim of management and drew administrators' attention to the importance of teamwork and such subjective factors as morale.[55] This emphasis on the importance of group harmony in the highly personalised environment of the office was taken to its extreme in Dale Carnegie's best-selling *How to Win Friends and Influence People* (1938). 'Dealing with people', Carnegie wrote, 'is probably the biggest problem you face, especially if you are a businessman', and he urged businessmen to apply such techniques as 'How to Make People Like You Instantly' and 'Making People Glad To Do What You Want' in order to infuse their organisation with 'new loyalty, new enthusiasm, a new spirit of teamwork'. The collective character of management and the pervasive insistence on general morale meant that the individual's needs and capabilities no longer enjoyed the primacy that individualism had enforced but were harnessed to the overriding needs and communal capabilities of the working group. 'There has developed today', David Riesman commented in *Individualism Reconsidered*, 'a great pre-occupation, less with specific needs, than with group mood – a feeling on the part of individuals that they wanted or felt they had to spend their energies, first in making a group, and second, in attending and improving its morale.'[56] It was more important, according to the new organisation philosophy, that an individual be able to fit into the team, to be 'one of the boys', even though his talents may be mediocre, than that he possess brilliant technical expertise and yet be an introverted isolate.

The subservience of the individual to the group, or what William H. Whyte called the Social Ethic, in contrast to the Protestant ethic, operated not only in the white-collar worker's place of work, but also in his place of residence, typically the suburbs. These housing estates on the periphery of the metropolitan centres were built to accommodate the mushrooming new middle class of 'organisation man'. His values dominated them and newcomers had to be prepared to jettison their old values and attitudes and conform to his if they wished to survive socially. The new arrivals to suburbia probably still possessed some traditional Protestant reserve and some principled self-reliance, but the suburbanite residential group, usually based on a cul de sac or crescent, would work upon their personalities to make them less reticent and more outgoing. Eventually, they would tend to lose all personal reserve and share the most intimate details of family life with other members of 'the gang'. As he handed over the guidance of his tastes and values to the other people with whom he lived and worked, the individual may actually experience guilt at efforts to secure privacy.[57] This is a far cry from Emerson's strident protest in 'Self-Reliance' against any form of social conformity. 'Check this lying hospitality and lying affection', he demanded, 'Live no longer to the expectation of these deceived and deceiving people with whom we converse.' Such powerful individualism would have seemed distinctly out of place among the neatly ordered suburbs that spread rapidly during the consumption phase to become the standard residential pattern.

The imperative of satisfying the expectations of other people and obeying social norms was nowhere more evident than in the field of consumption. The new recruit to white-collar work and suburbia had frequently moved from the small country town to the city and in the transition had lost his inner security and identification with traditional values. In the small community from which he typically came his social position was known to everyone through his personal history, but in the vast anonymity of the metropolis his social position had to be advertised by means of instantly recognised signs. Furthermore, the rootlessness of suburbia and job mobility forced him to rely solely on his pecuniary status for his self-esteem and self-image, and the widely accepted signs of this status were the consumer durables he was able to acquire and display.[58] The status system was a continuously graduated scale that was linked to an implicit class identification since only those commodities which approximated to the consumer preferences of the leisure class were considered honorific. At its heart lay the exploitation, by advertisers in their campaigns to maintain demand, of the anxious need for the approval of others and the drive to emulate those who seemed better off.

The mentality of self-advertisement embodied in the status symbol permeated the work-place as well, for in the corporation office success in the bureaucratic hierarchy depended upon the impression one made upon others. The white-collar worker's personality rather than his moral character became all important and a 'personality market' came to operate in the organisation.[59] Not only did he have to be good at his job and be a fully integrated member of the team but the salaried manager or executive had constantly to display this fact in order to get ahead. He had to be able to sell himself to those who decided on promotion, much as the salesman who was more and more a feature of the consumer economy had to be able to sell himself to the customer before he could sell his 'line'.

Much of the ideology of individualism was still competitive and propagated by teachers, parents and the media, but the new forces at work in the socialisation processes of home and occupation were effecting a great shift in the social character of the urban middle class. The prevalent ethos of salesmanship gave rise in Erich Fromm's view to a new character orientation, 'the marketing orientation', and David Riesman and his co-authors argued that the inner-directed character type (typical of the production-phase ideologies of individualism and Protestantism) was being displaced in the group-dominated environment of office and suburbia by the *other-directed* character type. For other-directed people in their typology the source of direction is not internalised but is located in the peer group, either those immediately known to them, or more distantly known through the mass media.[60] The values and attitudes with which an individual guided his or her life therefore ceased to be fixed on internalised principles and drifted instead with the fluid attitudes and values of the current peer group, at school, college, work or suburban community. The rise of the peer group as a significant agent of socialisation and the relative decline of the church and family can be traced to the emergence of a college-based youth subculture in the 1920s, a subculture that was pervaded by consumerism.[61] Many of the white-collar personnel that staffed the corporations' bureacracies were recruited, of course, from the college- and university-educated young.

In *Faces in the Crowd* Riesman pointed to some of the social changes that were associated with the rise of the other-directed character and to its strong connection with the consumption-oriented phase of American society, listing 'the rise of the "new" middle class; the preoccupation with consumption rather than production, and within the sphere of production with the "human factor"', and 'the weakening of parental assurance and control over children' as important related developments. And in *The Lonely Crowd* he and his co-authors contrasted the typical activities of the inner- and other-directed types: 'The other-directed person's tremendous outpouring of energy is channeled into the ever expanding frontiers of consumption, as the inner-directed person's was channeled relentlessly into production.'[62] Just as production and its technical concerns did not disappear with the onset of the consumption phase but merely became overlayered by newer concerns derived from selling and distribution, so the inner-directed character did not vanish from the scene but coexisted with the other-directed type, and both modes of direction often formed part of the personal development of individuals. Inner direction survived in the ranks of the old middle class constituted by the small tradesman, businessman and farmer, but other direction, with its premium on sensitivity to the wishes and responses of others, became the dominant mode of encouraging conformity in the new middle class, whose members worked mainly with people in jobs created by the rapid expansion of the corporation bureaucracies and the service and marketing industries.

Typically, these white-collar workers acted as key agents in the circulation phase of capital, turning commodities they never saw into money they never owned. Their characteristic occupation was not the manipulation of materials but the 'care of paper: numbering, ticketing, accounting, routing, manifolding, filing to the end that commodities and services thus controlled could be sold for the profit of the absentee owners of the corporation'.[63] The preoccupation with paper symbols and abstractions led them to become distanced from the objective, physical world. They experienced nature not as an opposing reality and a field for active intervention, as producers did, but as a resource for leisure and recreation, as consumers. The foreground of their lives was entirely taken up with the constructed totality of the city and the shifting problems of human relations they daily faced in the office. Their lifestyle allowed for no development of the instinctual certainties derived from continuous contact with natural materials and natural rhythms, but encouraged a sense that 'reality' had receded into an enigmatic distance to be reached only by mediating interpretations. The passive Lockean model of perception gave way to a more active projective model and the certainties of positivism yielded to a more problematic epistemological relativism. The heavy psychological emphasis of advertising – the President of the Public Relations Society of America announced that 'the stuff with which we work is the fabric of men's minds'[64] – combined with these tendencies to bring the individual's mentality and capacity for ordering his world to the fore as the main focus of interest and attention. The distance from nature and the 'real' world of men also created a sense of loss, of not being at home in the world, of alienation, and this led to a compensatory idealisation of, and nostalgia for, the simple unquestioned immediacy of physical activity and physical materials that obtained during the production phase.

The middle-class worker's alienation from the physical world was coupled with the self-alienation engendered by the personality market. Since the white-collar professional was engaged in trying to sell himself, he experienced his abilities and qualities as commodities estranged from him so that his sense of a hard core of self diminished and the externalised values of prestige, status and public image were seized upon as substitutes for a genuine feeling of identity.[65] The other-directed person, dependent upon the approbation of his peer group, tended to sacrifice any distinguishing individuation to the imperative of harmonising with the group. Since he was constantly undergoing this process of adaptation there soon disappeared any centre of self to which he could return and, in the face of the diverse roles that had to be adopted and the various customers and colleagues that had to be handled, he tended to become merely the succession of his roles and encounters.[66]

The shift of the American economy into its consumption-oriented phase in the 1920s then was accompanied by changes in the social structure, national ideology and dominant work experience. A new hegemonic group, the leisure class, demonstrated a lifestyle based on abundance and hedonism and generated a consumption ideology which came into conflict with the ideology of work and scarcity inherited from the earlier phase. The white-collar middle class grew greatly in numbers to man the bureaucracies of the corporations and the expanded functions of distribution and marketing. The working environment of the office and living environment of the suburban estate brought new pressures of socialisation to bear upon the individual and encouraged the formation of the other-directed character type. We now turn to examine the literary response to this complex social transformation.

6 The Literary Response (*ii*)

The First World War, despite the United States' comparatively limited involvement, acted as a watershed between the old and the new in American culture, bringing trends which reinforced those arising from secular economic development. It produced its own crop of parvenu millionaires to add to the leisure class, increased the centralisation of industry, hastened the opening up of wider job opportunities for women, and by its militarisation of thousands of men brought them into contact with modern authoritarian organisation. It led to increased Federal management of public information and provided a pretext for curbing traditional civil liberties and cracking down on the political radicals through the Espionage Act of 1917 and the Sedition Act of 1918. Also, as has frequently been noted, the carnage witnessed between 1914 and 1918 seemed to invalidate the nineteenth-century confidence in progress, reason and morality and encouraged instead a general cultural pessimism and a cynicism with regard to received pious notions.

The war's impact on American culture was rendered especially heavy by the fact that so many of that talented generation which came to prominence in the 1920s either, like Dos Passos, Cummings, Cowley and Hemingway, came face to face with the conflict or, like Fitzgerald and Faulkner, entered military training but never saw action. The European hostilities and associated army life provided the creative, serious temperament with a moral and social focus and compelling, vivid material, with the result that one powerful thread of 1920s fiction – Dos Passos's *One Man's Initiation: 1917* (1920) and *Three Soldiers* (1921), Cummings's *The Enormous Room* (1922), Faulkner's *Soldiers' Pay* (1926) and Hemingway's *A Farewell to Arms* (1929) – was spun from attempts to assimilate and interpret, for those who never knew what it was like, the full meaning of the war experience.

However, most of the fine fiction written in America between the wars – and it was a remarkable efflorescence of literary talent – was generated in response to traditional native material and native themes, and there were, inevitably, strong continuities with pre-First World War fiction. This was partly a matter of personal continuity, as Sinclair and Dreiser lived on to write and publish alongside 'the lost generation'; partly of formal continuity as an inherited realist conception of the novel was only slowly remoulded by modernist experimentation and the influence of other art forms; and mainly of social continuity as the city, class distinctions, ambition and corruption continued to exert their fascination as material.

In *An American Tragedy* (1925), Dreiser's narrative strategy and fictional techniques remain conservative and residual even as he tackles new subject-matter. Like many a naturalist novel, it is based upon an actual event – in this case the trial and execution in 1906 of Chester Gillette for the murder of Grace Brown at Moose Lake, Herkheimer County, New York – and upon documentary research. Dreiser visited the places involved and consulted the newspaper records, and parts of the lawyers' speeches and extracts from Grace Brown's letters appear almost verbatim in the novel.[1] The result may be fiction but in common with *The Financier* or Sinclair's novels it is a fiction heavily grounded in social and historical reality. Dreiser builds up his narrative slowly and methodically by the steady accumulation of realistic detail and provides the same specification of industrial work we find in *Sister Carrie* or *The Jungle*. There is a governing perspective of biological and social determinism, but fortunately this is neither too obtrusive nor too tendentious, although by 1925 it seems decidedly out of date. The presentation of character is external and objective in the naturalist manner and when he wishes to indicate the protagonist's mental processes and subjective responses he resorts to indirect discourse.

A similar conservatism of technique is evident in Sinclair Lewis's novels, *Main Street* (1920) and *Babbitt* (1922), which display the same externality of approach and also a sociological interest in the average and representative. Lewis, however, lacks any determinist perspective (though his plot developments do imply a limited notion of human freedom) and his realism is far from attaining a balanced objectivity since initially in both novels it is yoked to a satiric purpose that finally degenerates into sentimental affirmation. While Lewis's focus is on the small town and small city, Dos Passos reveals a familiar fascination with the spectacle of the metropolitan city in his *Manhattan Transfer* (1925). In its early part he depicts America's polarisation into rich and poor by the standard device (found also in Norris's *Octopus*) of dramatic juxtaposition. Reminiscent of Sinclair and Dreiser, he shows a poor working man, Bud Korpenning, being defeated by the harsh conditions of the big city and he contrasts this defeat with Ellen Thatcher's rise to success. Dos Passos also conceives of himself as a kind of historian, documenting and commenting upon social changes in America since the turn of the century. In *Manhattan Transfer* he restricts his focus to New York but in *The Forty-Second Parallel* (1930) and the other two novels that comprise his *USA* trilogy (1937), he broadens his vision to accommodate the whole of America taking in industrial conflict in the mining West and the experience of the war in France.

The war as 'watershed between old and new' could be temptingly specified within our particular perspective as the disjuncture between the historically identifiable production- and consumption-oriented phases of American capitalism, and there would be more than descriptive convenience to recommend this. For undoubtedly the organisation of manufacture first on a war footing and then, with the cessation of hostilities, its reversion to a domestic footing, accelerated the processes of reorientation and readaptation necessary to achieve the shift in the economy. However, these processes were not begun in 1914 or 1917; nor were they complete in 1919 as the depression of 1920/21 indicates, and the consumer economy did not get seriously under way until the upturn that ended that depression. There was no neat historical break, as I have already stressed, but rather, to introduce a metaphor of changing concentrations in a fluid mix, the feeding of powerful new currents into the economic stream as the practices and imperatives of one business sector gained in volume and dispersion over the practices and imperatives of the other.

'Social being determines consciousness' is the materialist proposition underpinning this study, and such 'currents' manifested in new social patterns, modes of work and lived experience could be expected to engender a changed consciousness. Literature, as one of the forms by which writers, with all their personal variation of theme and emphasis, define and articulate a current consciousness, would be expected to register this change. As we saw in the previous chapter, there were determinate changes in ideology and society accompanying the economic shift from production to consumption, and one literary commentator also points unequivocally to a connection between this shift and a shift in the contemporary mentality.

Malcolm Cowley, in his memoir of the 1920s, *Exile's Return* (1934), identifies in American society of that time firstly a set of conservative attitudes, 'the business-Christian ethic'. 'Substantially', he wrote, 'it was a *production* ethic. The great virtues it taught were industry, foresight, thrift and personal initiative.' This ethic had been congruent with the young and expanding economy, but with the end of the First World War a major change occurred. 'Our industries had grown enormously to satisfy a demand that suddenly ceased. To keep the factory wheels turning, a new domestic market had to be created. Industry and thrift were no longer adequate. There must be a new ethic that encouraged people to buy, a *consumption* ethic.' If his explanation of the economic shift is simplistic, his account of the ideological shift is familiar and corroborates the main thrust of our previous chapter. For Cowley, however, one important source of this consumption ethic was not the leisure class, as I suggest, but the subculture of New York's intellectual bohemia:

> It happened that many of the Greenwich Village ideas proved useful in the altered situation. Thus, *self-expression* and *paganism* encouraged a demand for all sorts of products, modern furniture, beach pyjamas, cosmetics, colored bathrooms with toilet paper to match. *Living for the moment* meant buying an automobile, radio or house, using it now and paying for it tomorrow. *Female equality* was capable of doubling the consumption of products formerly used by men alone.[2]

As a temporary member of that subculture Cowley rather naturally accords it more influence upon popular attitudes than it really enjoyed. Intellectuals did indeed lead the attack on Puritanism with Van Wyck Brooks's *America's Coming of Age* (1915) and Harold Stearns's *America and the Young Intellectual* (1921) but as Daniel Bell points out, it was capitalism itself which brought about the decline in traditional values and not the criticisms of the culturally progressive.[3] In the post-war climate the 'deracinated' young writers and commentators, separated like the members of the leisure class from the industrial productive processes, did find little to recommend itself in the inherited value-system, and in their rebellion against the old middle-class virtues of sobriety, thrift and rational foresight did insist upon the immediacy of the moment and the primacy of hedonistic gratification. They thus acted as cultural seismographs, registering the early tremors before the geological shift in American social values made its full impact upon the general public. However, whilst the impulse to imitate bohemian ways may have played a part in eroding Puritan restraint and encouraging a consumer mentality in the middle class, far more potent factors were the glamorous example of the leisure class, the status-system, consumer credit and pervasive advertising.

As well as the continuities already mentioned, there were then significant expansions of fictional content and adaptations of fictive form as writers sought to define, and to evolve adequate literary vehicles for, their vision of the historical conditions being created by consumer capitalism. Native American material came to include those social developments associated with the consumption phase and native themes came to mean those ideological conflicts and their implications for personal character created by the intrusion of the consumption ethic into a Puritan-minded and work-dominated society. In addition, the newly important social groups tended to displace the entrepreneur and the urban poor from the centre of the literary stage.

The manners and *mores* of the white-collar middle class form the subject of Sinclair Lewis's sociological fiction of the early 1920s as they do also of Dos Passos's central work. This new social formation was setting its imprint upon American society through its characteristic work and living patterns and values. Its growth and power attracted scrutinising attention, and literary representation formed an inevitable part of its cultural assimilation and definition. The delineation of its typical lifestyle and the exposure of its weaknesses and foibles, its philistinism and corruption, offered a demanding project to the realist author.

In *Main Street* Lewis, writing from the perspective of an aspiring young woman, Carol Kennicott, expresses the reaction of modern metropolitan youth against the constricting Protestant morality of the small Midwestern town. These desolate towns scattered across the prairies have, in Lewis's mainly iconoclastic

account, betrayed their frontier legacy of vitality and egalitarianism without achieving any compensating sophistication, and the
main abettors of their decline into dullness are the parochially
minded members of the local middle class. His next novel,
Babbitt, takes the standardised middle-class lifestyle based on
office work and suburban living and satirises it for its excessive
group conformity and half-hearted, half-guilty attempts at
hedonism. George F. Babbitt, real estate agent, is a little man
thoroughly saturated in the restrictive norms of his ironically
named city, Zenith, and in the modes of thinking generated by
consumerism. These novels delighted H. L. Mencken, who had
been lampooning the *boobus Americanus* from the pages of the
American Mercury, but their critical thrust is considerably
softened in the latter stages where Lewis, growing affectionate of
those very places and people he has earlier held up for derision,
changes his mood to one of gentle compromise.

'Gentle compromise' certainly does not figure as part of Dos
Passos's style, although 'compromise' in its broadest sense
amongst the white-collar middle class provides, perhaps, his
major theme. According to Cowley, individualism was dying in
the 1920s and there were no longer any individualists. Furthermore, the urban middle class, in his view, lacked both political
awareness and political power.[4] Dos Passos, an intellectual radical
associated with the *New Masses* and *New Republic*, held to much
the same view. *Manhattan Transfer* portrays the difficulty of
asserting any full individuality in the context of the mechanical
routine and unrelenting pressures of life in an urban mass society.
New York, in Dos Passos's jaundiced view, is dedicated to a
ruthless success ethic that drives the weak to suicidal despair and
imposes self-alienation on those lucky or single-minded enough to
rise in its status hierarchy. It is too huge and dynamic to combat
and the only valid response is tactical withdrawal, embodied in
would-be artist Jimmy Herf's thumbing out of the city at the
novel's close. In his long *USA* trilogy comprising *The Forty-
Second Parallel, Nineteen Nineteen* and *The Big Money*, he
presents the middle class's complacent acquiescence in the
destruction of democratic freedoms brought about immediately
by a repressive state apparatus, as in the focal trial and execution
of Sacco and Vanzetti, but more distantly by the rise of monopoly
capitalism. Significantly, the main character in the trilogy is not
an entrepreneur or manufacturer but a figure representative of

the new age of mass manipulation by advertising and 'image', the public relations counsel, J. Ward Moorehouse.

It is in Dos Passos's work, as in that of Scott Fitzgerald and, later, Arthur Miller, that we find expansions of literary form to accommodate the novel content of social experience in the consumption phase. The realists, secure in their empirical assumptions, devoted their art to mimesis, to the representation of reality as an objective, independent entity. But consumerism and white-collar work, with their heavy psychological emphasis, induced a less positivistic, more relativistic, subjectivist world-view. Modernism involved a 'disruption of *mimesis*' and a denial of 'the primacy of an outside reality, as given',[5] and these three writers adopted some of the emphases and techniques of literary modernism in order to qualify the mimetic impulse and communicate the more subjective nature of reality.

In *Manhattan Transfer*, for instance, the locale may be the familiar one of the big metropolitan centre, but the treatment of the city as subject is changed from what had appeared before. It has become more than mere setting and more than the awesome arena of vast Social Darwinian forces. Reflecting an awareness of the city as psychological environment, it has become an enveloping medium through which the characters move and which saturates every moment of their private being. Manhattan is presented not so much as a concrete reality mimetically rendered but rather as a symbolic and experiential reality rendered concrete. By means of the expressive, projective imagery developed by modern art and drawn upon by Dos Passos, the city's latent content, its hidden meanings for personal consciousness, is given form and made visible by a frequently brilliant, although occasionally shrill and strained, impressionistic prose.[6] His cityscapes offer fleeting sensuous details of scene and by his constant, almost stressful, shifting of attention he succeeds in conveying the incessant restlessness, accelerating pace, nervous tension and brassy quality of what Lewis Mumford called the 'negative vitality' inherent in metropolitan life.[7]

In *USA* the narration is flatter, more prosaic, and represents a reversion to a more naturalistic mode of presentation, but it is accompanied by radical innovations at the organisational level. In *Manhattan Transfer* Dos Passos had broken away from the constricting conventions of a unified narrative by adopting an episodic technique which depicted parallel events distributed amongst unrelated characters. In *The Forty-Second Parallel* and its sequels he moved even further from the textual coherence of the traditional realist novel to develop a structure in which the formal conflict of its diverse elements embodies his sense of social divisiveness and polarisation. The conventional narrative strategy is to interweave the life-histories of various characters into a single strand, so foregrounding the connections between people and their common participation in a larger whole, the 'community' of the book. But by laying out his characters' life-histories in twelve discontinuous narratives in *USA*, Dos Passos, in contrast, foregrounds the estrangement, the lack of relation, between people and communicates directly his vision of an atomistic society. Furthermore, *The Forty-Second Parallel* introduced alongside the narratives three innovative devices – the 'Newsreel', the biographical portrait and the 'Camera Eye'.

Dos Passos had inserted newspaper headlines and scraps of popular songs into *Manhattan Transfer* to help convey the texture of quotidian experience and he expanded this technique into the 'Newsreels'. A verbal collage of newspaper headlines, excerpts from speeches and reports, contemporary songs, they sketch in historical developments and indicate the flavour of mass culture, 'the common mind of the epoch'. They are thus comprised of those collective representations, formulated and transmitted by the mass media, which govern an average person's sense of his time and which tend to standardise all feeling and thought to their own superficial level. The portraits of real people 'are interlarded in the pauses in the narrative because their lives seem to embody so well the quality of the soil in which Americans of these generations grew'.[8] Their subjects can be divided into those Dos Passos considered 'useful people', 'producers', such as inventors and activists for democratic rights, and those he regarded as 'destructive people', 'exploiters', such as bankers, college-presidents and propagandists.[9] The portraits and 'Newsreels' together provide the documentary material which firmly grounds the fictional narratives in the context of the real historical and social changes taking place in America and Europe. They also play their part in Dos Passos's commentary on the direction of American civilisation by introducing themes, such as the rise of monopoly capitalism in 'Newsreel 6', and alerting the reader to the significance of developments in the narratives. Thus, the portrait of Thorstein Veblen, whose intellectual shadow falls across so much of *The Big Money*, is inserted into the narrative of Charley Anderson at the point where he begins to illustrate Veblen's dichotomy between production and business. By means of juxtaposition with these other elements then, the life-histories presented in the fictional narratives are endowed with a socially representative status.

The discontinuity evident in the novels of *USA*, their daring fragmentariness of construction, operates as a type of alienation technique, repeatedly breaking the illusion of a self-contained, aesthetically sealed, fictional world and keeping us at a distance. Dos Passos, rather in the manner of Brecht (the 'Newsreels' seem the equivalents of Brecht's placards and back-projections), discourages us from identifying emotionally with his characters and reasserts the writer's organising, indeed didactic, presence behind the work. He asserts his presence most obviously through the 'Camera Eye' device, which, he explained, 'aims to indicate the position of the observer'.[10]

In this way the principle of the relativism of perspective is foregrounded in the form and brought into problematic relation with that outer world of public fact, of consensual history, represented in the 'Newsreels' and portraits. The fictional narratives can be seen as mediating, not always satisfactorily, between the authorial-personal and world-historical realms. At times they deviate far from the 'Camera Eye' as in the 'Mac' sections, and at others they virtually replicate the same experience as in the sections concerning the war in France in *Nineteen Nineteen*. Dos Passos is writing history, personal and social, recording his evolution towards a bitter oppositional stance as well as general trends in American society. What his bold structure in *USA* attempts in a methodologically alert fashion is to embody the active processes of response, interpretation and representation (of self, and of real and imagined others) by which that history comes to be written and concretised in a received text. Hand in hand with the realist's attention to the object being recorded there exists the modernist's self-reflexive emphasis on the projective activity of the imaginative recording itself. This is also evident in Fitzgerald's *The Great Gatsby*, as we shall see below.

The importance of that other main social formation, the leisure class, and its associated status hierarchy is recognised by Dreiser in his *American Tragedy*. In this novel he chose a protagonist at the other end of the social and psychological spectrum from Frank Cowperwood. Clyde Griffiths, a weak and passive youth, is caught in the contradictions of a society in which both a production ethic and a consumption ethic operate at the same time. In his short and futile life is dramatised the ideological conflict and confusion which characterised post-First World War America. It is Scott Fitzgerald, however, who centres his fiction on the leisure class and who best evokes its bewitching combination of glamour and corruption. 'Beautiful and damned', nearly always young, and immeasurably rich, they moved in a world of Long Island mansions, transatlantic liners, and the best European hotels. They belonged entirely to the realm of freedom, enjoying infinite possibility, but they were aristocrats who possessed neither *vertu* nor virtue. Through 'The Rich Boy' and *The Great Gatsby* (1925) Fitzgerald renders his sense of the distinctiveness of that newly important social group and articulates the ambivalent response which its rise evoked in society at large. In *Tender is the Night* (1934), as we shall see, he uses the decline of the brilliant young psychiatrist, Dick Diver, to dramatise the corrosive effect of the leisure-class lifestyle upon such traditional American values as industry, independence and achievement.

The Great Gatsby could so easily have been a novel only of exposé, of a privileged glimpse of the rich and a rather self-righteous condemnation of them for the way they squandered their wealth and possibilities. It is partly this, of course, as we are made aware of the waste, vulgarity and 'carelessness' of the leisure class, but significantly, the realistic impulse merely to present the milieu is subsumed in the more complex impulse to embody in the form itself the processes of response, interpretation and evaluation by which the society at large (specificially the middle class) assimilates and comprehends these new social phenomena; hence the adoption of the Conradian narrative strategy of a narrator-participant and his sociological specification as a white-collar Ivy League graduate from the conservative Midwest, someone like Fitzgerald himself who has an *entrée* to the milieu but who is not of it. The persistent freshness of the novel, where an exposé would have staled, lies in the sense it gives of an active sensibility, at once impressionably absorbed and earnestly discriminating, trying to order and assess its experience of the leisure class, just as indeed Americans in the 1920s were trying to assess the meaning of their *nouveaux riches*. The real interest lies not in Gatsby's tawdry schemes and rather juvenile phantasy of regaining Daisy but in the process by which this dross is transmuted into the precious metal of Carraway's romantically lambent, morally judicious narrative. It is his imagination and the relativism of his perspective that are foregrounded by the form, as we view the 'world' of the novel only through his refracting consciousness.

Though in *Tender is the Night* Fitzgerald returns to third-person narration and the stance of the omniscient author, he also communicates a certain relativism of perception by writing the story from different points of view. In the revised edition the action is presented first from Dick Diver's perspective, then, in a section unambiguously entitled 'Rosemary's Angle', from that of Rosemary Hoyt, the young Hollywood actress, and finally in the last sixty pages from that of Nicole Diver, the rich heiress.[11] The technique of the single narrator had endowed *The Great Gatsby* with a tight, unifying coherence that the later novel lacks. Presumably, as he worked at what was to become *Tender is the Night*, work that was spread over some seven years with many interruptions, Fitzgerald felt the tensions in his view of the leisure class drifting too far apart to be encompassed within one consciousness. The magical enchantment of the leisure-class lifestyle on the Mediterranean seaboard did not accord well with the spiritual exhaustion which he also wanted to locate there, and so some distribution of response between distinct characters was necessary. The result is a novel which is more flawed formally but which enjoys more scope and is more penetratingly engaged with social and cultural change. Unfortunately, the critics failed to recognise the novel's qualities in 1934, tending to regard it from a post-Crash perspective as the evocation of an outdated and meretricious lifestyle.

The Great Depression put a brake on the rapid development of consumerism, and it seemed as if the age of scarcity had returned as material hardship and unemployment became widespread. In the 1930s the polarised character of American society was re-emphasised, and the glaring inequalities that the collapse of the 'system' brought to the fore radicalised many of the liberal intelligentsia.[12] Contemporary literature reflected the social crisis by reverting to more naturalistic modes and to those themes of class conflict and the condition of the poor that we met in the fiction of thirty or forty years earlier. One thinks here of Farrell's Studs Lonigan trilogy and Steinbeck's *Grapes of Wrath* in fiction and Odets's *Waiting for Lefty, Awake and Sing!* and *Paradise Lost* in drama. Dos Passos's *USA* is also symptomatic of the 1930s mood of animus against the American business system, a mood that is especially prevalent in the last volume of the trilogy, *The Big Money*.

After the end of the Second World War the consumption phase quickly regained momentum and Arthur Miller established himself as America's leading playwright with *All My Sons* (1947) and *Death of a Salesman* (1949). *All My Sons* arose out of a wartime incident in which a manufacturer had sold faulty engines to the airforce; in it Miller explored the tension between economic individualism and social responsibility. The play, he explained, 'lays siege to ... the fortress of unrelatedness' and is a social play in that 'the crime [of selling dangerously faulty parts] is seen as having roots in a certain relationship of the individual to society, and to a certain indoctrination he embodies'.[13] *Death of a Salesman* takes that archetypal figure of the consumer economy, the travelling salesman, as its central character, and lays bare his debilitating separation from the traditional roots of value and his self-alienation as a result of his dedication to the personality market and a hollow success ethic. In it we find not only a content determined by the consumption-oriented phase but also a significant adaptation of form.

All my Sons was entirely in the tradition of dramatic realism stemming from Ibsen. A detailed naturalistic setting is employed and the characters are presented only in the external, public world. In *Death of a Salesman*, however, Miller moved away from realism towards a more expressionist mode. The original title of the play, 'The Inside of his Head', indicates that Miller's concern was to represent not only the external, physical actions of a character on stage but also the private, subjective operations of that character's consciousness.[14] The set is only partly representational and the mood and action change according to Willy Loman's mental associations. Through this interiorised, subjectivist structure in which the boundaries between outer and inner, private and public, have been broken down Miller was able to convey the heightened interpenetration of the personal and the social in the consumption phase. With the operation of a personality market at work, the preoccupation of many kinds of white-collar vocations with handling people, and the use of depth psychology by advertising to manipulate consumer choice, the psychological dimension of social life had grown to unprecedented importance in the late 1940s.

In *Death of a Salesman* Miller could still draw upon the production values of working with one's hands in the great outdoors away from the urban status system as a powerful element in that ideological conflict and confusion which we find in both Willy and Biff and which Miller's dramatic mode presents with such immediacy. But through the 1950s and 1960s, as the consumption phase imprinted its stamp upon all aspects of American society, the early production values derived from the Protestant ethic, the frontier and the democratic tradition became an increasingly residual value-system, fading to only a nostalgic recall of what had once been. In his screenplay *The Misfits* (1961), based on one of his earlier short stories, Miller demonstrated with brilliant economy the tawdry decline of the Western agrarian myth before an omnivorous commercialism. What used to be a fine, independent way of life for Gay Langdon has been made base and corrupt, 'changed . . . all around', 'smeared . . . all over with blood, turned . . . into shit and money just like everything else'. Kurt Vonnegut in his *God Bless You, Mr Rosewater, or Pearls before Swine* (1965), uses the trap fisherman, Harry Pena, to show the irrelevance of self-reliance and independence and direct physical work in a world of consumer affluence. 'Real people don't make their livings that way any more', Bunny Weeks, the restauranteur, says of Harry's fishing. 'That's all over, men working with their hands and backs. They are not needed.' Indicating 'four, stupid, silly, fat widows in furs', Bunny points to the bland consciousness steeped in surfeit which has replaced those old values. 'And look who's winning,' he says. 'And look who's won.' For Vonnegut in this novel, as for Thomas Pynchon in his second novel, *The Crying of Lot 49* (1966), capitalistic development in America has led not to a rich efflorescence of personal possibilities but to a severe constriction of them, and the major cause is the amassing in a few hands of the nation's wealth. In Pynchon's novel the polarisation of American society is represented on the one hand by multimillionaire Pierce Inverarity who owns an entire city and on the other by the 'futureless' people who have been rejected by the economic sector he and his like control. Oedipa Maas, the executrix of Inverarity's estate, 'had heard all about excluded middles; they were bad shit, to be avoided; but how had it ever happened here with the chances so good for diversity?' Even those fortunate to have a place in Inverarity's business empire have to pay the price of conformity and stultified creativity.

The loss of the old values and the saturation of American society by consumerism became then an assumption in American literature rather than a point of exploration, and the lifestyle of the white-collar middle class became a favourite subject. Dos Passos in *Mid-Century* (1961) returned to some of the techniques of *USA* and adopted a marketing executive as one of his central characters, while Joseph Heller in *Something Happened* (1974) presents the confessional of a middle-ranking executive who in his lifestyle and anxieties is very much the other-directed organisation man, a fully qualified member of the lonely crowd. After this brief overview of the literary response to the consumption phase in which the significant adaptations of content and form have been indicated, we now turn to a detailed reading of selected texts to establish how the social changes and ideological conflicts brought about by the emergence of the consumer economy are articulated there.

7 Class and the Consumption Ethic: Dreiser's *An American Tragedy*

An American Tragedy is Dreiser's finest work. Sergei Eisenstein wrote that it was 'as broad and shoreless as the Hudson ... as immense as life itself', and that it could allow 'almost any point of view of itself'. Its rare quality of multifaceted massiveness has fathered a large number of critical studies which all acknowledge Clyde Griffiths's representative stature but make only vague gestures towards its origins. This imprecision is due to an individualist emphasis upon the character and fate of the protagonist and a corresponding lack of specificity in describing the given social structure and ideological framework with which that character interacts. Eisenstein regarded Clyde's crime as 'the sum total of those social relations, the influence of which he was subjected to at every stage of his unfolding biography and character', and from our adopted sociological perspective it becomes evident that the social relation of class and the emergence, particularly among the young, of a consumption ethic condition Clyde's character and fate to a large extent. A full understanding of the social context imaged in the novel is a prerequisite to a more exact identification of Clyde's representativeness and leads to a definite locating of *An American Tragedy* within that conflict of values characteristic of twenties America.[1]

Dreiser assumes a rigid polarisation of society, and the contrast between rich and poor – on the one hand the eastern Griffithses and the Finchleys with their power and affluence derived from the ownership of capital, on the other the western Griffithses and the Aldens with their penury and powerlessness – constitutes the shaping tension of the novel. Born of the one class, Clyde longs to be of the other, and *An American Tragedy* is essentially the story of his attempt and failure to cross the great divide.

In his early adolescence Clyde is eager to achieve success by means of the Protestant virtues. The only way to wealth he could see was Benjamin Franklin's – Work, Save and Prosper: 'He would work and save his money and be somebody.' But from the very beginning his adoption of that programme is undercut both by his motivation and the content with which his milieu imbues the notion of success. At the drug-store where he works as a soda-jerk he observes that it requires an expensive style of dress and hence a certain amount of money to win girls: 'Very often one or another of these young beauties was accompanied by some male in evening suit, dress shirt, high hat, bow tie, white kid gloves and patent leather shoes. ... No good-looking girl, as it then appeared to him, would have anything to do with him if he did not possess this standard of equipment.' His social ambition is thus initially fuelled by his sexual desire, and his conception of advancement is coloured by prospects of personal consumption and display. This commingling of erotic and pecuniary impulses generates a wholly sensuous appreciation of wealth in Clyde, a taste that is augmented by his first vision of the Green-Davidson Hotel in Kansas City where 'it was all so lavish' and there were 'lamps, statuary, rugs, palms, chairs, divans, tête-à-têtes – a prodigal [*sic*] display'. In the heavily itemised, almost caressingly detailed description of the hotel's lobby, Dreiser presents Clyde's wide-eyed discovery of the sheer opulence of the material realm of things. The deprived adolescent has begun to discover the rich variety of the world's commodities.

Dreiser draws attention to the corrosive effect the hotel has upon several features of Clyde's early psychology and values, and shows that his adherence to the Protestant scheme of life is seriously undermined during his period as a bell-hop. The generous tipping he receives, 'the steady downpour of small change', belies those twin propositions of the Protestant ethic – the necessity of hard work and the proper correspondence of reward to effort: 'Why, thirty-five cents – and for a little service like that. This man had given him a quarter and the other a dime and he hadn't done anything at all.' His unworldly parents, who still assume the traditional proportionality of work and payment, never suspect that such an untaxing job could pay so well. As a comparatively affluent bell-hop with a modest disposable income,

Clyde does not give his money to his needy family but spends it instead on smart clothes for himself or on his girlfriend, Hortense Briggs. The hotel also acquaints him with a hedonistic, leisure-dominated lifestyle: 'The talk and the palaver that went on in the lobby and the grill, to say nothing of the restaurants and rooms, were sufficient to convince any inexperienced and none-too-discerning mind that the chief business of life for anyone with a little money or social position was to attend a theater, a ball-game in season, or to dance, motor, entertain friends at dinner, or to travel to New York, Europe, Chicago, California.'[2] This is a lifestyle Clyde and the other bell-hops attempt to imitate, and which Clyde meets again in the Cranstons and Finchleys at Lycurgus.

Though he lies to his parents about his tips, Clyde initially draws upon the stock of Puritan values they have inculcated in him to criticise his fellow bell-hops' adventures and vices. He maintains some resistance to their attempts to rope him in, but the sensual appeal of their activities gradually overcomes his moral reservations and he joins in 'by degrees'. In Muncie, Indiana in 1925 the Lynds observed that 'the group has come to assume some of the intangible functions of parents' in establishing norms, this being due to changing patterns of youth relationships based on going to dances, movies and shows, driving cars and generally having more money to spend.[3] In tune with these newer patterns of youth relationships Dreiser has Clyde make the crucial shift of allegiance from his parents to his peer group as the main arbiters of his behaviour and values.

The conflict between the authority of the family and that of the peer group comes to a head over the supper outing. The other bell-hops persuade Clyde to accompany them first to a restaurant and then to a local brothel, but he is concerned about the outing's probable effect upon his relationship with his parents. He feels his loyalties divided, but his allegiance to 'the crowd' finally triumphs over his deference to his parents' repressive morality and he goes to the supper and the brothel. As a consequence of his rejection of parental authority and the older values that had been instilled in him, Clyde becomes an example of the other-directed character-type, taking his cues from others and using his contemporaries as models on which to base his own personality.

Imitation is his key mode of development. When he worked as a soda-fountain assistant his driving wish was to emulate the debonair young men he served: 'To be able to wear such a suit with such ease and air! To be able to talk to a girl after the manner and with the sang-froid of some of these gallants! What a true measure of achievement!' At the Green-Davidson he chooses another bell-hop, Doyle, as 'a youth to imitate', and although he appears to experience a resurgence of Protestant sobriety and earnestness while working at the Union League Club, this too is only brought on by his conviction that 'if he tried now, imitated the soberer people of the world, and those only, . . . some day he might succeed'. In the manufacturing city of Lycurgus when he is interviewed by Gilbert Griffiths, his cousin and an arrogant business manager, he does not measure him by any independent set of values but regards him simply as 'such a youth in short, as [he] would have liked to imagine himself to be'. (Indeed, Clyde's later scheme for drowning Roberta and faking an accident is an imitation of a crime he saw reported in a newspaper.)

In the main, Dreiser presents Clyde as being far too adaptable to his surroundings, taking on chameleon-like the moods, values and styles which he sees immediately about him. Such a mode of development and such a plasticity of character bespeak the absence of any substantial core of self and the improbability of any real growth. After Clyde, as a result of meeting his uncle at the Union League Club, has mortgaged his future on a return to the Protestant scheme of life and we know that the conjunction between himself and Lycurgus society is bound to take place, Dreiser heightens our premonitory apprehension of catastrophe by confirming this fundamental flaw in Clyde's character: 'For to say the truth, Clyde had a soul that was not destined to grow up. He lacked decidedly that mental clarity and inner directing application that in so many permits them to sort out from the facts and avenues of life the particular thing or things that make for their direct advancement.'[4] This analysis raises serious doubts as to Clyde's ability to fulfil either his own or his uncle's expectations. He is fixated at an adolescent stage of development and lacks inner direction and a moral centre from which to evaluate his environment critically. Incapable of making a mature assessment of social outlets and their relevance to his needs, he is headed for confusion and, ultimately, disaster in a society such as that of Lycurgus which will present him with a plurality of values and avenues for social advancement.

Samuel Griffiths, Clyde's rich uncle, conforms to the stereotype of the late-nineteenth-century entrepreneur. 'Long used to contending for himself, and having come by effort and results to know that he was above the average in acumen and commercial ability', he is the embodiment of self-reliant individualism. It is his faith in the myth of success, his conviction that a young man should be given the opportunity to show his merits and so rise, that partly motivates his offer of a job to his nephew. Like Howells's Silas Lapham, a principled man, and not an amoral financier like Dreiser's own Frank Cowperwood, Samuel Griffiths is a manufacturer directly engaged in the productive process and he holds to the traditional Protestant values. His own and his son's business credo is thus expressed:

> It was necessary when dealing with the classes and intelligences below one, commercially or financially, to handle them according to the standards to which they were accustomed. And the best of these standards were those which held these lower individuals to a clear realisation of how difficult it was to come by money – to an understanding of how very necessary it was for all who were engaged in what both considered the only really important constructive work of the world – that of material manufacture – to understand how very essential it was to be drilled, and that sharply and systematically, in all the details and processes which comprise that constructive work. And so to become inured to a narrow and abstemious life in so doing. It was good for their characters. It informed and strengthened the minds and spirits of those who were destined to rise. And those who were not should be kept right where they were.[5]

In this key passage Dreiser has cleverly brought together all the elements of the distinctively nineteenth-century ideology that was grounded in the production-oriented phase of American capitalism. There is the emphasis on 'material manufacture'; moral value is placed upon a disciplined and abstemious life; and the class hierarchy is legitimated by a belief in predestination adapted in such a way that economic success is taken as the confirmation of virtue, and failure, conversely, as the stigma of moral fault. This passage is placed immediately after Samuel Griffiths's offer to his nephew in order to alert us to the ideological context into which Clyde will be projected and by which he will be measured. The problem facing Clyde is more comprehensive than most critics' exclusive concentration on the moral aspects of his predicament would suggest.

For if this representation of their world by the business class ever corresponded to the real processes of social and commercial life, it certainly did not do so by the early 1920s. It is a residual world-view whose inappositeness to modern conditions is not confined to its moral rigidity alone but extends to all its elements. In that it constitutes a class-based ideology this credo represents a further impingement of social relations upon Clyde, for he has to come to terms not only with the social reality of Lycurgus but also with the myths that structure that reality. He fails to approximate his life to the Griffithses' credo in part – and herein lies one of the subtler aspects of his victimisation – because that credo as an explanation of social dynamics does not fully account for Lycurgus society and does not present an exclusively valid guide for personal conduct within it.

First, the individualist basis of success and failure which this version of the Protestant ethic assumes, and which appears confirmed in Samuel Griffiths's career, is undercut by subsequent information. We soon learn that the father of Asa and Samuel left the bulk of his 30 000 dollar estate to be shared between Samuel and one other son while Asa, Clyde's father, was left only 1000 dollars. Samuel thus began his business career with the advantage of inherited wealth, capital to the sum of 15 000 dollars. Clyde has no capital, of course, and in Lycurgus where capital is entrenched and wealth inherited he can only hope to make his way up by working for someone who has.

Secondly, as we have seen, the Protestant ethic was based upon a production-oriented economy in which the material problems of manufacture were the main concern. The Griffithses, as producers, inevitably adopt this emphasis, but Clyde, like a minor but growing proportion of the work-force of the time, has been employed not in the primary producing industries but in the service industries. The capacity to handle people rather than the ability to handle materials matters more in these latter occupations, and at the Green-Davidson Clyde has realised that the other-directed virtues of sensitivity and responsiveness to others may be more useful than hard work and self-denial: 'For the first time in his life, it occurred to him that if he wanted to get on he ought to insinuate himself into the good graces of people – do or say something that would make them like him. So now he contrived an eager, ingratiating smile.' He grows adept at being personable and making a good impression. To Samuel Griffiths he seems 'very adaptable' and to Gilbert Griffiths he seems suited to become a salesman, an occupation in which his agreeable presentation of self would be most useful. Clyde, for his part, does not think of working hard in order to prove himself to Gilbert but only of trying to 'win his way into his good graces'. Thus, as Dreiser carefully establishes, Clyde's formative years were spent under prolonged exposure to the styles and values of that consumption-oriented sector of the economy which had grown increasingly important since the beginning of the century and which rejected Puritan restraint in favour of a hedonism based on the gratification of personal wants. In particular, Clyde is the product of that youth subculture of consumerism represented by records, dancing, movies, parties, joy-rides in cars, pleasure parks and fashionable clothes which first flowered in the early 1920s.[6] As a result of such conditioning and his lack of 'inner directing application' Clyde is radically unfitted to meet the demands of the stern regimen imposed by the Griffithses' business ethic. Consequently, he gradually abandons his application to the long, gruelling climb through the factory hierarchy and comes to rely on a male version of the Cinderella myth with Sondra Finchley cast as a Princess Charming who will spirit him into the ranks of the rich by marriage.

Dreiser, well aware of the significance of such sociological information to the novel's themes, also indicates briefly that the economic base of Lycurgus is dominated by consumer industries, manufactories concerned with bacon, canning jars, vacuum cleaners, wooden and wicker furniture and typewriters. Indeed, Samuel Griffiths's own business is based on the consumer item of shirt collars. The emergence of consumerism as a way of life in Lycurgus is made additionally apparent during Clyde's walk around the city on his arrival when he notices the wealth of consumer commodities on display: 'such expensive-looking and apparently smart displays of things that might well interest people of means and comfort – motors, jewels, lingerie, leather goods and furniture'. It is partly Clyde's vulnerability to the appeal of things, to the barely resistible glamour of consumer durables, which leads to his eventual downfall, as the Reverend McMillan observes near the novel's end: 'This young boy – really –. His hot,

restless heart which plainly for the lack of so many things which
he, the Reverend McMillan, had never wanted for, had rebelled.'

Furthermore, Samuel Griffiths may point out to his family in
Lycurgus that Clyde is 'coming here to work – not play', but the
manufacturing city is neither so abstemious nor so work-oriented
as the Griffithses' Protestant credo pretends. Among young
members of the upper class in particular 'play' has become a prominent feature of their activities. The Lycurgus business
community, we learn, is composed of a conservative set, to which
the older, more established families such as the Griffithses
belong, and a 'fast set' led by the relatively parvenu Cranstons
and Finchleys who are 'given to wearing the smartest clothes,
[and] to the latest novelties in cars and entertainments' and who
are generally considered to be 'too showy and aggressive'. This
behaviour reveals that among one section of the business class
there has been an attenuation of the Protestant emphasis on thrift
and sobriety, but it is the second-generation rich in· the novel,
those born to wealth, who demonstrate most fully the decline of
Puritan restraint and the triumph of the newer hedonistic values.
In Dreiser's representative social image they exemplify what
Veblen called 'the substantial canons of the leisure-class scheme
of life', namely 'a conspicuous waste of time and substance and a
withdrawal from the industrial process'. Gilbert Griffiths, being
involved in the productive process, still holds largely to the older
values, but even so he and his sister take part in the group's characteristic pursuits of dancing, 'cabareting', parties, car-rides and
water-sports.

This, then, constitutes the social context into which Clyde is
projected. In the young rich of Lycurgus he recognises a lifestyle
both honorific and pleasurable which would cap his desires for
social advancement and the sensuous enjoyment of wealth. And
to his eventual detriment, his name together with the efforts of
Sondra Finchley and Bertine Cranston render it tantalisingly
accessible. It may seem improbable that Clyde should be so successful with Sondra and her set, but we have to take into account
both Clyde's ready adaptability to his immediate peer group and
his competence in that common youth subculture which formed
the basis of most of their activities. For the predominance of
youth among the main participants in the novel deserves
emphasising. Clyde is only 16 when he works at the Green-
Davidson, 20 when he arrives at Lycurgus, and 21, perhaps, when

executed. Gilbert Griffiths is 23 and his sister 18, while Sondra is 17 and Roberta Alden 23 during the central action of the novel. The story, consequently, is largely a tale of late adolescence and early adulthood, and the involvement of these characters in the youth culture is symptomatic of that rift between the generations which forms one of the sub-themes of *An American Tragedy*. With the possible exception of Ratterer's mother and father, the parental generation, regardless of social position, is portrayed as hide-bound by a restrictive code which looks askance at the entertainments and licence of the young. The youth in turn prefer to take their leisure not with their family but with their peers, and they look to one another and the mass media such as the movies for their tastes and values. The prevalent youth culture in some ways therefore transcends class boundaries – Clyde is able to dance so well with Sondra at the parties of the rich because of the practice he gains with Roberta in the dance-halls of the pleasure-parks – but it also comes into tension with the divisive class-structure of Lycurgus society.

Reliance upon the traditional bond of kinship emboldened Clyde to ask his uncle for a position, and a lingering sense of filial duty towards Asa inclined Samuel Griffiths to grant the request, but as Dreiser indicates, the family is very much a vestigial factor in modern social relations. The two brothers have not seen each other for thirty years, and their blood-tie is easily outweighed by class differences. Taken on at the Griffithses' factory, Clyde is set to the drudgery of the shrinking room, and Samuel Griffiths points out to his own family that Clyde, though a cousin, is by no means a social equal. Regarded then by the Griffiths as a potentially embarrassing poor relation, Clyde is treated with the same indifference as the other employees. Yet he cannot identify with the lower class because his name as well as his physical resemblance to Gilbert associate him in his own mind as well as in other people's with the factory-owners. His fellow workers in the shrinking room, for instance, look upon him as 'part of the rich and superior class' and are suspicious of him. Appearances thus dictate that Clyde adopt a social position to which he has only tenuous claims.

This ambivalence in his position is heightened by the fact that Samuel Griffiths's aloofness towards his nephew is qualified from time to time by a residual avuncular patronage. He looks after Clyde's welfare at the factory (when he remembers) and asks him to the house for dinner. This equivocation on the Griffithses' part is ultimately far more damaging than either full acceptance or complete ostracism. Had he been treated solely as an employee, Clyde would never have entertained dreams of entering the Lycurgus élite and marrying Sondra Finchley; had he been welcomed as a full member of the family, he would not have become so lonely and, as a consequence, involved with Roberta Alden. As it is, his relationship with his uncle, which seemed at first to expand the possibilities of his life, ultimately limits them by trapping him in an ambiguous class position. The full irony of this relationship becomes apparent during his trial when the most effective plea for the defence to make − that of temporary insanity − is disallowed by Samuel Griffiths on the grounds that it would cast a slur on the family name.

Roberta Alden, poor and aspiring like Clyde, soon discovers that 'the line of demarcation and stratification between the rich and poor in Lycurgus was as sharp as though cut by a knife or divided by a high wall'. All the social norms are drawn along strict class lines, but Clyde lacks a firm class position and as such is practically disbarred from society. Condemned to a *déclassé* limbo, he suffers a freezing isolation which he can escape only by transgressing some rigid norm. He can satisfy his all-too-human need for female companionship only by violating the strong social taboo on sexual relations between the classes, and it is his attempt to conceal that violation that leads to Roberta's death.

Since Lycurgus has evolved a young leisure class, 'the principle of status runs through the entire hierarchical system', and Clyde's uncertain class membership generates an uncertain status, a fluctuating social estimation of him by others.[7] His insecure position, together with his sensitivity to the actions and responses of others, render him extremely conscious of such differentiations as rank and status. Clothes provide an immediate mark of social position and when Clyde has his first interview with Gilbert he takes note of Gilbert's dress just as Gilbert takes note of his. Another mark is provided by others' reactions. When Clyde arrives at the factory he tells the receptionist his name and purpose and notices that 'her quite severe and decidedly indifferent expression changed and became not so much friendly as awed'. Due to the Griffiths connection he has been re-evaluated from a nobody barely worthy of consideration to someone of high social esteem. A reverse estimation takes place during his first dinner at the Griffithses' when Mrs Griffiths pointedly informs Bertine Cranston and Sondra Finchley that Clyde is poor and he observes the changes in their expressions. He soon realises after experiences such as these that his name and appearance are his sole claims to an elevated position on the status ladder.

Lacking any substantial core of self, Clyde has little defence against this status evaluation, and his identity is tightly bound to the social images of himself which he sees thrown back from other people. In the words of a contemporary psychologist:

> Unconsciously [the individual] is at every moment taking stock of his reactions as they appear in the eyes of others. In this way the persons about us have to represent unconsciously a sort of social foil against which we watch the outline of our own image. Thus in his social relationships the individual *sees* himself in the light in which those relationships reflect him. All of them give back his personal image in the social mirror they present to him. To the servant we play the master; to royalty we play the slave.[8]

The employees at the factory expect Clyde to behave as their social superior, and Clyde responds by being condescending. Later, after his promotion to a white-collar position, he feels it incumbent upon himself both to consolidate his new image, by spending his leisure 'in some way befitting his present rank', and to protect it by 'keeping out of sight of those who were imagining that he was being so much more handsomely entertained than he was'. Nowhere is Clyde's vulnerability to the estimation of others more apparent than in his relations with Sondra and Roberta. To princess Sondra, the focus of his social and sexual desires, he plays the slave; to the worker, Roberta, he plays the master.

Roberta, like her sister machinists, views Clyde in a more glamorous light than he warrants and he comes to represent 'paradise' for her in much the same way that Sondra represents 'paradise' for him. Clyde contributes to this exaggerated notion of his social position by falsely intimating that his povety-stricken parents in the West are quite wealthy, a fabrication that epitomises his alienation from his actual social roots and demonstrates his readiness to sacrifice an honest relationship for the sake of public esteem. While it brings him closer to Sondra on the status scale, it distances him from the only person with whom there is the possibility of genuine rapport, namely Roberta. She and Clyde are from similarly impoverished and repressive backgrounds and they share the loneliness and frustration of the young mobile worker. At first, they enjoy a warm mutual affection, but this is later vitiated by the social images that govern their perception of each other. She casts him in the role of a suave male of the Lycurgus élite, an image of himself that he intensely wants confirmed and that he cannot resist playing to the full. At the dance-hall of the Starlight pleasure-park he rises to her expectations, 'carried away by a bravado that was three-fourths her conception of him as a member of the Lycurgus upper crust and possessor of means and position'. Since Clyde evaluates himself according to the criteria of status and means, he inevitably rates Sondra and Roberta by the same social scale. 'As contrasted with one of Sondra's position and beauty', he asks himself, 'what had Roberta really to offer him?' He views Roberta as a mere factory girl, someone he might win and be happy with for a while but never marry, and he regards it as part of his social privilege to desert her and then deny any past relation with her. The element of role-playing in his attitude towards her gradually increases until he is cynically simulating affection and concern when he is 'disposed to re-enact the role of lover again'.

One of the novel's strongest ironies lies in the negative effect Clyde's propensity for role-playing has upon the possibility of his acquittal at the trial. The social image he has carefully nurtured of the young, well-to-do socialite generates nothing but hostility among the rural people of Cataraqui County, and the prosecuting attorney, who has suffered a poverty-smitten boyhood remarkably like Clyde's, bears a fierce prejudice against the upper class, so that he casts Clyde in the role of rich-boy seducer and murderer and affects to identify with Roberta as a poor, deprived girl. Belknap, the senior defence lawyer, on the other hand, sympathises with Clyde since he is from a comfortable background and was once caught himself in a similar predicament over two girls. Also, Clyde's legal defence at the trial is dependent upon his successful enactment of a false role. At the time of Roberta's drowning, Dreiser makes plain, Clyde experienced a change of heart or, more accurately, a failure of the will and did not carry out the killing as he had planned. This version of events, for all its truth, would not, so the lawyers decide, provide a credible platform for the defence. So Belknap and his assistant concoct a story which portrays Clyde's 'change of heart' taking place over a longer period. They drill him in this version of events, drawing up a long list of possible questions with the answers type-written beneath, and they 'teach him to act it out'.

The lawyers base their general strategy for Clyde's defence on their recognition of his deficiency in the inner-directed virtues of moral principle and personal integrity. He is a 'mental and a moral coward', they assert, and they emphasise his vulnerability to external influences. Earlier in the novel Dreiser used the similarity of appearance between Clyde and Gilbert to highlight these aspects of Clyde's character by contrast.[9] Gilbert shares his father's business ideology and is capable of independent judgements and putting himself and his conclusions before anyone else. He has force and energy, we are told, whereas Clyde is soft and vague, and the contrast between Gilbert's ordering of life according to ethical principle and Clyde's pragmatic adaptation to prevailing norms is neatly registered in a short exchange. Gilbert explains to his cousin that a supervisor as a trusted representative of management has to maintain an irreproachable reputation and, consequently, cannot have any relations with the girls below him:

> And Clyde replied: 'Yes, I understand. I think that's right. In fact I know that's the way it has to be.'
> 'And ought to be,' added Gilbert.
> 'And ought to be,' echoed Clyde.[10]

Clyde thus agrees to follow the institutional rule but his understanding of its ethical aspect is only an 'echo' of Gilbert's. His blindness to the principled basis of conduct for some people is further illustrated during his early relationship with Roberta. In order to facilitate a meeting between himself and her, he suggests that she change her church. He has taken to going to church but solely out of other-directed motives, because 'he thought this might please his uncle and cousin and so raise him in their esteem'. Roberta, however, possesses that strong moral sense which Clyde lacks – 'I wouldn't feel right about it. And it wouldn't be right, either' – and his suggestion offends her.

After Roberta's death Clyde rarely feels the guilt that would afflict a morally principled character; instead, he is more concerned with the likely opinion of others. When he is arrested,

he begs not to be taken in front of his rich, young friends for he
fears the reaction of his peers, and later it is the opinion of the
wider society that gives him pain: 'All those people in Lycurgus
when they should hear in the morning. His mother eventually,
everybody.' His attitude towards his mother is 'a mixture of fear
and shame', because she would see his 'moral if not social failure'.
Significantly, it is her perception of his moral failure, and not his
own, which causes him most anxiety. His conscience, Dreiser indicates, seems to have externalised itself, first in the figure of his
mother and then in that of the Reverend McMillan. Just as at the
Union League Club, Clyde seemed to manifest a revival of seriousness and purpose under its austere influence, so, impressed by
the minister's magnetic personality, he seems to experience a
resurgence of moral awareness and a sense of guilt. But the
Reverend McMillan, it transpires, is just one more powerful, destructive force – an absolutist moralism in his case – in a life that
is oppressed, and ultimately ruined, by external forces.

In the Cowperwood trilogy, *The Financier, The Titan* and *The
Stoic*, Dreiser dealt with the dynamic social and economic forces
of the late nineteenth century, and chose as his representative
figure an aggressive individualist who thrust his way to power and
wealth. In *An American Tragedy* he presents a completely contrasting protagonist. Clyde Griffiths, unlike Frank Cowperwood,
is born poor and remains so. He is certainly no powerful individualist. He seems to lack both a centre of volition and a centre
of independent judgement, and it is in this hollowness which
occupies the heart of his personality that the secret of his representativeness lies. His very passivity, his uncritical adaptability to
the prevailing social norms, make him a waxen seal of the society
in which he lives and dies. 'After all, you didn't make yourself,
did you?' Jephson, the assistant defence lawyer, demands
rhetorically when Clyde is testifying in court. His development, as
laid before us by Dreiser, exposes the forces that mould
adolescent character and values, particularly those new forces
brought into being by social and cultural change.[11]

Clyde's dilemma does indeed arise from the demands made
upon him by the nineteenth-century, work-oriented moralism of
the Griffithses and his failure to meet them. But that failure,
Dreiser shows, was largely conditioned by developments which
rendered obedience to that moralism increasingly difficult. The

Protestant ethic, drawing on a Puritan code of moral restraint and delayed gratification for its sustaining discipline, legitimated social advancement and laid down a programme by which the poor aspirant ought to be able to rise in the class hierarchy. In the post-war period, however, American capitalism itself was effecting an attenuation of those values which it had hitherto depended upon for its functioning as well as its justification. As has already been outlined, the emergent consumption-oriented sector of the economy emphasised spending and gratification, not saving and denial, and the leisure class promulgated a lifestyle of conspicuous idleness and hedonism. Furthermore, the Puritan code was traditionally instilled in children by parents and the church but post-war changes in the mobility and economic independence of the young severely weakened these influences.

Clyde Griffiths's career registers the declining impact of Puritanism upon a generation whose rejection of parental authority went hand in hand with immersion in a youth culture based on consumerism. Lacking any internalised ethical principles, Clyde, an other-directed character-type, adopts those values he sees being currently endorsed. While he retains the traditionally legitimated ambition of social advancement, he imbues it with a content derived from contemporary developments as they are represented in the young leisure class. Within the sphere of industrial production, however, the Protestant ethic continued to be asserted, as represented by the Griffithses' business credo. Thus, as *An American Tragedy* dramatises, a contradiction came into being between the two value-systems – the one emergent, the other residual – encouraged by the two different sectors of the economy. Clyde's representativeness lies in his entrapment within this tension: the compliant product of a consumption-oriented value-system, he is yet the reluctant victim of the Protestant values of a production-oriented ideology.[12]

8　The Rich Are Different: Scott Fitzgerald and the Leisure Class

The emergence of the leisure class in early twentieth-century America was a social development of major ideological significance. Its aristocratic features belied the image of the republic as a fluid, democratic society, and led to the propagation of luxury, idleness, pecuniary emulation and conspicuous consumption as honorific pursuits, in contradiction to the Protestant ethic of work, thrift and abstinence. The economic boom of the 1920s (increased profits together with rising share values) financed a more extravagant leisure-class lifestyle and brought it by means of the mass media into social prominence. This stratum of elegant and not-so-elegant high-livers proved problematic for the dominant middle-class culture. In particular a tension was set up by the dual response of admiration for and envy of the glamorous life of the rich on the one hand, and moral condemnation of that life according to traditional values on the other. Scott Fitzgerald saw more clearly than some of his literary contemporaries that the leisure class was a social phenomenon of great importance, and he was particularly well placed by means of his own social position to sense acutely and then fully articulate that ambivalent response which the society at large was experiencing.

One of the opening paragraphs of his short story 'The Rich Boy' provides a neat model for much of his fiction:

Let me tell you about the very rich. They are different from you and me. They possess and enjoy early and it does something to them, makes them soft where we are hard, and cynical where we are trustful in a way that unless you were born rich, it is difficult to understand.[1]

150

Here, concisely expressed and in close conjunction, are some of those elements that contribute to his novels' fullness and seriousness of effect: the knowing tone of authoritative experience; the distanced assessment; the attempt at definition of this social group; and, most important of all, his adopted stance of intermediary, interpreting one section of American society – the leisure class – to another section – the middle class. This, of course, is very much the stance of Nick Carraway in *The Great Gatsby*. When Fitzgerald told Hemingway that 'The rich are different from us', Hemingway is supposed to have retorted dismissively, 'Yes, they have more money.' But Fitzgerald's assertion of a qualitative distinction of personality between the wealthy and the rest, over and above the quantitative one of money, is evidence not of sycophancy as Hemingway and others seemed to think, but of insight.[2] He recognised that the inheritance of wealth, the regarding of it as a natural-born right rather than as a just reward for victory in the business struggle, conditioned a new aristocratic spirit in America; to be *born* rich was what counted.

The Fitzgerald family itself had risen to affluence on the wave of nineteenth-century expansion. Scott's grandfather, an Irish immigrant, had established a successful grocery business in the growing Midwestern city of St Paul, and left at his death in 1877 a personal fortune of over 260 000 dollars and a business with a turnover of millions. The daughter married Edward Fitzgerald, a local small businessman, and on her mother's death in 1913 their capital rose to 125 000 thousand dollars. These sums, large as they were, were sufficient to obtain them a place in only the bottom ranks of the Midwestern rich. Scott's father's business failed in 1898 and he was dismissed from Procter and Gamble in 1908, when the young Fitzgerald prayed silently that they might not have to go to the poor-house. Such events, together with the fact that his education was paid for by Aunt Annabel, impressed the family's precarious financial and class position upon the socially conscious boy. As a son of the bourgeoisie he was able to move in élite circles – there was no question of his having to mix with the lower classes – but he was constantly accompanied by the shadow of economic insecurity and an awareness of his relative poverty. 'That was always my experience', he wrote near the end of his life, '– a poor boy in a rich town; a poor boy in a rich boy's school; a poor boy in a rich man's club at Princeton. ... I have never been able to forgive the rich for being rich, and it has colored my entire life and works.'[3]

He was not born rich, and in that long, depressing summer of 1919 he almost lost the love of his life because of it. He had met Zelda Sayre at Montgomery, Alabama, while he was in the army, and had got engaged, but back in New York after the war he was unable to sell his stories and, apart from a dull job at Barron Collier's advertising agency, unable to make a living. In May 1919 Zelda broke off the engagement because he had no money, and it was only after the publication of *This Side of Paradise* in March 1920 had brought him fame and prosperity that they married.[4] The episode was formative, shaping his preoccupations for the remainder of his life:

> The man with the jingle of money in his pocket who married the girl a year later would always cherish an abiding distrust, an animosity, toward the leisure class – not the conviction of the revolutionist but the smouldering hatred of a peasant. In the years since then I have never been able to stop wondering where my friends' money came from, nor to stop thinking that at one time a sort of *droit de seigneur* might have been exercised to give one of them my girl.[5]

The financial rewards of his writing, particularly from his dollar-earning short stories, secured him entry into the ranks of the wealthy, but he never lost either the bitterness of that comparative social deprivation which stared him in the face before the publication of his first novel, or the awareness it had driven home that money was the dynamo which powered the bright lights of the leisure class.

It is significant, given Fitzgerald's identification of the power of wealth with sexual possession and the consequent pain at the possibility of his personal loss, that he does not condemn the choice that Zelda made. Her insistence that wealth, luxury and status should accompany deep human relationship is accepted unquestioningly, and his distinction between the 'revolutionist' and himself as 'peasant' has a striking accuracy. The revolutionary questions the social order and demands the overthrow or supersession of the hierarchy of wealth and power which characterises it. The peasant, on the other hand, sees society purely in personal terms. It is not the order itself which he questions but only his position within it, and his 'animosity' is thus a species of jealousy.[6] Amory Blaine expresses this kind of 'peasant' mentality during his ostensible defence of socialism in *This Side of Paradise*, written, of course, while Fitzgerald was fearful of losing Zelda to some wealthier suitor. 'I'm sick of a system where the richest man gets the most beautiful girl if he wants her', Amory exclaims, and later continues: 'My position couldn't be worse. A social revolution might land me on top.' As George Orwell once remarked, an equivocal class position tends to induce an intensified class identification.[7] So for Scott Fitzgerald, brought up on the lower borders of the rich, the qualities of glamour, ease and status which the leisure class possessed were eminently desirable, and Zelda's rejection of him because he could not guarantee these attributes himself paradoxically gained his sympathetic understanding, for her ambitions in their material aspects at least closely mirrored his. As a young man, he did not wish for the abolition of the very rich but simply for an extension of their privileges to himself, and when his writing provided the financial basis he assimilated his lifestyle to theirs – a Long Island mansion, parties, sojourns in Paris and on the Mediterranean seaboard. Fitzgerald's upbringing and early experience thus made him acutely aware of the importance of social class, and they determined that his attitudes towards the leisure class would be characterised by both an identification with, and a distrust of, that social group.

We find this creative tension articulated in his writings, and the success of his early novels may have been partly due to the fruitful coincidence of this personal ambivalence with the widespread ambivalence felt by the society at large towards the leisure class. Amory Blaine in *This Side of Paradise* largely embodies and expresses the sensuous and prestigious appeal. 'I think of Princeton', he says, 'as being lazy and good-looking and aristocratic', and he reverses traditional moral values by exclaiming his contempt for the poor and asserting that 'It's essentially cleaner to be corrupt and rich than it is to be innocent and poor'. He gives up his job writing copy for an advertising agency and in his new state of social desperation expounds socialism to a rich man who belongs to 'the class I belonged to until recently; those who by inheritance or industry or brains or dishonesty have become the moneyed class'. This closing section represents the undertow of disavowal, the critical, negative aspect of his dual attitude towards the rich, but it is not prepared for, is peremptory, and carries little real force since, as we have seen, Blaine is only interested in putting himself 'on top'.

The Beautiful and the Damned (1922) neatly encapsulates this ambivalence in its title, presenting the rich as the middle class liked to view them, as a bewitching combination of glamour and corruption, as, enviably, the physically blessed upon earth and, comfortingly, the morally degenerate who would suffer in the hereafter. Anthony Patch is a thoroughgoing member of the leisure class; he 'drew as much consciousness of social security from being the grandson of Adam J. Patch as he would have had from tracing his line over the sea to the crusaders. This is inevitable; Virginians and Bostonians to the contrary notwithstanding, an aristocracy founded sheerly on money postulates wealth in the particular.' As an expression of this aristocratic consciousness engendered by inherited wealth, Anthony prefers to live off his bonds and make a desultory attempt at writing a history of the Renaissance popes rather than take on a job of work. When his funds are exhausted and he is forced to try several jobs, he finds that his nature is too indolent to be capable of sustained effort and they are abruptly terminated. His final words – 'It was a hard fight, but I didn't give up and I came through.' – express his pride, as he sails for Europe a rich man once more, in remaining loyal to the values and behaviour of the leisure class during the long legal battle over Adam Patch's fortune. Fitzgerald's presentation of his leisure-class protagonist here is far more ironic than that of Amory Blaine, and he uses Anthony's crippled physical state to symbolise the considerable moral degradation that accompanied such fidelity to 'aristocratic' principles.

In *The Great Gatsby* (1925) he adopted the most effective and economical technique for conveying the tension in his own perspective on the wealthy – a narrator-participant who would himself through his story evoke both the sensuous attraction of the life of the rich and bring a moral consciousness to bear on their waste and corruption. Nick Carraway, a young man like Fitzgerald from the supposedly undegenerate Midwest, brings a discriminating and evaluating sense of decency to bear on his story of Jay Gatsby, who though he 'represented everything for which' Carraway had 'an unaffected scorn', eventually wins his respect. Gatsby with his Long Island mansion and lavish parties and dubious wealth, partakes of both the glamour and corruption of the leisure class of the 1920s, when bootlegging and speculating, not industry and thrift, were the most effective ways to wealth. The Protestant code dismissed such a figure as Gatsby as a criminal and a waster; conservative taste, too, dismissed such a figure as a flashy and vulgar upstart. And Fitzgerald honours both these responses in Carraway. Yet the middle-class imagination was also irresistibly drawn to the powerful trinity of youthful beauty, doomed love and great wealth (the stock ingredients of popular romance fiction), and Fitzgerald honours this impulse too through Carraway's vicarious participation in the lives of the rich and his growing imaginative involvement in Gatsby's obsession. Carraway steadily disengages Gatsby from his milieu and clothes him in the imagery of fairy-tale as a knight in quest of the princess in the tower, both of whom are magically locked in a timeless world. His pursuit of Daisy Buchanan, representing the sensuous attraction of the leisure class to a poor boy, is romanticised into a complex cultural symbol for the discrepancy between the great promise of America and its latter-day realisation in the lifestyle of the leisure class. Gatsby is redeemed in Carraway's eyes by the fact that in the midst of corruption he maintains an 'incorruptible dream', and this contradictory conjunction of an idealising vision with a sordid and inhospitable social reality has inevitably led to influential interpretations of *The Great Gatsby* in terms of the materialism that has beset 'the American Dream'.[8]

Yet not only do we need to go beyond this cultural interpretation by bringing the social and class specificity of Fitzgerald's fiction into proper relief, but we also need to be alert to the degree to which Fitzgerald may be distancing himself from Carraway's presentation. Carraway's favourite epithets are 'romantic' and 'enchanted', and surely the vacuous repetition of 'romantic' by Daisy and Tom early in the novel implies a debasement of meaning.[9] There is a satirical thrust in Fitzgerald's revelation of the tendency to excess in Carraway's imagination, which, like one of Walt Disney's animated paintbrushes, quickly paints any receptive scene in glowing hues. Even Wilson's grubby little garage has 'sumptuous and romantic apartments' projected into it, and the image of 'a great flock of white sheep' on Fifth Avenue, while brilliantly summoning the Jeffersonian Republic of agrarian virtues before us in this world of decadent plutocrats, also suggests an imagination that (for a bond salesman!) is remarkably free of the domination of the literal. Carraway's poetical attitudinising – 'I was within and without, simultaneously enchanted and repelled by the inexhaustible variety of life' – seems deliberately adolescent, and to the generation brought up on Mencken and the *Smart Set* may have seemed risible. Such indications, then, of Carraway's impulsive romanticism throw into doubt his valuation of Gatsby when in the famous closing passage he associates Gatsby's quest with the promise and wonder that the New World held. Gatsby is too insubstantial a figure to carry the heavy weight of that association, but Fitzgerald, in reaching out ambitiously for a larger cultural resonance, is presenting the yearning of the middle class to place within and assimilate to a noble national tradition that seduction by the values of glamour, ease and wealth which they guiltily felt within themselves.

The 'American Dream' was, of course, at root merely the promise of material advancement held out by virtually unlimited expansionary capitalist development, but it became idealised, mythicised, mystified, until the sense of possibilities for the individual became dematerialised, detached from the basic business of getting and making. The leisure class represented the efflorescence of American capitalist development and, since its members wholly inhabited the realm of freedom, the final realisation of the promise of the new continent. Yet, as already suggested, the leisure class presented a problematic social formation to the middle class. Haunted by the ghosts of Puritanism and egalitarianism and subject themselves to the daily demands of work and getting ahead, the members of this class could reconcile the tensions in their attitudes only by legitimising the sensuous attraction of the leisure class through its assimilation to an acceptable cultural complex – the 'American Dream'.

While Fitzgerald's imagination felt the sensuous appeal and the mystique of the life of the rich and his prose evoked those qualities with delicate, lambent images, there was also in that complex dualism of his response an opposing, unromantic, materialist perspective. His early experience and his precarious social position had instilled in him an awareness of the centrality of money and class to the social structure, and late in his career his personal insights were corroborated by his reading of Marx. In a letter to Maxwell Perkins he wrote, '[Spengler] and Marx are the only modern philosophers that still manage to make sense in this horrible mess', and he urged his daughter to read *Capital*.[10] Furthermore, his explicit avowal in his 'Notebooks' that he was 'essentially Marxian' indicates that a reading of his fiction which pays particular attention to Marxist emphases – class, amongst others – is justified and is likely to be illuminating.[11] 'I have never been able to stop wondering where my friends' money came from', he said, because he realised with the intensity of his own financial insecurity that the very getting of the money, the how and the why of where it came from, the economic dimension of individual life, profoundly determined the perspectives and values of the recipient. The institution of the leisure class *seemed* to revolve around higher aesthetic concerns connected with art and elegance and grace, but ultimately, Fitzgerald saw with clear-eyed realism, it was based on how the dollars came to be in people's pockets.

Running hand in hand with the evocation of the life of the rich through Fitzgerald's novels, then, is a concern to demystify wealth, to tie the lifestyle to its roots in the prosaic, amoral processes of American capitalism. He frequently provides biographical details which reveal his characters' class origins, or he specifically indicates how they obtain their living, so grounding them firmly in the economic substructure. In *The Beautiful and the Damned* Anthony Patch, we learn, lives by selling his bonds while waiting for the settlement of the will of his grandfather, Adam Patch, a Gilded Age financier who, after the Civil War, 'charged into Wall Street, and . . . gathered to himself some seventy-five million dollars'. Carraway is a bond salesman, an occupation which immediately alerts us to the material basis of the leisure-class lifestyle he observes at Gatsby's and the Buchanans'. This basis is further alluded to in the telling detail about Ferret, the gambler – 'when Ferret wandered into the garden it meant he was cleaned out and Associated Traction would have to fluctuate profitably next day'. Fitzgerald thus trenchantly associates the operations of Wall Street with the moral corruption of gambling, an invidious comparison we have met before in Howells's Silas Lapham and Norris's Cressler.

Gatsby, himself, represents wealth mystified. He appears from nowhere, buys an expensive mansion, throws lavish parties, and apparently has an inexhaustible source of money. Such mystery generated, and was in turn augmented by, the numerous rumours that crossed back and forth over his party tables. Yet it is one of the rich ironies of this mysterious figure that he is also a demystifier. He and Carraway discuss Daisy's voice:

> 'She's got an indiscreet voice,' I remarked. 'It's full of —'
> I hesitated.
> 'Her voice is full of money,' he said suddenly.
> That was it. I'd never understood before.[12]

The romantic response to the sensuous appeal of Daisy's voice has been Carraway's; it was he who found in it 'a singing compulsion, a whispered "Listen", a promise that she had done gay, exciting things just a while since and that there were gay, exciting things hovering in the next hour'. In a startling insight, given his emotional involvement with Daisy, Gatsby cuts through all this mystique to ground her appeal firmly on money, to place her once more in direct relation with the economic substructure that provides the material basis for her luxurious lifestyle. The revelation is wasted on Carraway who, giving full rein to his romanticising imagination, immediately proceeds to remystify her voice: 'It was full of money — that was the inexhaustible charm that rose and fell in it, the jingle of it, the cymbals' song of it. ... High in a white palace the king's daughter, the golden girl.' Gatsby's motive, the appeal of Daisy for *him*, has to be interpreted and articulated, apart from rare instances of direct speech, by Carraway and thus it is that he projects the aura and elusiveness that he felt the socially elevated Daisy held for the aspiring Gatsby. The contrast between Gatsby's matter-of-factness and Carraway's effusiveness reveals the degree to which Carraway's imagination is constantly at work transforming Gatsby's pursuit of Daisy into the stuff of romance and myth.

Gatsby himself may have no illusions about wealth and can penetrate the mystique of the leisure class, but he has, nevertheless, submitted to the mystification of sexuality by class. For Gatsby, as for Clyde Griffiths, sexual attraction and social ambition have become powerfully fused in a young woman of the leisure class. All his parties and his money are but a means to the consummation of his early romance with Daisy. Gatsby realises that wealth and sexual possession are closely associated in a class-bound society and that the consummation can take place only when he has proved himself her social equal. He had started life poor and, as his 'Schedule' reveals, with Franklinesque resolutions for self-improvement. But the Protestant path to prosperity is quite irrelevant to the consumption-oriented society of the early 1920s, and Gatsby resorts to bond forgery to provide the money that will bring Daisy to him. Showing her his mansion and displaying his many shirts constitute the ritual presentation of his credentials for membership of the leisure class, and hence for socially legitimate possession of her: 'He took out a pile of shirts and began throwing them, one by one, before us, shirts of sheer linen and thick silk and fine flannel, which lost their folds as they fell and covered the table in many coloured disarray. ... Suddenly, with a strained sound, Daisy bent her head into the shirts and began to cry stormily.'[13] Daisy's oddly emotional response to this rich display of conspicuous consumption betrays her recognition that Gatsby has overcome the social barriers that separated them and is now directly asking for her favour. That Gatsby's dedication is misplaced is made evident through the general portrayal of the worthlessness and meretriciousness of the rich which the novel contains.

The long list of names that Carraway jots down on an old timetable – 'the Leeches, and a man named Bunsen ... and Doctor Webster Civet ... and a whole clan named Blackbuck ... the Chromes ... and S. W. Belcher and the Smirkes and the young Quinns' – is reminiscent of Dickens in its sharp, economical satire, and it reminds us too that in this novel the demands of mimetic realism have yielded to those of interpretative effect. As members of the leisure class, Tom and Daisy Buchanan belong to 'a rather distinguished secret society', behind whose barriers of class and wealth they retreat after the débâcle of Myrtle's death and Gatsby's murder. Their 'difference' lies in being cynical where Carraway and Gatsby are curiously naive and trusting, and Carraway sums them up dismissively as 'careless people'. The novel's tone of distaste for the rich would have been all the more forceful had Fitzgerald entitled it 'Trimalchio' as he subsequently wished he had.[14] The extended comparison of Jay Gatsby with Trimalchio, the vulgar, upstart emperor of Petronius's *Satyricon*, would have considerably undercut the attraction and stature of his romantic quest. As the novel stands with only the residual reference,[15] Carraway, the imaginatively involved advocate and judge, easily exonerates him of the taint of the prevailing corruption by emphasising his role as an innocent with 'an extraordinary gift for hope, a romantic readiness'.

Gatsby is presented as a primitive, a man who in the midst of the sophistication of the twenties still has faith in the omnipotence of wishes and the power of dreams. His dream of himself and Daisy elevated to the realm of eternal, absolute love possesses, he believes, an irresistible force that though incapable of denying the reality of class is capable of overcoming time. Carraway tells him that he can't repeat the past: '"Can't repeat the past?" he cried incredulously. "Why of course you can!"' So demanding has his dream become that no mortal woman could have completely fulfilled it, for it has 'gone beyond' Daisy, beyond Daisy's merely 'personal' love for Tom, to attain an impersonal purity and dynamic of its own. It has become a personal myth shaping Gatsby's entire world, providing it with order and endowing his possessions – his shirts and his parties – with reality and significance. When this myth collapses, betrayed by Daisy, then the material world, no longer organised into any pattern of meaning, becomes unreal, and Gatsby feels only his alienation: 'He must have looked up at an unfamiliar sky through frightening leaves and shivered as he found what a grotesque thing a rose is and how raw the sunlight was upon the scarcely created grass. A new world, material without being real, where poor ghosts, breathing dreams like air, drifted fortuitously about.'[16] This destructured, suddenly strange, world is associated directly by plot development and imagery with one of the major symbols in the novel – the valley of ashes. The lines which conclude the above passage – 'like that ashen, fantastic figure gliding toward him through the amorphous trees' – refer, of course, to the vengeful Wilson who has spent much of his life in that barren wasteland which, like Locke's realm of primary qualities, represents a material world untransformed by any creative imagination. No redeeming myth presides there to lend significance to experience; only the huge eyes of Doctor T. J. Eckleburg stare down from their abandoned hoarding and provide the single point of reference.

The genesis of this striking image from a projected dust-jacket for the novel is well known,[17] but its appositeness, its undoubted power as a symbol is due to its integration in two closely related aspects of the theme embodied dramatically in the rise and fall of Gatsby. First, Gatsby's dream, his self-making imagination, was a way of *seeing*, of which the two eyes of Doctor T. J. Eckleburg are but the literalised metaphor. And if the valley of ashes is read as the urban-industrial world of everyday experience, we can understand his story as the dramatisation of the irresistible impulse towards, and the inevitable failure of, a romantic vision in such an inhospitable environment. The second aspect of the hoarding symbol is revealed by Wilson when, looking at the eyes, he tells Michaelis that 'God sees everything'. The omniscient God was the basic premise of the Puritan religion, and His symbolisation in a faded advertisement is eloquent of the reduced stature of the faith built upon that premise, for the decline of Puritanism has moral implications which become apparent to Carraway through Gatsby's fall. The all-seeing God in whom Wilson still believes was the final tribunal, the source of all moral absolutes, but in the modern industrial wasteland which includes the life of the leisure class, there are no longer any secure moral absolutes by which the actions of men can be judged. In their stead there are only personal ethical standards and the inevitable relativism that accompanies them. It is in reaction against the collapse of such imaginative and moral orders that Carraway desperately asserts the need for some general moral standard in society: 'When I came back from the East last autumn I felt I wanted the world to be in uniform and at a sort of moral attention forever.'

The monetary rewards and the prestige that his early novels together with his stories brought Fitzgerald enabled him to adopt the lifestyle of the leisure class and to become accepted by that status group.[18] He did not, however, belong to the same *class* proper as other members of the group since his income did not arise from property or capital. Ironically, his position in an élite which attached great social honour to the life of leisure was maintained only by repeated hard work on his part turning out the profitable *Saturday Evening Post* stories. His own life, therefore, registered on an individual scale that tension between the old ethic of asceticism, work and achievement and the new ethic of consumption, hedonism and living for the moment which the leisure class was propagating on a social scale. In 1924 Fitzgerald, after finishing *The Great Gatsby*, met Gerald and Sarah Murphy who were independently wealthy and who invited him and Zelda (with their daughter) to spend the summer with them at the little colony of the American leisure class they had founded at Antibes on the French Riviera.[19] Fitzgerald drew on his Mediterranean sojourn for the setting and atmosphere of the novel he began on the Riviera in the late summer of 1925, the novel that after many revisions became *Tender is the Night* (1934). In it he further explored the tensions – the romantic versus the moralist and Marxist, the work ethic versus the consumption ethic – which composed the ambivalences in his attitudes to very rich. The background, he wrote in his 1932 outline for the novel, was to be 'one in which the leisure class is at their truly most brilliant and glamorous'.[20]

The sensuous appeal of the life of the leisure class is articulated through the responses of Rosemary Hoyt, the young Hollywood parvenue, who comes into contact with the wealthy Divers on the French Riviera and falls in love with Dick Diver. To her, the Divers' ease and grace and encompassing charm make them exemplars of the civilised life of the leisure class, and *externally*, Fitzgerald assures us, they represented 'the exact furthermost evolution of a class, so that most people seemed awkward beside them'. Rosemary endows their lifestyle with Parnassian qualities. During the outdoor dinner party at the Divers' villa, for instance, her impression of its flattering exclusiveness and quality of magic is vividly conveyed, as the table seems to rise 'a little toward the sky like a mechanical dancing platform, giving the people around it a sense of being alone with each other in the dark universe, nourished by its only food, warmed by its only lights'.[21] Rosemary represents the highly paid artist who by means of the financial rewards and status of her profession is able, like Fitzgerald, to share the lifestyle of the leisure class while still basing her value-system upon work. She had, we are told, 'been brought up with the idea of work', and she envies the Divers their unhurried days, having known 'little of leisure' but having 'the respect for it of those who have never had it'.

At one point Rosemary and Nicole Diver go shopping together and Fitzgerald uses the occasion to highlight their different relationship to money. Nicole, living on the proceeds from a multi-million dollar estate, has made no personal investment of time or effort in order to secure her income, so she spends freely, limitlessly. Rosemary, however, 'thinking now through her mother's middle-class mind,' is conscious that she is spending money 'she had earned'. Thus Fitzgerald indicates how the leisure class obeys values antithetical to the middle-class values of work and commensurate reward. Nicole is the romantic epitome of the leisure-class woman, the very acme of the social system, and her shopping presents the opportunity for one of Fitzgerald's most extended and most forceful demystifications of wealth and glamour:

> Nicole was the product of much ingenuity and toil. For her sake trains began their run at Chicago and traversed the round belly of the continent to California; chicle factories fumed and link belts grew link by link in factories; men mixed toothpaste in vats and drew mouthwash out of copper hogsheads; girls canned tomatoes quickly in August or worked rudely at the Five-and-Tens on Christmas eve; half-breed Indians toiled on Brazilian coffee plantations and dreamers were muscled out of patent rights in new tractors – these were some of the people who gave a tithe to Nicole.[22]

This passage explicitly makes those linkages between the attractive luxury of the leisure class and the ugly toil of industry which more sycophantic portrayals of the rich seek to conceal. It makes plain that Nicole stands at the peak of the pyramid formed by the expropriation of surplus-value, her hedonistic lifestyle supported by the 'tithes' paid to her and the 'feudal' Warren family. Fitzgerald could hardly be more Marxist here.

Since he did not complete the novel until October 1933, he was able to endow his account of the late 1920s with the benefit of hindsight. The 1929 Wall Street Crash and ensuing Depression had brought the 1920s' profit and stock boom to an abrupt end and demonstrated the fundamental instability of the capitalist system. Fitzgerald closes the passage on Nicole with apocalyptic overtones and the suggestion of a close interconnection between the sickness of the economy and her characteristic leisure-class activity of conspicuous consumption: 'and, as the whole system swayed and thundered onward, it lent a feverish bloom to such processes of hers as wholesale buying, like the flush of a fireman's face holding his post before a spreading blaze. She illustrated very simple principles, containing in herself her own doom.'

In his 1932 outline for the novel Fitzgerald wanted it to 'show a man who is a natural idealist, a spoiled priest, giving in for various causes to the ideas of the *haute bourgeoisie*, and in his rise to the top of the social world losing his idealism, his talent and turning to drink and dissipation'.[23] And it is in the life-history of

Dick Diver as we see it between the closing stages of the First World War and the beginning of the Depression that Fitzgerald fully dramatises the antithetical relationship between Protestant values of work and achievement and consumption values of hedonism and the primacy of personal interaction. He is elevated into a figure representative of social and cultural change in the 1920s, and his decline and ultimate exhaustion embodies a moral comment on the leisure class and acts as a heavy counterweight to Rosemary's romantic approbation.

After beginning a brilliant career in psychiatry with total dedication to the values of intellectual asceticism and achievement, burning his textbooks for warmth 'with the fine quiet of the scholar which is nearest of all things to heavenly peace', Dick Diver becomes involved with Nicole Warren, the schizophrenic daughter of one of the richest families in Chicago. With marriage he enters the leisure class and finds himself with some unease adopting its contrasting lifestyle of conspicuous consumption: 'He felt a discrepancy between the growing luxury in which the Divers lived and the need for display that apparently went along with it.' His presence in the leisure class, like Rosemary's, is ultimately based on work, for his marraige to Nicole, it emerges, is largely a protracted course of psychiatric therapy to cure her of the traumatic effects of incest with her father. At the conclusion of Nicole's 'treatment' when he has abetted if not engineered the transference of affect from himself to Tommy Barban, we are told that 'the case was finished' and 'Doctor Diver was at liberty'. That title, 'Doctor', signifies with quiet force Dick Diver's return to the professional middle class from which he was originally recruited. By returning Nicole to health and wholeness he has performed a useful service for the 'feudal' Warrens; as Baby Warren remarks with aristocratic *hauteur*, 'That's what he was educated for.' Having served his therapeutic service, he could be discarded. It is sociologically appropriate that he is replaced by Barban, a full-fledged member of the leisure class whose name suggests 'barbarian' and whose occupation of waging war is, according to Veblen, 'chief among the honorable employments in any feudal community'.[24]

If the marriage was restorative for Nicole, for Dick it was a corrosive experience, causing him to lose his values of work and asceticism and leaving him intellectually and spiritually bankrupt. The felt loss of his personal integrity brings him guilt and a self-searching puzzlement as to the direction he took in squandering his talent, as to how 'he had been swallowed up like a gigolo and had somehow permitted his arsenal to be locked up in the Warren safety-deposit vaults'. The psychological explanation he is searching for does not become apparent until a later incident – the arrest of Mary North and Lady Caroline Sibley-Biers – reveals a crucial flaw in his character and brings to the surface the latent content of the motivation that underlay his marriage. Dick's self-analysis prompted by this incident, that is strategically placed immediately after we have been given notice of the marriage's breakdown, reveals that the seed of his subsequent decline lay in his all-too-human need for love and approval, 'because it had early become a habit to be loved, perhaps from the moment when he had realized that he was the last hope of a decaying clan'. Transposed into social terms, his desire for love and acceptance could best be satisfied by the upper class since its members were the leading arbiters of social worth. The opportunity, therefore, to earn love from representatives of the leisure class was difficult to resist. The tragic irony of Dick's response and motivation in the case of the night arrest lies in the fact that the two representatives whom he compulsively assists are, like the Warrens, incapable of giving him love. They are cynical where he is trustful, and the futile investment of effort and concern he makes in their case is but a miniature recapitulation of the investment he made in, and the emotional bankruptcy he derived from, his marriage to Nicole.

Dick Diver's mistake then, Fitzgerald suggests, was to shed the lonely assurance of his own integrity and to allow himself to be seduced by the ephemeral pleasures of social success and leisure-class acceptance. He embodies in fictional terms – and herein lies his social representativeness – the cultural change influentially described in characterological concepts by David Riesman and his collaborators in *The Lonely Crowd*. Applying Riesman's categories once more to a figure in a novel, we can characterise Dick Diver's personal transformation as the erosion of his earlier inner-directed values of individual achievement and personal ideals, and his adoption under the influence of the leisure-class lifestyle of the other-directed values of social acceptance and group harmony and approval.

Inner direction, as we have seen, was the mark of the earlier Protestant mentality, with which was also associated an ethic of asceticism and hard work. Dick's father, significantly a Protestant minister, is of this type. He never lost *his* integrity, but died with it intact. 'His father', Dick reflects, 'had been sure of what he was', and he had held to the inner-directed virtues of '"good instincts", honour, courtesy, and courage'. But as Fitzgerald indicates in his deft sketching of the cultural context, that type of mentality had lost its social dominance by the late 1920s. The Jazz Age was in full swing, 'the whole upper tenth of a nation living with the insouciance of grand ducs and the casualness of chorus girls'.[25] The leisure class, marked by hedonism and other direction with its emphasis on display, peer-group acceptance and social evaluation, had appeared at the apex of the status pyramid and as the harbinger of an increasingly diffused consumption ideology. Thus, although *Tender is the Night* grew out of autobiographical sources – Fitzgerald's admiration for the Murphys and their Mediterranean life, his experience of psychopathology and psychiatry through Zelda, a preoccupation with his own possible emotional exhaustion – it was also informed by Fitzgerald's acute sensitivity to his time, and he was able to reach out ambitiously for a larger resonance by making Dick Diver's life serve as a focus for such large-scale cultural change. His use of his protagonist to dramatise his awareness that a phase of American life has come to an end in the 1920s is markedly evident in the scene in which Dick, in a restaurant with Rosemary and Nicole, sees a party of gold-star mothers – American women who had lost sons in the Great War. They possess 'dignity' and in them he 'perceived all the maturity of an older America'. 'Momentarily, he sat again on his father's knee, riding with Mosby while the old loyalties and devotions fought on around him. Almost with an effort he turned back to his two women at the table and faced the whole new world in which he believed.' And when, later in the novel, he kneels at his father's grave, he bids him farewell with the strong historical sense of bidding farewell to the whole American tradition that stemmed from the early Puritans: 'Good-bye, my father – good-bye, all my fathers.'[26]

The very rich of whom Fitzgerald wrote were remarkably few in number – perhaps 50 000 individuals received one half of all national share income in 1929[28] – but they were powerful and influential and raised a tension between admiration and distrust on the part of the middle class. Through his own environment and experience Fitzgerald was particularly well fitted to feel the duality of response to the wealthy and this creative tension is repeatedly articulated in his writings. His work is thus particularly expressive of that ideological conflict which the rise of the leisure class and the growth of consumption-oriented hedonism was generating in American society in the 1920s. Wealth for him became a Janus figure, with one face innocent and wondering looking toward the unformed future that offered so many exciting possibilities, and the other, callous and calculating, looking back to the sordid grind of work and commerce from which it had come. Fitzgerald the romantic loved the mystique, the magical promise of wealth, and painted it in haunting images, but Fitzgerald the social critic, in whom the moralist and Marxist combined, condemned it as the efflorescence of a corrupt class structure which ruined the best in men. It was the very contradictions in his relationship with the very rich that enabled him to perceive such tensions in his society and to articulate them in his stories and novels in a way that no American contemporary could match.

9 Satire and Sentiment: Sinclair Lewis and the Middle Class

Few writers can have staked a claim for the national representativeness of their fiction so boldly, so arrogantly even, as did Sinclair Lewis in his short preface to *Main Street* (1920). '*This is America*', he begins sweepingly, and claims that Gopher Prairie's Main Street is '*the continuation of Main Streets everywhere*'. And in the novel he attributes to his protagonist, Carol Kennicott, a representativeness that is both regional – as 'the spirit of that bewildered empire called the American Middlewest' – and broadly social – as 'commonplaceness, the ordinary life of the age, made articulate and protesting'. *Main Street* sold 180 000 copies in the first six months of 1921 and its phenomenal success, making it 'the most sensational event in twentieth-century American publishing history', seemed to justify Lewis's boldness and to indicate that he had deeply plumbed the national mood.[1]

Lewis's concern to depict the 'ordinary life of the age' and his attention to process and physical detail establish a certain continuity between him and the Naturalist novelists of the previous generation. He did not share their determinist philosophy, however, and unlike theirs, his realism of presentation is in the service of an iconoclastic intention. The social *mores* of the white-collar middle class and the triumph of business values in the small town, the small city, the medical profession or evangelical religion constitute his favourite targets.

With the growth of the industrial towns and cities in the late nineteenth and early twentieth centuries the American village no longer played a significant role in the capitalist economy. The census for 1920 revealed for the first time that the majority of Americans could be defined as urban dwellers and so America had ceased being a predominantly rural nation. Despite its

168

reduced sociological status the small town continued to be viewed conventionally as the real America, as the unquestioned, natural seat of all that was best in the Republic. It was a comforting, but residual, image rendered obsolete by social change, and Lewis, who ten years later in his Nobel Prize speech was to continue criticising the persistence of sentimental, outmoded literary versions of America, attacked it in *Main Street*.[2]

Lewis, himself a product of Sauk Center, Minnesota, identifies two traditions of the American small town: that 'the American village remains the one sure abode of friendship, honesty, and clean sweet marriageable girls', and that 'the significant features of all villages are whiskers, iron dogs upon lawns, gold bricks, checkers, jars of gilded cat-tails, and shrewd comic old men who are known as "hicks"'. These folksy traditions, Lewis insists, passed out of actual life forty years before, and the current reality is the rather tawdry mass consumerism of the post-First World War years, 'cheap motor cars, telephones, ready-made clothes . . . kodaks, phonographs'. Gopher Prairie, Minnesota, has lost whatever regional distinction it once possessed and has merged, like other small towns, into a standardised, commercial culture which extends in deadening conformity across the nation.[3] Its world is dominated by 'silos' and 'alfalfa' and consumer items, and its characteristic working group is not composed of producers working with their hands but of white-collar workers in the service trades. The problems facing the individual in this environment, Lewis suggests, are not those of production and physical survival but of adjusting to one's social group and finding a way of life commensurate with the promise of material prosperity.

Dreiser in *Sister Carrie* portrayed Carrie Meeber as a migrant from the small town to the big city, for that was the common social pattern as the urban-industrial centres expanded and sucked in labour from the surrounding hinterland. But in *Main Street* Lewis reverses the direction of migration as part of his strategy for exposing the shortcomings of the small town. In 1912 and 1913 the new waves of modernist thought and art from Europe were penetrating metropolitan America with remarkable speed, and the bohemias of Greenwich Village and Chicago, the locations of the new arts, were rapidly expanding.[4] Carol's contact with bohemia in Chicago and her work in the library in St Paul have given her an interest in, and acquaintance with, the current intellectual ferment. She is thus portrayed as having attained a certain taste and sophistication before arriving in Gopher Prairie, and her first reaction, extensively and sympathetically delineated by Lewis, is an aesthetic revulsion at the small town's bleakness and desolate sense of temporariness. To her critical, urban eyes it seemed 'a frontier camp', and her revulsion gradually extends from the town's physical arrangement to encompass the thinness and narrowness of its social existence as she discovers with deepening dismay that it is a cultural backwater.

It is essential for Lewis's purpose, of course, that Carol be a sympathetic figure – cultured but not a snob, critical but not shrewish – and to this end he imbues her with a combination of optimism and altruism that at times leads to a loss of psychological credibility. Filled with missionary zeal, she attempts to introduce the community to aesthetic diversity and the latest developments by means of Japanese decor, modern poetry, experimental drama and schemes for civic improvements. But Gopher Prairie's stolid citizens rebuff each attempt, as Lewis builds up his portrait of a middle class that is Puritan and provincial, hostile to the arts, and devoted solely to material values, a portrait that was vigorously endorsed by H.L. Mencken in the pages of the *American Mercury*. Some of Carol's aesthetic ideas seem quite fatuous today. Her imagination, as conveyed by Lewis, is excessively literary and derivative in part of stale, late-Victorian romanticism. As she leaves for Washington with her son she tells him they are going to 'find elephants with golden howdahs from which peep young maharanees with necklaces of rubies, and a dawn sea colored like the breast of a dove, and a white and green house filled with books and silver tea-sets'. If Lewis had established a proper distance between himself and his protagonist, he could have subjected such immature whimsy to the irony it deserves, but by allowing Carol's flights of fancy to escape his satire and receive his endorsement he weakens the authority of his criticism of the town's jejune existence.

That aspect of Lewis's criticism which draws on Carol's metropolitan perspective may be compromised then, but there are other aspects which retain their trenchancy. These draw upon her regional representativeness and are historical and nativist in perspective. Carol, having failed to imbue the villagers with a taste for the beautiful and cosmopolitan, turns to the frontier tradition as an indigenous source of value for the town, deciding that 'in the history of the pioneers was the panacea for Gopher Prairie'. From the opening description of Carol standing 'on a hill by the Mississippi where Chippewas camped two generations ago', the close historical presence of the pioneering period in the West is a reiterated theme and the frontier myth plays a central role in the novel.[5]

This myth had been largely shaped and articulated by Frederick Jackson Turner who, in the years since he had read his famour paper, 'The Significance of the Frontier in American History', to the American Historical Association in 1893, had expanded and popularised his 'Frontier Thesis' in various papers and lectures which he collected together in *The Frontier in American History*, published the same year as *Main Street*. Whether or not Lewis was directly influenced by Turner (his biographer makes no reference to the historian), or whether he drew upon ideas that were 'in the air', Turnerian views of the frontier seem to provide the nativist base from which he directs his second attack upon the worth of the American small town. Turner's main points were that the frontier promoted individualism, egalitarianism and democracy, and that it had largely formed the striking characteristics of the American intellect. He painted the pioneers as a vigorous race, intelligent and energetic, fiercely independent and full of 'the buoyancy and exuberance which comes with freedom', full, in fact, of that 'sturdiness' which Carol now looks back to in the folk tradition of the barn dance and the western pioneer and hero, Lincoln. The frontier in Turner's view had also kept alive the American promise of a new, egalitarian social order: 'The entrance of old society upon free lands meant to the pioneer opportunity for a new type of democracy and new popular ideals. The West was not conservative: buoyant self-confidence and self-assertion were distinguishing traits in its composition. It saw in its growth nothing less than a new order of society and state.'[6]

This promise of a new society that the West held preoccupies Carol as she journeys into Minnesota with her husband for the first time. The Northern Middle West is 'the newest empire in the world', 'a pioneer land', and what is to be its future, she wonders? 'A future of cities and factory smut where now are loping empty fields? Homes universal and secure? Or placid chateaux ringed with sullen huts? . . . The ancient stale inequalities, or something different in history, unlike the tedious maturity of other empires?'[7] There are echoes here of Jefferson's distaste for industrialism and of Crèvecoeur's praise of an American egalitarianism based on the freeholder in contrast to feudal Europe, as Carol invokes the early hope for agrarian democracy as a new type of social organisation. But 1920 was not 1780 nor indeed 1870, and although the frontier as an image of hope and renewal lived on in American myth well into the twentieth century, as a material fact it passed out of American history in 1890 when the Superintendent of the Census declared it officially closed. As Lewis emphatically expressed it at the beginning of *Main Street*, 'The days of pioneering . . . are deader now than Camelot', and the impossibility of recovering the frontier spirit across half a century of social change exists in tension with its tantalising historical closeness. The Middle West, Lewis makes plain, no longer enjoys the fluidity or vitality of frontier social conditions and has already settled into 'the tedious maturity of other empires'.

Carol's resort to cultural nostalgia is, therefore, doomed to disillusioning failure. Just as she discovers that the town has lost whatever pioneer vigour it once enjoyed without attaining any compensatory refinement – that it is 'neither the heroic old nor the sophisticated new' – so she discovers that it has betrayed its social and political promise too. In Lewis's jaundiced image of the American small town the native tradition of openness and democratic sentiments has completely faded away. In its stead there reign social inequalities and a status system based on middle-class income and the strength of one's claim to be of early white Anglo-Saxon American stock. The only person in the town to exemplify the exuberance and independence of the pioneers, Miles Bjornstam, is ostracised by the members of the middle class because his contempt for convention and his socialist beliefs threaten their conservatism and business values.

Above all, Gopher Prairie, and by implication, America, has failed to fulfil the frontier promise of personal freedom and a higher, more satisfying type of life for all. Once the problems of production had been overcome and scarcity eradicated, then it seemed American life could begin to realise those possibilities for individual development which, unhampered by European traditions and inequalities, it had always held. As we have seen, however, the fruits of the New World's development were not shared among the many but concentrated in the hands of a few, so producing a stratified society just like that of Europe. Lewis

brings together Carol's regional and social representativeness in
the key political speech she makes to Guy Pollock:

> I believe all of us want the same things – we're all together, the
> industrial workers and the women and the farmers and the
> Negro race and the Asiatic colonies, and even a few of the
> Respectables. It's all the same revolt, in all the classes that have
> waited and taken advice. I think perhaps we want a more
> conscious life. We're tired of drudging and sleeping and dying.
> We're tired of seeing just a few people able to be individualists.
> We're tired of always deferring hope till the next generation.
> ... We want our Utopia *now* – and we're going to try our
> hands at it. All we want is – everything for all of us![8]

Identifying herself with all those social groups which have been
excluded from those opportunities which America, and the West
in particular, promised, Carol generalises her youthful personal
disaffection into a widespread upsurge of utopian expectations.
Lewis thus temporarily introduces a tone of broad social protest
into the novel.

He once joined the Socialist Party and spent some time at
Upton Sinclair's co-operative experiment at Helicon Hall.[9] He
had considerable sympathy, therefore, with radical critiques of
American society and no doubt socialist thinking informs the
main demand in Carol's minor manifesto that the inequalities of
capitalism give way to an egalitarian utopia. Another probable
influence was Progressivism, the most important development in
American politics between 1900 and 1920, which was closely
associated with such Middle-Western senators as Clapp and
Nelson of Minnesota, Cummins and Dolliver of Iowa, and
Robert La Follette of Wisconsin.[10] Progressive reformers were
optimistic that social and political injustices could be solved by
returning economic, political and social institutions to a larger
degree of popular control, and this confidence in the imminence
of reform is evident in Carol's attitude. As Lewis indicates, such
hopeful anticipation of the fruition of the American social
promise is frustrated by the political conservatism, the single-
minded commercialism, the vested interests and class divisions of
small towns like Gopher Prairie. The pioneers' idealistic hope that
something fine and grand might come out of the Middle West
once the crude work of settlement was completed has, according

to Lewis's critical portrait, been overwhelmed by a barren combination of conservatism, materialism and philistinism, and in
Main Street he thus voices a social and political, as well as
aesthetic, disillusionment with the civilisation of abundance that
has come to pass there.

Even the small town's economic function, which Carol eventually considers its only justification, is exposed as a hollow sham.
Gopher Prairie makes its living by selling retail services to the
agricultural producers in the surrounding countryside and Lewis
several times reiterates his charge that the town's middle class is
parasitic upon the farmers. The town is founded on exploitative
commercialism, and both its social sterility and its physical
ugliness proclaim the dispiriting triumph of business values.
Economically unjustifiable, hostile to the arts, socially divided,
bigoted and prurient, Gopher Prairie represents Lewis's damning
indictment of the Middle West and the small-town mentality.

At long last, it seems, Carol escapes, fleeing like thousands of
young Americans in those years from the village to the city in
search of independence and broader horizons. During the years
of the First World War the expansion of office work created new
career opportunities for women as clerks, typists and secretaries,
and Carol's disaffection and her escape to a white-collar job with
a government agency in Washington also contain an element of
feminist revolt against the limited sexual roles of housewife and
mother in an era of growing professional independence among
women. Once she has left the stifling atmosphere of Gopher
Prairie, however, Carol's attitude shifts from critical rejection of
the small town to affectionate idealisation. Not that Lewis's
portrait of her life in the Middle West has been all negative; there
have been positives such as the duck-shooting and fishing
expeditions, and Kennicott, in Lewis's rather eulogistic account
of the country-doctor's practice, has shown qualities of quiet
heroism and pioneer self-reliance which Carol admired. In the
last stages of the novel, then, Lewis relinquishes his satirical tone
for a sentimental one, as from the perspective of the national
capital in the East Carol 'saw Main Street in the dusty prairie
sunset, a line of frontier shanties with solemn lonely people
waiting for her, solemn and lonely as an old man who has outlived
his friends'. Lewis thus begins to reclothe Gopher Prairie with the
folksy hues of that jaded frontier tradition which he has so
effectively demolished in the earlier stages of the novel. That

Carol should finally return to the small town after experiencing independence and a career in Washington seems a violation of her characterisation and is an unconvincing plot development.

The novel's final effect, consequently, is an unsettling ambivalence of satire and sentiment in Lewis's view of the small town. Despite the keenness of his earlier criticisms of Gopher Prairie, he eventually seems to endorse its values against those of the sophisticated metropolitan centre, so, ultimately, helping to sustain that myth of the American small town which he set out to undermine. This ambivalence, according to his biographer, reflects the tensions within his temperament between convention and freedom, crudity and refinement, but perhaps it can also be related to a change in the political climate.[11] By 1920 Progressivism had become a dead letter, as the urge for reform seemed to fade away with the coming of post-war prosperity and consumerism. This was registered in 1920 with the election to the Presidency of Warren G. Harding, a Midwesterner from a small town in Ohio, who promised not to embark on spectacular idealistic programmes but to favour business and the pursuit of prosperity and so bring about a return to 'normalcy'.[12] There is sociological appropriateness, therefore, in having Carol, the 'spirit' of the Middle West and representative of 'the ordinary life of the age', abandon her hopes of a richer, more exciting life and settle, like the nation, for conformity and dull abundance.

In *Babbitt* (1922) Lewis once more attacks the conformity and limitations of the white-collar middle class. Unlike *Main Street*, this novel carries no grandiose rubric, but it is evident nevertheless that Zenith is meant to stand for small American cities everywhere and George F. Babbitt, like Carol Kennicott, for the person in the street, the sociological average. Lewis originally intended the book to be a record of twenty-four hours in Babbitt's life from alarm clock to alarm clock and this early conception remains for the first seven chapters.[13] The remaining twenty-seven chapters are assembled set-pieces covering such topics as Politics, Leisure, Club Life, Marriage and Family, Work, Class Structure and Religion, that taken together provide an almost complete sociology of middle-class life. There is no real plot to unite these episodes which are held together only by Babbitt's progression through them in his development from acceptance to rebellion and then compromise. *Babbitt* is thus a rather static novel with little over-all structural coherence, and the first section enjoys a unity of conception and sureness of tone lacking in the remainder of the book.

In these early chapters Lewis establishes his distance from his protagonist in a way he had failed with Carol Kennicott. He treats Babbitt objectively as a social specimen to be turned this way and that for the reader's amusement, such phrases as 'he was, to the eye, the perfect office-going executive' and 'he may be viewed tonight as . . .' indicating the general externality of approach. The satiric tone is maintained by the two devices of the mock-heroic and comic-hyperbole. Babbitt's success in parking his car in the morning, for instance, is 'a virile adventure masterfully executed', and his preparations for leaving his office during his lunch-period 'were somewhat less elaborate than the plans for a general European war'. By such means Lewis is able both to endow his account of a mundane existence with colour and humour and to suggest the degree of his real-estate agent's immersion in the stifling and essentially trivial routines of the office-worker. In *Babbitt* Lewis created an altogether larger and more appealing character than Carol Kennicott, although even this, his most successful and most famous creation, suffers from burlesque exaggeration and embarrassing sentimentality.[14]

In Zenith too, Lewis has created a setting that is more comprehensive and modern than Gopher Prairie. The opening description alerts us to the fact that we are in a mainly post-industrial environment. Zenith's business centre is dominated by skyscraper office-blocks and the peripheral hills are covered with the new suburban homes of the white-collar middle class. Its economic base is composed not of primary, but of secondary industries – 'factories producing condensed milk, paper boxes, lighting-fixtures, motor-cars' – and even these industries are inconspicuous in the city landscape. Although Lewis occasionally reminds us of the continued existence of an industrial working class, his attention is almost totally devoted to middle-class businessmen involved in distribution, service trades and selling. Babbitt 'made nothing in particular, neither butter nor shoes nor poetry, but he was nimble in the calling of selling houses for more than people could afford to pay'. Zenith, Lewis makes plain, is economically and socially immersed in the consumption phase of American capitalism, and in *Babbitt* he documents those features of post-war prosperity which made an impact upon

American values and character in the 1920s.

The main business imperative in this consumption phase is selling, and Lewis alludes to its centrality in the new economy by means of two travelling salesmen. To them 'the Romantic Hero was . . . the great sales-manager . . . who devoted himself and all his samurai to the cosmic purpose of Selling – not of selling any-thing in particular, for or to anybody in particular, but pure Selling.'[15] As an aid to selling, Zenith is saturated with the pre-eminent institution of consumerism – large-scale advertising. On his way to work every morning Babbitt passes 'hoardings with crimson goddesses nine feet tall advertising cinema films, pipe tobacco, and talcum powder', and Babbitt, as a property sales-man, also writes advertisements for his own agency. Lewis alludes to the advertising in newspapers and magazines several times and he casts Cholmondeley Frink in the role of an advertising copy-writer.

The documentary accuracy of Lewis's Zenith as a typical mid-western city is evident from comparison with Robert and Helen Lynd's sociological study of Muncie, Indiana in 1925, published as *Middletown* in 1929. So close are the parellels between the two portraits that had not *Babbitt* been published seven years ahead of *Middletown*, Lewis might well have been accused of plagiar-ism. Both fictional Zenith and real-life Muncie share such features of consumerism as advertising and the prevalence of electrical goods of all kinds in the home; both share a deep-seated conservatism of attitude; and both indulge in self-advertisement, an organised activity of city-boosting which insists the city must be kept to the fore and its shortcomings played down in order to attract business. This activity provides Lewis with one of his richest satirical opportunities as he portrays the brash buffoonery which Babbitt and other members of the Boosters Club commit in order to promote Zenith at Monarch, the state capital.

Two observations the Lynds made of Muncie are particularly germane to *Babbitt*'s main theme: 'Never was there more pressure in the business world for solidarity, conformity, and wide personal acquaintance than exists today'; and 'Standardized pursuits are the rule; with little in their environment to stimulate originality and competitive social life to discourage it, being "different" is rare even among the young.'[16] Lewis keenly satirises this relentless pressure for conformity and the tedious standardi-sation of middle-class life in his portrait of George F. Babbitt. It is not the Protestant ethic that rules as a scheme of behaviour in Zenith but the Social Ethic, as William H. Whyte termed that subservience of the individual to the group which he observed in white-collar occupations and on suburban estates. For much of the book Babbitt is a thoroughgoing conformist, eagerly responsive to all the social group's exhortations and compliant with all its restraints. He is shown being proudly competent in the suburban rites of cocktails and dinner parties, and in unquestioned accord with his business class's WASP prejudices against unions, socialists, immigrants, Catholics and Jews. This desire, as well as capacity, for conformity is, Lewis indicates, part of a larger personality pattern.

W. E. Leuchtenberg pointed out some implications for the American character with the rise of a consumption-oriented society in the 1920s: 'The nineteeth-century man, with a set of personal characteristics adapted to an economy of scarcity, began to give way to the twentieth-century man with the idiosyncrasies of an economy of abundance. Agressively optimistic, he was friendlier but had less depth, was more demanding of approval, less certain of himself.'[17] In Babbitt Lewis created the stereotype of just such a twentieth-century man. Like many recruits to the suburban middle class, Babbitt has migrated from the country to the city, and in the transition has lost what inner security and identification with traditional values he once had. He lacks any strong principles or personally established convictions; even his religion is merely practical, for 'it was respectable, and beneficial to one's business, to be seen going to services'. Having no independence of mind, he finds 'it hard to form an original opinion' and so adopts whatever attitudes are fed to him by the organisations to which he belongs. He is also portrayed as being extremely dependent on the approval of other people; he 'liked to like the people about him' and 'was dismayed when they didn't like him'. And when he has caused some friction in his office, 'he was distressed by losing that approval of his employees to which an executive is always slave'. With his lack of independence and inner strength, his conformity to the group, his need of the approval of others, Babbitt is another fictional representative of the other-directed character-type.

The source of direction for other-directed people is not internalised but is located in the peer group, either known directly to them or through the media. Thus Babbitt adopts not only those values imparted directly to him by his social group through its organisations, but also passively accepts those values and styles purveyed to him by advertising: 'the large national advertisers fix the surface of his life, fix what he believed to be his individuality. These standard advertised wares – toothpastes, socks, tyres, cameras, instantaneous hot-water heaters – were his symbols and proofs of excellence; at first the signs, then the substitutes, for joy and passion and wisdom.'[18] Here Lewis highlights the effect upon, and the cost to, the personality of too heavy a reliance upon those closely inter-linked features of consumerism – advertising and status symbols. In the competitive milieu of Zenith 'a family's motor indicated its social rank precisely', and an individual must rely solely on his pecuniary status and the signs of that status for his self-esteem. Veblen was among the first to point to the significance of consumer durables in the status-system, and Lewis seems to be following him in his characterisation of Babbitt who is shown immersed in the world of commodities. Objects dominate his life, supplying him with reassurance and an identity. His backyard 'was the neat yard of a successful business man of Zenith, that is, it was perfection, and made him also perfect'; his Boosters Club button makes him 'feel loyal and important'; and his office water-cooler and expensive ties confirm him in his sense of social superiority. Lewis skilfully builds up the impression that Babbitt must repeatedly take stock of his possessions in order to remind himself of who and what he is.

Despite the apparent solidity of Babbitt's existence, therefore, there is a hollowness at its centre with these commodities becoming 'substitutes' for, instead of signs of, autonomous feelings. Babbitt's repression of the private, noncommercial aspects of his personality, and his reliance on externals for his sense of self mean that he has not generated any inner core of security and identity. The regressiveness of his bath-time play, and his fantasy of the fairy child deliberately alert us to the immaturity of his real emotions. Lewis's external approach to his subject, with a great deal of attention paid to surface detail, is thus particularly apposite to his character and theme, since most of Babbitt's inner life is expressed in objects, and surfaces count for so much in the lives of Zenith's middle class. The coherence of Lewis's conception of Babbitt is evident in that whenever he is shown acknowledging his real desires to himself, such as his sexual attraction to his secretary or his wish to go away without his wife, the feeling which oppresses him is not guilt but loneliness. For these desires transgress not a moral, but a social, code, and Babbitt is intuitively aware that the behaviour they urge could lead to ostracism from his group.

Babbitt would be little more than an early image of 'one-dimensional man' were it not for the element of disaffection which Lewis introduces into his personality. What differentiates him from his fellow conformists, deepening him as a fictional character and generating the tension in the novel, is his growing apprehension beneath his willed joviality and automatic obeisance that his standardised lifestyle is barren and futile. Initially, he harbours only intermittent 'doubts regarding life and families and business' but these wax into confusion and, finally, outright revolt.

'Wish I'd been a pioneer, same as my grand-dad', Babbitt wistfully says to himself, and one avenue of escape from the sterility of socialised living that offers itself to him is a return to nature and the accompanying frontier qualities of self-reliance and freedom. For the real-estate agent, as for white-collar workers at large, the foreground of experience is entirely taken up with the constructed totality of the city and shifting problems of human relations. Having no active contact with the hard, unambiguous natural world creates a sense of loss, which is represented by Lewis as a nostalgia on Babbitt's part for that immediacy of work and physical reality which obtained during the early production phase. Babbitt and Paul Riesling, having gleefully achieved independence from their wives, go fishing in Maine, where, amongst more primitive conditions, they briefly lose their group-oriented ways and enjoy a regenerative spell of naturalness and comradeship. When he returns a year later with the same nostalgic urge to be a pioneer, to 'take up a backwoods claim with a man like Joe, work hard with his hands, be free and noisy in a flannel shirt', he discovers that as the product of a highly commercialised, highly socialised environment he is bound to it as if by chains, because he has internalised all its patterns and concerns, 'because in his own brain he bore the office and the family and every street and disquiet and illusion of Zenith'.

Having exhausted his one means of escape from the Midwestern city, and the crisis of Riesling's imprisonment having rendered him temporarily indifferent to his group's sanctions and beliefs, he engages in a mild rebellion, which reaches its high-point when he refuses to join the Good Citizens' League, yet another organisation for ensuring political and social conformity. As a result of this he begins to feel, and fear, the power of the group's sanctions. Furthermore, he deserts his usual company, abandons his customary sobriety, and becomes an enthusiastic member of Tanis Judique's group of hedonistic friends. This represents no assertion of independence, however, but only subservience to a new set of social demands, as he finds himself 'bound by the exceedingly straitened conventions, the exceedingly wearing demands, of their life of pleasure and freedom'.

The writing curiously sags during these episodes of Babbitt's 'revolt', partly due to the fact that Lewis, intent upon securing sympathy for his real-estate agent, loses his former sureness of tone and attitude of detachment. Also, Lewis seems to agree with his character in believing that this short burst of half-hearted liberalism, mild flirtation and heavy drinking has more significance than it really does. Babbitt's 'rebellion' is so conditioned by the *mores* of Zenith that it offers no real alternative or opposing set of values, thus implying a failure on Lewis's part to conceive of any positive content for the notions of 'freedom' and 'independence' in the context of middle-class America. Even this overrated revolt does not last long, however, as the old conformist Babbitt reasserts himself, dropping liberalism and Tanis Judique, joining the Good Citizens' League, and finding himself accepted back into the fold. *Babbitt* thus ends disappointingly as a sentimentalised tribute to that middle-class conformity which it had so vigorously attacked earlier, and so suffers from the same failure of nerve which mars *Main Street*.

'The mass of men lead lives of quiet desperation', Thoreau noted, and the quality of muted disquiet in Babbitt's character, overshadowed as it is by the exuberant satire, constitutes Lewis's main psychological insight in the novel. The most serious and most affecting passages in *Babbitt* are those in which he portrays the middle-aged realtor's slow realisation of the sterility of his life, his growing confusion, and his eventual, painful alienation from everything about him that had previously given comfort. There is a desperation in conformity too, as Lewis effectively indicates the status ranking, competitiveness, restlessness and insecurity that beneath all the aggressive optimism and camaraderie haunt these middle-class members of 'the lonely crowd'. In Babbitt, Lewis gives us the first complete image of a new social type, the white-collar office-worker and suburban resident, characteristic of the consumption-oriented phase of American business. George F. Babbitt is, perhaps, the first fully documented Consumer Man in American fiction.

10 Undemocratic Vistas: Dos Passos, Mass Society and Monopoly Capital

The strong historical impulse behind John Dos Passos's work has long been recognized, particularly since he himself emphasised the closeness of fiction to history. In 1928 he wrote that he regarded the novelist as 'a sort of second-class historian of the age he lives in', and in 1935 he told the American Writers' Congress, 'American writers who want to do the most valuable kind of work will find themselves trying to discover the deep currents of historical change under the surface of opinions, orthodoxies, heresies, gossip and journalistic garbage of the day.'[1] Like Norris and Dreiser before him, Dos Passos sought to document a whole period and to dramatise its shaping forces. His important novels of the 1920s and 1930s constitute a highly selective 'history' of his time and reveal a critical, oppositional perspective which acted as an interpretative principle for his fiction.

As the son of a wealthy corporation lawyer, Dos Passos was technically of the professional middle class, but his irregular early life – his parents did not marry until he was fourteen and he spent his childhood moving from hotel to hotel[2] – gave him little opportunity to develop a firm sense of class membership, and since he was not a member of a fixed community he was not socialised into the normal middle-class conventions and ideologies. The only community he could be said to belong to was that loose fraternity of mobile, deracinated intellectuals who after their 'exile' in Europe during the war and after returned to invade American letters. As for many of his generation, the experience of the European battlefields (as an ambulance driver in his case) was formative and shocking. It destroyed his residual Harvard aestheticism, heightened his belief in the importance of individual liberties, intensified his hatred of officialdom and the conventional pieties, and led to a deep disillusionment with the character of American society. He generalised his disgust with the military into a comprehensive social pessimism which embraced business civilisation. 'Everywhere it seems to me,' he wrote to a Spanish friend early in 1918, 'there is nothing, either for the rich or poor, but slavery; to industry, to money, to the mammon of business, the great God of our times.'³ When he returned to America, he allied himself with the radicals, associating himself with the left-wing *New Masses* and voting in 1920 for the Socialist Party presidential candidate, Eugene Debs.⁴ The recurrent themes of his wartime correspondence – an identification of military organisation with the organisation of industrial society, the curtailment by both of individuality and the finer, aesthetic aspects of life, and a despairing sense of entrapment, futility and frustration – surfaced in his first two novels, running like dark threads through the immature *One Man's Initiation: 1917* (1920) and the more achieved *Three Soldiers* (1921).

Three Soldiers contrives, not too successfully, to present a representative picture of the experience of soldiers in the American Expeditionary Force. The diverse geographical origins of the three main characters – 'That's goddam funny. You're from the Coast, this feller's from New York, an' Ah'm from ole Indiana, right in the middle' – suggest an attempt at a national comprehensiveness, and the section titles – 'Making the Mould', 'The Metal Cools', 'Machines', 'Rust' and 'Under the Wheels' – point to the compression of the free individual into a standardised component of the military war-machine and identify this process with the general dehumanisation of men in a machine-dominated society. (The mechanisation of the human by the war is also evident in the paintings of Fernand Léger, who treated the body itself as a metallic automaton.) For this war was the first fully mechanised conflict and it forcefully contrasted the helplessness of men with the technical efficiency of modern armaments. The war demonstrated too the arrival of the mass age, as tens of thousands of soldiers, mobilised by mass propaganda and recruited by general conscription, were subjected to a slaughter that was ignoble, impersonal and indiscriminate. Dos Passos's concern for the greatly reduced stature of the individual in the face of such crushing developments becomes explicit in the artist-figure Andrews's meditation on the contrast between the bold individualism of the Renaissance and the crippling conformity of the present:

Men seemed to have shrunk in stature before the vastness of the mechanical contrivances they had invented. Michael Angelo, da Vinci, Aretino, Cellini; would the strong figures of men ever so dominate the world again? Today everything was congestion, the scurrying of crowds; men had become ant-like. Perhaps it was inevitable that the crowds should sink deeper and deeper in slavery. Whichever won, tyranny from above or spontaneous organization from below, there could be no individuals.[5]

Here, in simple, direct statement are enunciated several of Dos Passos's obsessive, pessimistic themes: the aridity of contemporary life, the dwarfing of the individual before his own collective and industrial creations, and his absorption into urban mass society.

From the last quarter of the nineteenth century in America the processes and products of mass manufacture had steadily permeated society, shaping a standardised, routinised existence that was dominated by images of the dynamo and conveyor belt. Thorstein Veblen in *The Instinct of Workmanship* (1914) drew attention to the pervasive impact of the machine on modern life, pointing out that 'the ordinary routine of life is more widely and pervasively determined by the machine industry and by machine-like industrial processes today' and that 'no one can wholly escape or in any sensible degree deflect the sweep of the machine's routine'. He highlighted the mechanical routine of life at large and the growing depersonalisation wrought by the accelerating pace and heightened tension of urban-industrial living. In *The Vested Interests* (1919) also, he wrote of the way in which industrialism enforces a mechanistic conception of things and processes and generates a materialistic frame of mind.[6] Veblen was probably the leading, if officially neglected, liberal social analyst of his day, and his thought, rather than Marx's, influenced Dos Passos's perspectives on American society.[7] Dos Passos, like Dreiser, was aware of, and depicted, the polarisation of America into rich and poor, but more than in class conflict, he was interested in the many subtle and insidious ways by which an overarching economic system, monopoly capitalism, mediates its effects upon the individual. Dos Passos took for granted the materialistic temper of urban man in his characterisation and showed how people themselves can become automata. In *Manhattan Transfer* (1925) he sought to demonstrate how the dense overcrowding of the metropolitan centres and the rhythms of a highly mechanised environment were dehumanising the people who suffered them and pre-empting that proud individualism associated by Andrews with the Renaissance, but also espoused in the native American tradition by Jefferson, Emerson and Whitman among others.

The swarming city, huge in scale, anonymous and impersonal, was the natural focus for mass society, and *Manhattan Transfer* opens with an image of congestion and ant-like scurrying, as the crowd disgorges from the harbour ferry to '*press through the manure-smelling wooden tunnel of the ferryhouse, crushed and jostling like apples fed down a chute into a press*'. A few pages on there are further images, 'the annihilating clatter of the L trains overhead', 'the rancid sweet huddled smell of packed tenements', to suggest the physical density of urban life. His trilogy *USA* opens with images of mass urban society too: 'People have packed into subways, climbed into streetcars and buses; in the stations they've scampered for suburban trains; they've filtered into lodgings and tenements, gone up in elevators into apartment houses.' This constitutes the limiting context within which the muted, compromised lives of his characters take place. By repeated references throughout *Manhattan Transfer* to the crowding, the noise and the smells and the gritty wind, Dos Passos succeeds in creating an atmosphere of physical oppression, of a continuous environmental pressure acting upon the vulnerable individual and frustrating his self-creating energies.

In *Manhattan Transfer* Dos Passos documents with considerable economy the social history of Manhattan from the beginning of the century to the early 1920s, and presents the city as a huge symbol of twentieth-century tendencies.[8] In the early part of the novel there is a sense of promise generated by the rapidly rising city as the immigrants pour in and the skyscrapers take shape. At the beginning of the 'Metropolis' chapter he presents a vision of New York as an architectural wonder, as a city to rival the great cities of old but made from new materials and according to revolutionary designs: 'Steel, glass, tile, concrete will be the materials of the skyscrapers. Crammed on the narrow island the million-windowed buildings will jut glittering, pyramid on pyramid like the white cloudhead above a thunderstorm.' We recall how often in the novel we are made to feel the presence of 'the tall buildings' which squeeze out the sky and dwarf the individuals, like Jimmy Herf, walking in their shadow. For Dos Passos, as for Lewis Mumford writing at the same time, the skyscrapers expressed

American civilisation and reflected the dominance of business enterprise over social and artistic needs. They represent, Mumford wrote, a mechanical 'architecture fit only for lathes and dynamos to dwell in', and they had created a dehumanised environment which suppressed creative fulfilment and crushed the individual.[9] Because of this dominance of business values the city fails to fulfil its promise. Urban growth and social change did not bring more freedom and equality and a richer quality of life but a distinctive metropolitan lifestyle characterised by greed, conformity and barrenness that sets the mad tramp raving with a vision of apocalypse at the novel's close. Dos Passos's distaste for the metropolis permeates the whole book, and is in a long tradition, stemming from Jefferson, of American intellectuals' negative response to the city.[10]

He presents a fairly comprehensive social panorama, embracing the working, middle and upper classes, and indicates that New York is class- and status-ridden with money and appearances paramount in importance. His main focus, however, is on the members of the new white-collar middle class who are divorced from the productive processes and who inhabit what Dos Passos once called with disgust 'an all pervading spirit of commerce'.[11] While the problem that defeats Bud Korpenning in the beginning and faces Dutch Robertson at the end is that of material scarcity, the problems facing the middle-class characters are typical of abundance and satiety. They are freed from real need; yet their lives are blighted with anxiety, tension, disillusionment and loss of direction. The traditional ideologies, Puritanism and individualism, no longer carry much force in a mass society based on commercialism and consumption. The middle-class characters are shown indulging in a hedonistic lifestyle and drifting according to the behaviour patterns of their peer group in an amoral progression of drunkenness, infidelity and hypocrisy. In this light George Baldwin's bland espousal of the work ethic in regard to the leisure-class male, Stan Emery – 'I guess all he needs is to go to work and get a sense of values' – is heavy with authorial irony, since in Dos Passos's critical view the only 'values' taught by work in Manhattan are the subordination of the individual to alienating routine and the primacy of 'getting ahead'. The whole city is firmly committed to a success ethic, but the dedication to material ambition as Dos Passos presents it in the lives of George Baldwin and Ellen Thatcher leads only to boredom and spiritual emptiness. Stan Emery enunciates the futility of such ambition: 'But what can you do with success when you get it? You can't eat it or drink it.'[12] Only Jimmy Herf is endowed with sufficient capacity for individualistic rebellion to reject the business way of life with its tyrannical money values, and his departure from Manhattan, a *declassé* outcast thumbing down the highway to an unknown destination, represents a muted victory for the forces of life.

The single-minded drive for money success, coupled with the pursuit of sensual gratification had, in Dos Passos's view, corroded a once-rounded individualism into a harsh egotism shorn of all communal dimensions. The result was a social atomism in which the normal nexus of human sympathy was broken. This failure of common feeling is markedly illustrated several times through the novel. It is there in the tugboat captain's selfish response to Bud Korpenning's suicide, and in Ellen Thatcher's callous reaction to a girl's serious burns in a fire at her dressmaker's: 'Just somebody's bad luck, the sort of thing that happens every day.' With such lack of feeling and such an inflexible egotism dominating their make-up, Dos Passos's characters enter into relationships that are only transient and tenuous and that lead to neither real joy nor real grief. The traditional loyalties and ties, to the family, the church, to a local community, have dissolved entirely, leaving people free but isolated, drifting on the tides of the city. Despite the close physical proximity of individuals enforced by urban crowding, strong barriers of indifference and impersonality, Dos Passos indicates, keep people apart in a mass society.

The novel shows people being dehumanised not only by their environment but also by their acquiescence in a greatly limited range of emotional experience. For the sake of material considerations they frequently repress their own spontaneity and deny their deep inner impulses. This process of petrification, leading to eventual dissociation, is dramatically instanced in Ellen's reaction to George Baldwin's proposal of marriage:

Through dinner she felt a gradual icy coldness stealing through her like novococaine. She had made up her mind. It seemed as if she had set the photograph of herself in her own place, forever frozen into a single gesture. An invisible silk band of bitterness was tightening round her throat, strangling. . . .

Ellen felt herself sitting with her ankles crossed, rigid as a porcelain figure under her clothes, everything about her seemed to be growing hard and enameled, the air bluestreaked with cigarette-smoke, was turning to glass.[13]

This is a superbly evoked and chillingly detailed process of emotional anaesthesia, as Ellen denies her instinctual refusal of his offer in favour of a calculated course of action. Such dissociation from her authentic responses is achieved only at the cost of becoming mechanical. She has turned herself into an object thoroughly assimilated into the hard materiality of her environment. The inner emptiness and automata-like state of these two characters is directly alluded to in George Baldwin's pitiful admission that he has 'been like a tin mechanical toy, all hollow inside'. Ellen, oppressed by this image that comes so close to the truth of her own condition, replies in a strangled voice, 'Let's not talk about mechanical toys.' Ellen has earlier been assimilated to the inanimate in the description of her dance with Jimmy Herf at the roadhouse, in which her voice is compared to 'a tiny flexible sharp metalsaw' and she becomes 'an intricate machine of sawtooth steel whitebright bluebright copperbright in his arms'. With her hard-edged egotism she is never presented in organic terms but only in terms of the machine.

In *Manhattan Transfer* Dos Passos is mainly concerned with the negative tendencies towards dehumanisation and the saturation of business values embodied in Manhattan's social change. His focus is not on the economic or political system as such (though we are shown glimpses of the corruption of ward politics), and that political dimension which Dos Passos introduced into Andrews's expression of cultural despair does not enter the foreground until *The Forty-Second Parallel* (1930). During the 1920s Dos Passos was active in leftwing causes such as the Sacco–Vanzetti Defence Committee (1927) and this involvement grew in the early 1930s with the Harlan County miners' strike of 1931 and his support in 1932 for William Z. Foster, the communist candidate for the Presidency. Despite his participation in communist-led protests, however, he was never a Party member and always maintained a sceptical distance.[14] For his political radicalism, which informed the three novels of *USA*, really had its roots in native American sources: a Whitmanesque concern for, and ultimate faith in, American democratic values;

a Veblenian analysis of contemporary society; and the anarchism of Emma Goldman and Max Eastman and the Industrial Workers of the World.[15]

When Dos Passos looked at the America of the 1920s and 1930s, it seemed to him that the values and ideals of Jeffersonian democracy were under sustained attack, an attack that was begun during the First World War. He came to regard the war as a plot of the big interests, based on financial greed and mass deception. After the war, the 'Red Scare', the assaults on labour, the lynching of Wobblies, the shooting down of strikers, and government-initiated anti-Bolshevist purges, all seemed to be overt signs of a concerted effort to suppress the people while securing the economic and social supremacy of the big, monopolistic concerns. No incident exemplified so clearly to radicals like Dos Passos a violation of America's ideals and historical origins as did the trial and eventual execution of the two Italian anarchists, Sacco and Vanzetti, in an atmosphere of anti-foreign and anti-radical rage. 'When we took up for Sacco and Vanzetti', he explained years later, 'we were taking up for freedom of speech and for an evenhanded judicial system which would give the same treatment to poor men as to rich men, to greasy foreigners as to redblooded Americans.'[16] He wrote a pamphlet, 'Facing the Chair', on their behalf, and began writing *The Forty-Second Parallel* after the case was over. *The Big Money* (1936), and thus the trilogy, draws to a close after Mary French's return from the execution, and the most deeply felt writing in *USA* is Dos Passos's own commentary on the case in 'The Camera Eye (50)'.

The Forty-Second Parallel covers the period from 1900 to 1917 and traces the rise of big business and economic imperialism through the 'Newsreels' and biographies. In the early part the themes of social inequality and class struggle are prominent, labour militancy being portrayed directly through Mac, the Wobbly, or indirectly through the many references in the 'Newsreels' and the biographies of labour activists. 'Newsreel 6' introduces the rise of monopoly capitalism in a headline heavy with a latent irony that Dos Passos makes manifest during the remainder of the trilogy: 'PRAISE MONOPOLY AS BOON TO ALL.' The biographies are divided between those who represent aggressive entrepreneurial capital – Minor C. Keith and Andrew Carnegie, useful men like Edison, and those representing the fight for democratic ideals in industrial America – Debs, Haywood, La

Follette and Bryan. Through the account of Mac's picaresque adventures and his Wobbly activities there runs an undercurrent of socialist hope for a revolutionised America, a hope that is sustained in *Nineteen Nineteen* (1932) by the advent of the October Russian Revolution.

In 1932, in a reply to Malcolm Cowley, who had enquired about the general trend of the trilogy as well as about the attitudes in *Nineteen Nineteen*, Dos Passos wrote, 'I don't know if there's any solution — but there's a certain amount of statement of position in the later Camera Eyes. I think also . . . the latter part of the book shows a certain crystallization (call it monopoly capitalism?) of society that didn't exist in the early part of 42nd Parallel (call it competitive capitalism?).'[17] This general trend towards monopoly capitalism is presented with gathering tempo in *The Big Money*, which takes Dos Passos's chronicle up to 1929. In the first 'Newsreel' an excerpt encapsulates the novel's thematic concern with the usurpation of traditional democratic freedoms by a government dominated by the monopolies: 'they permitted the Steel Trust Government to trample underfoot the democratic rights which they had so often been assured were the heritage of the people of this country'. Later 'Newsreels' present both the ominous atmosphere of strikes and political upheaval and the increasing roar of the business boom leading up to the Crash and the Depression. Class warfare is featured directly in the trilogy once again with the account of the Pittsburgh steel strike supplied in the narrative of the activist, Mary French. The passages relating her involvement in the Sacco–Vanzetti case resonate with the rhythm of passionate protest, a rhythm that bursts out in the climactic chord of 'The Camera Eye (50)':

all right we are two nations
America our nation has been beaten by strangers who have
bought the laws and fenced off the meadows and cut down the
woods for pulp and turned our pleasant cities into slums and
sweated the wealth out of our people and when they want to
they hire the executioner to throw the switch

Out of the bitter realisation that American society could send two immigrants to the electric chair for their opinions came Dos Passos's conviction that the once egalitarian republic had become polarized into the haves and the have-nots, into those who bought and wielded police power and those who made up the great mass of the people. As well as this experiential source for Dos Passos's sense of class division and the erosion of basic rights in American society, there was a powerful intellectual source in Veblen, who also taught that the American population 'falls into two main classes: those who own wealth invested in large holdings and who thereby control the conditions of life for the rest; and those who do not own wealth in sufficiently large holdings, and whose conditions of life are therefore controlled by these others'.[18] Dos Passos was reading Veblen at the time of writing *The Big Money* and it is Veblen's vision of America with its neo-Marxist tone which so thoroughly informs the conception of society in this final volume.[19] In Dos Passos's thematically central portrait, Veblen

established a new diagram of a society dominated by monopoly capital,
etched in irony
the sabotage of production by business,
the sabotage of life by blind need for money profits.

As for Veblen's radical hope that the worker-technicians would take over production and run it for use and not profit, 'War cut across all that: under the cover of the bunting of Woodrow Wilson's phrases the monopolies cracked down. American democracy was crushed.'[20] This, orchestrated through all the different formal elements of 'Newsreel', autobiographical 'Camera Eye', biographical portrait and fictional narrative is the politico-economic theme of *USA*. Closely allied with it is the second of the two co-axial themes running through the trilogy: the barrenness and corrupt complicity of the middle class.

Although alternative lifestyles and viewpoints are present in *USA* in the figures of Mac, Joe Williams and Mary French, it is the white-collar middle class which dominates the trilogy through the central group of characters composed of J. Ward Moorehouse, Eleanor Stoddard, Eveline Hutchins, Janey Williams, Richard Savage and Charley Anderson. It is these people – uprooted and deracinated, in an ambiguous class position, atomistic individuals in a competitive society, lacking any tradition or culture of their own – who are most representative of social change in America up to 1930. The middle class was at the centre of the crisis of values which beset American culture after

the First World War, and in Dos Passos's despairing view it failed
to sustain the most vital elements of the American tradition in the
face of that crisis.

His characters' experience of the war seemed to destroy all their
learned moral inhibitions and certainties, and post-war affluence
offered no ethical guidance except the pursuit of money and
success and a selfish hedonism. As in *Manhattan Transfer*, it is
the amorality of Dos Passos's figures, their lack of direction and
robust integrity, and their loss of Puritan restraint and inner-
directed goals which are most evident. The temporariness and
tenuousness of familial and emotional/sexual relationships are
emphasised, and the dominant impression to be gained from the
narratives is one of a basic sameness as Dos Passos deliberately
eschews stylistic impressiveness in favour of a flattened prose
which, allowing for variations between the narratives, communicates the narrow range of his characters' consciousness.
From Joe Williams to Moorehouse there are no flights of lyricism,
nor deep tragic broodings; rather there is a tightly reined play of
feelings often dully expressed. Whilst the 'Camera Eye' sections
and the biographical portraits bristle with intelligence, alertness,
responsiveness, the fictional portraits (apart from the 'Mac' and
Mary French episodes, perhaps) convey little sense of richly felt
life; instead, there is the pervasive impression of people with
calloused sensibilities who are alienated from their own
experience. As in the case of the Manhattan characters, this
alienation seems largely due to a denial of inner impulses and
authentic responses carried out in order to harden the personal
defences and preserve the possibility of 'getting ahead'. Thus
Janey Williams, after Alec's death, undergoes a dissociation of
feeling rather similar, if less articulated, to that of Ellen
Thatcher: 'After that Janey never cried much; things upset her,
but she got a cold hard feeling all over instead.' Moorehouse
represses his impulse to leave Ocean City because he sees an
opportunity to capitalise on his connection with the Strangs, and
both his marriages are mainly motivated by material ambition.
Richard Ellsworth Savage experiences deep disgust at the war,
but he resists the impulse to make his separate peace in the
manner of Andrews in *Three Soldiers* because it would destroy his
career chances.

Once again, Dos Passos devotes his narrative to exposing the
vitiation and degradation of character in a commercial culture

and a mass society. The general meaninglessness of life in modern society is suggested almost at a subliminal level by the many references in the 'Newsreels' to murder and suicide, and is repeatedly dramatised in the narratives: in Joe Williams's directionless existence and arbitrary end in a bar-room brawl; 'Daughter's' senseless death in an airplane crash after a drunken night with a French aviator; Charley Anderson's dissipation and death; and Eveline Hutchins's suicide. Their lives possess no dignity or significance, but simply reveal characters adrift who have no strength at the core of their being. Like Dreiser's Clyde Griffiths, Dos Passos's middle-class characters readily adapt to prevailing norms and so manifest the social forces moulding personality and values in the war and post-war years.

Those forces are revealed to be the pressures created by commercialism and a consumer economy: the office environment, advertising and an ethos of personal consumption. 'Neither the gentle spinster stenographer from Washington, the amiable publicity director from Wilmington nor the sharp woman interior decorator from Chicago', Edmund Wilson wrote, 'has an intimation of any other values than those of the American business office, of the American advertising game, of the American luxury trade, out of which they make their salaries and in terms of which they conceive their ambitions.'[21] For the secular cause of that crisis of values, that ideological confusion, of the war and post-war years derived from the complex social transformation that accompanied the shift of the American economy from its production-oriented to its consumption-oriented phase. Three of Dos Passos's figures – Margo Dowling, Charley Anderson and J. Ward Moorehouse – are significantly representative of this crucial shift.

Margo Dowling, who begins a stage-career as a child actress in vaudeville and who eventually becomes a star of the Hollywood 'silents', represents the new popular idols of the consumer age – the movie star and show-business personality. These social roles and their contemporary importance are given further prominence in the biographies of Isadora Duncan and Rudolph Valentino which are strategically placed in close conjunction with Margo's narrative. Social heroes of this type were famed for their extravagant consumption, hedonistic lifestyle and mass appeal. When Margo becomes involved in the Hollywood mass entertainment industry, a director points out that the basis of a star's appeal lies in the ordinary person's capacity for identification with her: 'They all feel they are you, you are loving for them, the millions who want love and beauty and excitement.' Dos Passos here indicates the fashion in which mass culture tends to operate as a surrogate for real emotional enrichment, as a vicarious participation in others' more glamorous lives, and he points to the source of that popular hysteria manifested at Valentino's death: 'Jammed masses stampeded under the clubs and the rearing hoofs of the horses. The funeral chapel was gutted, men and women fought over a flower, a piece of wallpaper, a piece of broken plateglass window.' The biography comes to a close with an ironic comment on the ephemerality of the public's reaction to the screen idol's death. The spectacle and sensation provided by the entertainment industry, it seems, may be widespread but it is only shortlived as a rapidly bored public hungrily moves on to the next 'event'.

Charley Anderson, brought into close relation with Margo Dowling at one point, begins his post-war life as an aero-engine technician and Dos Passos strongly identifies him at this stage with the world of production. 'Good old Bill,' Charley says to his mechanic, 'the pilot's nothin' without his mechanic, the promoter's nothin' without production. . . . You and me Bill, we're in production.' And a little later Charley is shown identifying with the technicians against the bosses: ' "Hell, I ain't no boss," said Charley. "I belong with the mechanics . . . don't I, Bill?" ' In case we miss the point, Dos Passos rather heavy-handedly introduces a letter from Charley's rich girlfriend in which he is described as living 'in the real world of business and production and labor'. Then Charley, abandoning his friend and partner, moves to Detroit to work for a competing firm where he is warned by Bledsoe to make his choice between working as an engineer and behaving like a financier. Charley protests that he is 'only a mechanic', but Dos Passos has already intimated his vulnerability to the lure of easy money through his dabbling in stocks on Wall Street.

As we have already noted, Veblen's intellectual shadow falls across so much of *The Big Money* and his biography is inserted into the Charley Anderson narrative just at that point where Anderson illustrates the central tension in Veblen's social analysis between industry and business, between production – the technological institutions for making the goods, and finance – the pecuniary institutions for making the money. According to the Veblenian schema, Anderson loses 'the instinct of workmanship' and ceases to be a technician on the workers' side; he becomes, instead, an owner immersed in the pecuniary culture with its invidious distinction, competitiveness and property values.[22] Charley learns the leisure skills of the middle-class executive (in secret at first, like J. Ward Moorehouse) and becomes more and more involved with the stock market: 'What he enjoyed outside of playing with the kids was buying and selling stocks and talking to Nat over the longdistance. Nat kept telling him he was getting the feel of the market.' The stockbroker's dismissive remark, tellingly allowed to pass by Anderson, about Bill Cermak's death – 'After all . . . he was only a mechanic' – neatly expresses the contempt with which the men of money and business regarded the men of things and production. Anderson's material ambition hardens and coarsens and he is strongly associated with the novel's theme as he gets 'a kind of feel for the big money'. Deflected from his genuine desire to be a designer and a useful man of production by the lure of finance and wealth that so dominates *The Big Money*, he becomes an investor and speculator, his moral decay and loss of authentic meaning powerfully imaged in his accelerating dissipation and decline.

Finally, J. Ward Moorehouse, 'the public relations counsel', is very nearly the presiding genius over the whole trilogy, becoming a kind of giant who almost gains entry into the pantheon of the biographical subjects.[23] He is a Horatio Alger figure, the ambitious, all-American boy who rises to wealth and success through his own efforts, but the avenue he chooses is not entrepreneurial capitalism but public relations and advertising. No biographical subject looms over him in the way that the Wright brothers loom over Charley Anderson or Isadora Duncan over Margo Dowling, and yet he was based on a real-life model. In Moscow in 1928 Dos Passos had met the Rockefellers' publicity chief, Ivy Lee, who told him tales of his early life and whom Dos Passos admired for 'his dedication to his trade'. According to an interview Dos Passos gave, Lee was the original source for Moorehouse.[24]

Public relations and advertising are, of course, key features of the consumption phase of the economy, and they represent a major source of direction and value in a modern society where traditional ideologies such as Protestantism and individualism have lost their prescriptive force. As Dos Passos makes plain, not only do advertising and public relations promote consumption through the propagation of saleable 'images', they also provide an effective means of social control in a mass society. Many of the public relations practitioners received their early training and experience with George Creel's Committee on Public Information which had manipulated public opinion during the war, and they took the skills they had learnt there into the post-war world of marketing and commerce. As Dick Savage, Moorehouse's aide, remarks, 'Whether you like it or not, the molding of the public mind is one of the most important things that goes on in this country. If it wasn't for that, American business would be in a pretty pickle.' Through this ideological aspect of his work and influence, Moorehouse, as a representative of a developing social force, is closely bound up with the decay of American democracy and the triumph of monopoly capital.

His narrative begins in *The Forty-Second Parallel* with his rather pointedly significant birth on 4 July, and so he is associated from the beginning with the historical promise of America's democratic ideals. 'Clean cut young executive', he says to himself with satisfaction on looking at himself in a mirror, and his exploitation of his personal attractiveness in the service of his single-minded drive to get ahead becomes the keynote of his personality. Alert to the importance of advertising and the psychology of selling, he originates the idea of public relations on the part of big business to combat criticism from the liberal press and smoothe over antagonisms between the classes. Believing himself free of any ideology, he conceives of himself as a mediator between capital and labour, but as Dos Passos demonstrates, he becomes a dealer in false consciousness as he slips into the role of apologist and propagandist for corporate capitalism.

Moorehouse is one of those who, in the words of 'Camera Eye (50)', have 'turned our language inside out who have taken the clean words our fathers spoke and made them slimy and foul'. He has repeatedly assimilated the terms of Jeffersonian democracy to the undemocratic activities of big business, so corrupting them and associating them with oppression and inequality. During the bitter Homestead strike at Pittsburgh when the bosses used violent measures to break the workers' resistance, Moorehouse, as spokesman for the steel industry, claims that 'the great leaders of American capital' are 'firm believers in fairplay and democracy'.

Several times he equates democracy with monopoly capitalism and at a press conference defends the formation of an international oil cartel as 'a proof of a new era of international cooperation that was dawning in which great aggregations of capital would work together for peace and democracy'. *The Big Money* comes to a close with Moorehouse and Savage planning an advertising campaign that shamelessly exploits traditional American values in order to promote spurious home medicines. 'Of course,' Moorehouse gloats to his aide, 'selfservice, independence, individualism is the word I gave the boys in the beginning. This is going to be more than a publicity campaign, it's going to be a campaign for Americanism.'[25] In a sense, the struggle between labour and capital as envisaged by Dos Passos was not so much a conflict between ideologies as a contest *over* an ideology. The activists of the Left were striving to realise the full, liberating content of American democratic ideals, while the monopolists and conservatives were employing the beguiling phraseology of democracy to mask their expropriation of political freedom from the mass of the people.

The two co-axial themes of *USA*, then, are intertwined in the life history of Moorehouse, but the barrenness of middle-class existence and the dominance of monopoly capitalism are further interrelated during the final pages of the trilogy by the juxtaposition of Eddy Spellman's and Eveline Hutchins's deaths. Spellman, a labour activist, is murdered while working for a humanitarian cause, while, in contrast, Eveline Hutchins, socialite and hostess, commits suicide in despair at her aimless, party-giving existence. Mary French's criticism of the lives of the affluent middle class, represented by Eveline and, by association, Eleanor, Moorehouse and Savage, points to their dominant quality: 'It's the waste . . . the food they waste and the money they waste while our people starve in tarpaper barracks.' They fill out their days with egotistic hedonism and shelter behind a smug complacency while all the time other Americans are being beaten or shot in the struggle against exploitation, and American political institutions are being corrupted. In Dos Passos's unflattering portraits of his white-collar characters it is not only the inner emptiness and personal disintegration that are remarkable but also the conspicuous lack of social responsibility and political awareness. The new middle class in *USA*'s projection, far from being the reservoir of traditional democratic values in the manner of the old middle class, had become instead the willing agent of big business, countenancing the decay of civil liberties in return for material prosperity and secure careers. The real object of Dos Passos's disgust seems to be the complicity of this influential social group in the corrosion of American ideals and the coercive sway of monopoly capital.

The prevailing note at the end of *The Big Money* is one of political and cultural despair as big business becomes entrenched, advertising and public relations usurp the once-liberating terms, and the bitter industrial war continues with the Pennsylvania miners' strike. Allowing for the variations in tone and stance between the three constituent novels, there is a sense in which *USA* is one long *Tendenzroman*, orchestrating through its diverse formal elements a particular, pessimistic thesis about the direction of social change in America. The Depression had undoubtedly emphasised the polarisation of American society and the degree of social divisiveness, and the sense of a nation betrayed by its business system informs the last two novels. But, compellingly rendered as it is, Dos Passos's gloomy perspective was not entirely justified by historical events.

It is true that in 1920 the Supreme Court had not dissolved the United States Steel Corporation, despite the anti-trust policy formulated in the Clayton Act of 1914. This decision left the way clear for the continuation of the merger movement in the 1920s, and provided the spectre of the 'Steel Trust Government' which looms over the trilogy as an instance of the monopolies' power. Yet, apparently, the degree of monopoly control did not increase significantly in the 1920s, and on the positive side, legislation was passed in the early 1930s greatly increasing the rights of labour. The Norris–La Guardia Anti-Injunction Act of 1932 was a major landmark in the legal history of American trade unions, making illegal the 'yellow-dog' contracts by which workers were engaged on condition they did not join a union and forbidding federal courts from issuing injunctions against organised labour. This was followed by the National Labor Relations Act of 1935 which forbade employers to refuse collective bargaining and prohibited them from interfering with trade unions in their establishments. Such moves laid the legal foundation for the great rise in trade-union power which American industry saw during the 1930s and 1940s.[26]

In Dos Passos's historical interpretation monopoly capital had abrogated power to itself through the repressive arm of the State and in its thrust towards an unassailable economic position had severely compromised the civil freedoms of workers and left-wing activists. But, although the Harding, Coolidge and Hoover administrations were thoroughly pro-business, the Roosevelt union legislation demonstrated that countervailing power could make an impact and held out hope for the future. Yet, Dos Passos's position at the point of completing the trilogy is one of utter despair, even though shortly after he was to reaffirm his faith in the American democratic tradition.[27] Perhaps he felt too much the lone, liberal intellectual, alienated from the bourgeois establishment on the one hand and distrustful of the Communist-dominated Left on the other, powerless, oppressed by the thought that in an age of business and labour organisation 'there could be no individuals'. 'Camera Eye (46)' comes directly after the Mary French narrative and picks up the mood of liberal indecision and ineffectiveness dramatised in George Barrow, and in it Dos Passos honestly examines the doubts about, and the contradictions in, his actions, as he urges others to collective protest while retreating, himself, into the solitary pleasures of high literary culture and cerebral speculation, there to ponder 'the course of history and what leverage might pry the owners loose from power and bring back (I too Walt Whitman) our storybook democracy'.

Dos Passos must rank as a central figure in any discussion of the relationship between modern American literature and society. He possessed the historian's impulse to identify and record the dominant social and ideological forces at work in the first three decades of this century, but he realised that the conventional realist novel was inadequate to the portrayal of the texture of modern social experience and to the rendering of a definite historical interpretation. His best work, therefore, drew upon modernist experimentation, literary, artistic and filmic, in a rare and powerful fusion of artistic boldness and serious social commentary. *Manhattan Transfer* provides an unflinching portrait of the dehumanisation suffered by individuals in a mechanised mass society. With its episodic structure it possesses pace and economy, symbolic suggestiveness, and a prose that dazzles at times with its evocation of the spectacle of city life. The novels that comprise *USA* lack these memorable impressionistic qualities but they display a wider sweep and are expressive of a more comprehensive ambition. Dreiser, in his Cowperwood trilogy, had attempted to present a whole phase of capitalist development – the phase of the individualistic entrepreneur – but his narrative strategy of grounding his fictional representative in the real events and processes of American business history led to an excessive inclusion of documentary material within a form that could accommodate it only with strain. Dos Passos, in his strategy for rendering the phase of the monopolistic corporation, broke away from the individualistic in favour of the collective subject and introduced the devices of the 'Newsreel' and portrait to carry the selected documentary material. By means of the 'Camera Eye' he also introduced his own presence as narrator into the work, thus foregrounding the trilogy's relativist perspective and setting up relationships and tensions between his subjective impressions, real historical figures and events, and his imagined life-histories. His target, as in *Manhattan Transfer*, is the materialism of the white-collar middle-class lifestyle, but in *USA* that is brought into damning inter-relation with the anti-democratic rise of monopoly capital. To the charge of moral corruption Dos Passos adds that of political complacency as the members of that class acquiesce in the repression and loss of civil rights and play their part in the formation of an America of 'two nations'. Behind the disgust and despair that inform the trilogy (and deepen especially in *The Big Money*) there lies a Whitman-esque identification with the common man and a concern that a full, democratic individualism should be preserved in a hostile business world.

11 Consumer Man in Crisis: Arthur Miller's *Death of a Salesman*

With the end of the Second World War, after being held in check by the 1930s recession and the imperatives of war production, the consumption-oriented phase of the American economy surged forward once more. Fuelled at first by large personal savings accumulated during the war years, the consumer boom of the late 1940s established those features of a consumer society which emerged during the 1920s on a much larger scale. Automobile and consumer durable sales expanded at an enormous rate, as did consumer credit and advertising. Recruitment into white-collar occupations and the service trades continued to increase, as selling became a pervasive activity directly involving over three million people, some 38 per cent of whom were mobile salesmen.[1]

Arthur Miller, in the 'Introduction' to his *Collected Plays*, speaks of his responsiveness to social change and of its shaping effect upon his art, and his *Death of a Salesman* (1949) seems especially at grips with the human problems of psychology and ideology thrown up by consumerism in the post-war period.[2] He speaks, too, in his 'Introduction' of his shifting choice of forms according to the themes he wished to communicate, and the shift from the well-executed realism of *All My Sons* to the more expressionist mode of *Salesman* reflects Miller's awareness of, and desire to present, a new, historically conditioned consciousness. 'I wished to create a form', he wrote, 'which, in itself, as a form, would literally be the process of Willy Loman's way of mind', and in accordance with this subjectivist emphasis the set has only token representational aims.[3] Miller has always been concerned with the interpenetration of personal and social existence, and through the interiorised structure of *Salesman* he was able to convey the heightened intensity of that interpenetration during the post-war period. Then, the psychological dimension of social life seemed to gain especial importance. The growth of white-collar personnel matched an increase in work which involved handling people rather than materials. A lifestyle of suburban residence and consumer hedonism led to an emphasis on personal wants and their gratification. Those wants were exploited and the consumer's mind manipulated by advertising. The spirit of independence and self-reliance declined and a hierarchical status system created an anxiety-producing interpersonal assessment of social worth. The dominant social values and the individual's sense of himself were interrelated in an intimate manner and *Death of a Salesman* explores the destructive effects upon one vulnerable man of that relationship.

In *All My Sons* the main action hinged upon the intensity of a father–son relationship and demonstrated the loss of moral integrity that accompanies a dedication to a business ethic. In the doctor, Jim Bayliss, Miller reinforces this theme by presenting a minor character who has lost his best self because of a compromise with material values. 'And now I live in the usual darkness,' Jim tells Kate, 'I can't find myself; it's even hard sometimes to remember the kind of man I wanted to be.' This theme of the loss of direction and the search for identity is brought to the fore in *Salesman* and centred on a similarly intense father–son relationship.

Made aware from the beginning of a tension between Willy Loman and his son, Biff, it is not until near the play's end that we learn its root cause: Biff's discovery seventeen years before of Willy in a Boston hotel bedroom with a strange woman. The event was traumatic for them both. Willy lost his moral authority as a father and was filled with repressed guilt, and Biff from that time on could never see him as anything but a 'fake'. Their estrangement from each other and their search for some relatedness embody in their uniquely personal predicament their estrangement from themselves and their search for relatedness with the larger society.

Having lost faith in his father, Biff himself becomes 'lost', as though he never grew beyond the 17-year-old who flunked maths and found that his father was not a paragon of family virtue. He seems fixated at an adolescent stage of development. 'I'm like a boy,' he tells Happy, 'I'm not married, I'm not in business, I just – I'm like a boy.' He has taken to the aimless life of the migrant worker, a life of low status and low wages, rather than the career ladder of college and business which Willy had hoped for him. This choice was partly motivated out of rebellion against the draining routine of office work and commercial standards of success, but Biff still suffers from a degree of inner conflict and his rejection of those standards is far from complete. At the play's beginning his own impulses and attempts at self-identification are still under partial subjugation to the attitudes conditioned in him by his father, and although he has returned to the city, the locus of commercial opportunity and metropolitan notions of success, he remains confused. 'I don't know – what I'm supposed to want,' he confesses in ethical bewilderment. Biff's confusion, however, is but a faint echo of Willy's own perplexity.

Willy's life has been dominated by two images of success: that of Dave Singleman which has governed its direction, and that of Ben which returns at crucial moments to highlight Willy's sense of inadequacy and insecurity. In Willy's family history we are offered a cameo of social change in America, from the pioneering father who drove his waggon and horses westward across the continent, to the elder brother who gained a fortune in the great outdoors, and finally to the travelling salesman hemmed in by the towering tenement blocks of the modern big city. 'Success incarnate', Willy calls Ben, and in Willy's image of him he becomes a caricature of success, exaggerated and simplified as Willy's mind would like success to be. Ben possesses the stern individualism and ruthless competitive spirit of the stereotyped entrepreneur. 'Never fight fair with a stranger, boy,' he instructs Biff. 'You'll never get out of the jungle that way.' 'Jungle' is used here, of course, as the stock Social Darwinian metaphor for the city under *laissez-faire* capitalism, and Charley's closely allied remarks about business competition recall Willy's protest near the beginning of the play that 'the competition is maddening!' Willy, it is evident, is not tough enough for the business struggle while Ben is. For all his urge to success Willy remains one of the exploited, a victim, while Ben is one of the exploiters. As the representative of the pioneer and entrepreneur, Ben embodies the avenues to success of the earlier, more individualistic, production phase of the American economy.

Willy elevates him into a father-figure but he is incapable of taking his advice or following his example. Ben's appearance in Act II signifies Willy's memory of his lost opportunity when, offered a challenging job in Alaska, he chose instead security, urban life, selling. 'You've a new continent on your doorstep, William', Ben tells him, urging him to adopt an aggressive pioneering attitude. 'Get out of these cities, they're full of talk and time payments and courts of law. Screw on your fists and you can fight for a fortune up there.' But as the interview with Howard Wagner immediately before Ben's appearance alerts us, Willy had already opted for Dave Singleman and the salesman ideal of success in a consumer society:

> And old Dave, he'd go up to his room, y'understand, put on his green velvet slippers – I'll never forget – and pick up his phone and call the buyers, and without ever leaving his room, at the age of eighty-four, he made his living. And when I saw that, I realized that selling was the greatest career a man could want.[4]

Willy counters Ben's competitive individualism with a naive faith in the power of personal attractiveness as the new Way to Wealth in the highly personalised consumer economy: 'It's who you know and the smile on your face! It's contacts, Ben, contacts! . . . a man can end with diamonds here on the basis of being liked.' Willy has based his life on the credo, 'Be liked and you'll never want', so abandoning that self-reliance embodied in Ben and represented by his father. As he becomes increasingly conscious of the failure of that credo, the image of Ben haunts him with the possibility of what he might have been.

Willy chose the pre-eminent activity of the consumer phase – selling, and so negative is the impression of salesmanship fostered by Willy's disintegration that it is easy to forget that he was drawn to it by the prospect of genuinely human, if finally illusory, rewards: "'Cause what could be more satisfying than to be able to go, at the age of eighty-four, into twenty or thirty different cities, and pick up a phone, and be remembered and loved and helped by so many different people?' Unfortunately, the personal, local markets and friendly contacts of Dave Singleman's days and Willy's own early career have given way under the pressure of urbanisation to the large, anonymous mass market, and nobody in New England knows him any more.[5] But since Willy accepts the ideology of selling so wholeheartedly, the superficial values inculcated by salesmanship have a debilitating effect upon his character.

In selling, the presentation of personality is all-important, since the salesman can best sell his product by impressing the buyer, by winning his confidence and trust, by making himself likeable, by selling himself. (When asked what Willy was selling, Miller writes that he could only reply 'Himself'.)[6] This emphasis gives rise to a character orientation which Erich Fromm, writing at the same time as *Salesman*, called the 'marketing orientation'.[7] A salesman, like Willy, is not concerned with the attainment of some objective achievement but with the creation of a pleasing personality that will be saleable, and since he is trying to sell himself, he experiences his qualities and abilities as commodities estranged from him. This self-alienation has serious consequences, as David Riesman, following Fromm, points out. It diminishes the individual's sense of a hard core of self and, consequently, the externalised values of prestige and public image become substitutes for a genuine feeling of identity. For it is not the genuine self that is put in the market for economic success but the cosmetic self that is free from any nonsaleable idiosyncrasies. When this artificial self succeeds, Riesman suggests, doubts about the loss of identity may be quieted, but since self-evaluation has been surrendered to the market, failure in the market will be translated by the individual into self-contempt.[8] Miller indicates through Willy's frequent self-contradiction that he has no personal centre, a fact which Biff confirms when he says that Willy has no character. Willy has seized upon the notion of commercial success as a substitute for genuine identity, and when he begins to fail in the market he translates this failure into self-contempt and insecurity:

WILLY: Oh, I'll knock 'em dead next week. I'll go to Hartford. I'm very well liked in Hartford. You know, the trouble is, Linda, people don't seem to take to me.
LINDA: Oh, don't be foolish.
WILLY: I know it when I walk in. They seem to laugh at me.[9]

Since the salesman experiences himself as a commodity, he will inevitably experience others in the same way and assess their worth according to their success in the market. Thus Biff is a 'lazy bum' on this basis because his farm jobs lack status and he has yet to bring home thirty-five dollars a week.

Willy's main idea in bringing up his sons was not to instil moral principles in them, as a nineteenth-century Puritan-minded parent might have done, but rather to encourage them to depend upon their personal attractiveness and so equip themselves for successful careers in selling. Willy's emphasis on being 'well liked' and his dependence on others' approval distinguish him as an other-directed person. More accurately, he is an other-directed 'adjusted' person who is in the process of becoming 'anomic'. A person who has the appropriate character for his time and place is 'adjusted' even when he makes mistakes and deviates from what is expected of him. But 'utter conformity in behavior may be purchased by the individual at so high a price as to lead to character neurosis and anomie: the anomic person tends to sabotage either himself or his society.' This, together with some other remarks of Riesman and his co-workers, seems particularly apposite to Willy's personal crisis: 'The anomics include not only those who, in their character, were trained to attend to signals that are either no longer given or no longer spell meaning or success. They also may be . . . those who are overadjusted, who listen too assiduously to signals from within or without.'[10] Willy seems to share the features of both categories. He trained himself to be a certain type of salesman that has been overtaken by social change, and so he no longer receives those signals that indicate meaning or success. Also, he seems overadjusted, especially sensitive to signals both from without – others' reactions – and from within – his anxieties and fear of failure, as the interiorised form emphasises. Finally, of course, he does 'sabotage' himself.

Opposed to the ethic of material ambition and success represented by both Dave Singleman and Ben, but related to Ben's pioneering spirit, is a set of positive values associated with the outdoors and working with the hands. Willy's condition of alienation is partly due to the fact that he does not make anything. He is completely divorced from the fundamental productive processes which create the merchandise he sells; hence the omission of the name and nature of the product he carries in his sample cases. Since he has no connection with it, but is alienated from it, the 'line' is immaterial. As a salesman, Willy handles people, not materials. Yet, repeatedly, the play suggests his capacity for creativity and his practical skill in the handling of materials and things. The point is driven home in the elegiac lines near the play's close:

CHARLEY: Yeah. He was a happy man with a batch of cement.
LINDA: He was so wonderful with his hands.

Furthermore, in isolated, passing remarks Miller indicates that residing in Willy is a powerful love of the outdoors. He speaks longingly to Linda of nature, the country, the open-air life: 'But it's so beautiful up there, Linda, the trees are so thick, and the sun is warm. I opened the windshield and just let the warm air bathe over me.' That this incident later turns out to be an illusion, a memory transposed into the present, indicates the thrust of personal wish-fulfilment that lies behind it. Willy's repressed love for the tangible, concretely productive life is expressed in his desire – one that takes on the aspect of a cultural nostalgia – for a simpler, agrarian lifestyle divorced from commercialism and the city. Overshadowed by tenement blocks that squeeze out the sky above them, they dream, as do so many city-dwellers, of that 'little place out in the country' where they will 'raise some vegetables, a couple of chickens'. Willy has suffocated his own inner impulses towards an open-air life and craft satisfaction for the sake of the external rewards of status and business success offered by the urban-commercial world. His desperate, torchlit seed-planting at the end of Act II represents a pathetically belated attempt to establish an organic, instrumental relationship with the natural world and to give vent to those desires for active contact with the physically real.

Miller said of *Death of a Salesman* that he was trying 'to set forth what happens when a man does not have a grip on the forces of life and has no sense of values which will lead him to that kind of grip'.[11] Willy has adopted the lifestyle and values of the travelling salesman but, bewildered by the discovery, he finds that in the end they are incapable of sustaining him in his life. His confusion is manifest in his unsure, questioning attitude, prompted by his pained awareness that others have triumphed while he has failed. 'What's the answer?' he asks Ben. 'What – what's the secret?' he later asks the mature and successful Bernard. While conveying his insecurity and bewilderment, such questions also betray the limitations of his salesman's consciousness as he seems to search for a kind of Dale-Carnegie-style injunction which will point him on the path to success. His crisis arises in part from the fact that he is not 'one-dimensional' but is painfully conscious of the vacuum at the heart of his life. 'Had Willy been unaware of his separation from values that endure', Miller points out, 'he would have died contentedly while polishing his car, probably on a Sunday afternoon with the ball game coming over the radio.' But he was 'agonized by his awareness of being in a false position' and 'constantly haunted by the hollowness of all he had placed his faith in'.[12] His desperation and his inner contradictions are compounded by the knowledge of other, former values in the American tradition, values represented by his father, the itinerant flute-maker, who was a combination of pioneer, craftsman and artist (and travelling salesman of a kind, but one who was not alienated from his product nor dependent on the personality market). The passages of flute music poignantly recall that earlier, freer, simpler period, and at the same time they remind us of all that aesthetic experience of life expressed in music and art which is absent from Willy's existence. He has no protection against the undiluted commercialism of his working career and he has no resources – cultural, religious or familial – to draw upon for support and spiritual nourishment. Having chosen his values, he has come to the unbearable realisation that not only has he failed them but that he has chosen wrongly.

'The persuasive atmosphere of the play', Raymond Williams points out, 'is one of false consciousness – the conditioned attitudes which Loman trains in his sons – being broken into by real consciousness, in actual life and relationships.'[13] Here again, Miller's choice of the interiorised form is remarkably apposite, as we view Willy's shifts of consciousness directly. Not only past and present, but also subjective wish and objective situation are confused in his mind. He increasingly resorts to repression or fabrication in order to buffer his awareness against the slow penetration of his knowledge of failure. At the end of Act II the finally more grounded Biff insists on breaking through the miasma of false consciousness to seize on a few 'facts'. Willy's sense of reality, throughout the play, is shown to be relativistic, shifting with his momentary perspectives and the particular psychological demands he is trying to satisfy. In this instance, however, under the pressure of Biff's insistence, Willy's resort to wish-fulfilling invention seems to become a conscious act, more the deliberate taking of an anodyne than an unconscious evasion: 'I was fired, and I'm looking for a little good news to tell your mother, because the woman has waited and the woman has suffered. The gist of it is that I haven't got a story left in my head, Biff. So don't give me a lecture about facts and aspects. I am not interested.' Biff is almost swept up into the make-believe account constructed by Willy (with Happy's collaboration) of his meeting with Oliver, but he holds on to his new-found sense of things.

For, if the main process of the play is Willy's steady disintegration, there is a positive counter-current in Biff's achievement, out of confusion and contradiction, of a vital degree of self-knowledge. In the exchange between Biff and Happy in the restaurant we hear how the disillusioning meeting with Oliver has brought him to a real consciousness of his past status. But we do not learn the full extent of his clearer sense of things until later, at home, when he tells Willy how he recognised his real desires, rejected the white-collar lifestyle and its status hierarchy, and opted instead for the health and simplicity of outdoor work:

> I stopped in the middle of that building and I saw – the sky. I saw the things that I love in this world. The work and the food and time to sit and smoke. And I looked at the pen and said to myself, what the hell am I grabbing this for? Why am I trying to become what I don't want to be? What am I doing in an office, making a contemptuous, begging fool of myself, when all I want is out there, waiting for me the minute I say I know who I am![14]

With his rebellion against his own cultural conditioning complete, Biff is able to recognise that Willy's tragedy lay in his choice of the false values, 'the wrong dreams', encouraged by commercialism.

By his insistence in the restaurant scene on the truth of his own experience and his refusal to participate in any more comforting illusions, Biff precipitates a psychological crisis in his father. Early in the play we have heard a woman's laughter and, later, seen a brief exchange between Willy and a woman, but they are both cut short and left in enigmatic abeyance. It is not until Willy's capacity for evasion, for false consciousness, has collapsed before the combined weight of his being fired and Biff's failure with Oliver that the main 'fact' he has repressed for so long – the traumatic meeting with Biff in the Boston hotel – wells up irresistibly into his consciousness, its literal enactment on stage embodying the unfaded intensity of that crucial confrontation seventeen years before.

At the end of the second act Biff tries to re-establish the contact with Willy that was lost as a result of the Boston exposure. He tries to generate a new relatedness between them, based not on obfuscating personal images and on inflated notions of their own importance, but upon a realistic acknowledgement of their shared ordinariness. 'Pop! I'm a dime a dozen, and so are you', he tells him, but Willy takes on an heroic dimension as he rebels against the diminishment of the individual enforced by urban society (imaged in the towering apartment blocks). 'I am not a dime a dozen!' he claims defiantly and, still driven by the vital need for some distinction to rescue him from the anonymous obscurity of the lower-middle-class employee, he protests the dignity of his name: 'I am Willy Loman, and you are Biff Loman!' Biff's heartfelt appeal that he be accepted simply as a son and not as a potential social success restores Willy to his fatherhood, but so immersed is Willy in dreams of his son's glory that he immediately reimposes that onerous expectation which Biff has just sloughed off. 'That boy – that boy is going to be magnificent!' he proclaims, misplaced hope welling up in him once more. It seems odd that Willy should kill himself after experiencing a new relatedness to Biff after all the years of estrangement, but as Miller remarks, the suicide had no single cause but was complex in motivation: 'Revenge was in it and a power of love, a victory in that it would bequeath a fortune to the living and flight from emptiness.'[15]

Both within *Salesman*, in Linda's plea that 'attention must be paid' and Charley's gloss on the psychology of the salesman, and in other writings, Miller made claims for the representativeness of Willy and his predicament. 'The assumption was that everyone knew Willy Loman', he wrote in his 'Introduction', and in a symposium on the play he said, 'Willy Loman is, I think, a person who embodies in himself some of the most terrible conflicts running through the streets of America today.'[16] In the face of Miller's assertion in his 'Introduction' that he had 'not the slightest interest in the selling profession', we are forced to ask who or what Willy represents and why it is that his dilemma has struck such a resonant chord in modern audiences?

In general terms we can recognise that while Joe Keller of *All My Sons* belonged to the old middle class and possessed the independence and secure, if limited, viewpoint of the self-made man, Willy Loman is situated in the new middle class of white-collar employees who are dependent upon others for their livelihood, values and self-esteem. Miller's shift of sociological focus demonstrates his awareness of the growing importance of this rapidly expanding occupational group. It was establishing the general texture of American social life and bringing to the fore problems associated with the discontinuity of social change such as the need for new modes of identity and new values in a greatly altered environment. Miller presents Willy in all his social relations – as employee, as erring husband, as failed father, as less successful brother, as modern consumer harassed by mortgage payments, insurance premiums and credit instalments on machines that suffer from in-built obsolescence. He is thus shown being victimised both in his capacity as worker and his capacity as consumer. Two major ironies present themselves in Willy's commitment to bourgeois values: first, he does not become a property-owner until after his death, and secondly, as a failure in selling, as a cast-off functionary in the distribution system, he is worth more dead than alive. Since he has only ever obtained monetary reward at the cost of self-negation, there is a perverse logic in his receiving the highest financial reward for his most extreme act of self-negation.

Yet Miller is by no means a complete determinist. He does not allow Willy to be just a passive victim, a human atom driven by forces much larger than himself. He shows him making choices – selling, not Alaska – so that he must share some of the blame for his condition. Willy's crisis, then, is a personal one, but through the realm of values, through its ideological aspect, emphasised by Miller, it connects with the crisis of values in the society at large. Willy's problem, in a similar way to Clyde Griffiths's, is due not to a lack of values but rather to the plurality of value-systems operating in a society undergoing rapid change. That society was losing contact with a residual set of production-oriented values as it committed itself wholeheartedly to mass consumerism, and the resultant ideological conflict led to anxiety and disorientation among individuals living through that social change. Miller indicts the commercial ethos of success for its lack of any nourishing values, but the only solution he offers his characters is escape – death for Willy, and back to the land for Biff, back to an agrarian, productive life. In *Salesman* he does not really face the vexing question of how one is to live and work and retain integrity – attain 'autonomy', to adopt Riesman's term – in an urban society where all the pressures are towards false consciousness and the loss of selfhood. Not until *The Misfits* did he tackle the decline of agrarian life in the West as an ideal of freedom and wholeness, and not until *After the Fall* and *The Price* did he confront the dilemmas involved in preserving some notion of individual integrity in a complex social world where simple personal solutions are no longer available.

The changed work pattern and lifestyle associated with the growth of commerce, the character structure encouraged by these developments, and the emphasis the consumption economy placed on the personal and interpersonal, the newly evolving social being in short, fostered a new phase of consciousness. This new phase, Miller percipiently recognised, required an interiorised, non-realistic theatrical form to give it adequate expression. Both George F. Babbitt and Willy Loman represent in their respective ways the sterility of lives given over entirely to business values.[17]   But, while Sinclair Lewis saw Babbitt as only an externally drawn vehicle for mild satire at the expense of Middle America, Miller saw Willy Loman first in terms of a drama of consciousness and, secondly, as the focus for a drama of values. He also regarded his salesman as possessing a tragic stature of a particularly modern kind.[18] This deepening of mood, together with Miller's greater muscularity of intellect and responsiveness to the demands of art, mean that *Death of a Salesman* is a much richer, less woodenly articulated, presentation of Consumer Man than *Babbitt*. It also constitutes the capstone text in our overarching theme of the transition from a production-oriented to a consumption-oriented economy and the ideological conflicts and literary responses generated by that transition.

Notes and References

INTRODUCTION: PRODUCTION TO CONSUMPTION

1. 'Consumerism' is not used here in the sense, common in marketing circles, of an aggressive campaigning on behalf of consumers' interests, represented by Ralph Nader, say. It is used here to denote a type of economy which derives its dominant character from the sale of goods and services for personal consumption and which, consequently, relies heavily on the maintenance of consumer demand through such means as advertising, salesmen and instalment credit.
2. Fredric Jameson, *Marxism and Form: Dialectical Theories of Literature* (Princeton: 1971) pp. 377–8.
3. Frederick Engels, 'Socialism: Utopian and Scientific', in Karl Marx and Frederick Engels, *Selected Works* (London: 1968) p. 415; Karl Marx, *Selected Works*, p. 182. See Jean-Paul Sartre, *Search for a Method*, translated by Hazel E. Barnes (New York: 1968), and Raymond Williams, *Marxism and Literature* (Oxford: 1977) for a theoretical discussion of the deterministic relation between literature and society.
4. Karl Marx, *Capital* (London: 1971) II, pp. 399, 434.
5. Ibid., pp. 25–64.
6. Karl Marx, *Capital* (Chicago: 1909) III, pp. 85, 283.
7. *Capital*, II, p. 36.

CHAPTER 1: HARDWARE: THE ECONOMY, SOCIETY AND IDEOLOGIES OF PRODUCTION

1. Charles H. Hession and Hyman Sardy, *Ascent to Affluence: A History of American Economic Development* (Boston: 1969) pp. 420, 424.
2. United States Department of Commerce, *Historical Statistics of the United States – Colonial Times to 1957* (Washington: 1960) pp. 74, 140. Hereafter abbreviated to *HS* and incorporated in the text with the page number.
3. Karl Marx, *Capital* (London: 1971) II, p. 255.
4. Simon Kuznets, "The Proportion of Capital Formation to National Product", *American Economic Review*, 42 (1952) 507–26, Table I; Simon Kuznets, *Capital in the American Economy: Its Formation and Financing* (Princeton: 1961) pp. 408, 401. Net balance of foreign capital inflow is the amount of capital flowing into the country from abroad minus the amount of capital flowing out of the country.
5. Hession and Sardy, op. cit., p. 416; Kuznets, *Capital in the American Economy*, p. 64.

6. R. B. Nye and J. E. Morpurgo, *The Growth of the USA* (Harmondsworth: 1970) p. 578; Stewart H. Holbrook, *The Age of the Moguls* (New York: 1953) pp. 7, 301, 360. See also Matthew Josephson, *The Robber Barons: The Great American Capitalists 1861–1901* (London: 1962).

7. Hession and Sardy, op. cit., p. 469.

8. Nye and Morpurgo, op. cit., p. 631.

9. See Maurice Dobb, *Studies in the Development of Capitalism* (London: 1946), p. 290.

10. Railway mileage rose from 403 000 in 1919 to 429 000 in 1929, a rise of only 6.5 per cent, and slowly declined thereafter. *Historical Statistics*, p. 429.

11. Hession and Sardy, op. cit., p. 533.

12. Kuznets, *Capital in the American Economy*, p. 401; Dobb, *Studies*, p. 332.

13. R. H. Tawney, *Religion and the Rise of Capitalism* (Harmondsworth: 1938) p. 249.

14. Max Weber, *The Protestant Ethic and the Spirit of Capitalism*, trans. Talcott Parsons (London, 1971) p. 55; see Christopher Hill, 'Protestantism and the Rise of Capitalism', in *Capitalism and the Reformation*, edited by M.J. Kitch (London: 1967) pp. 3–8.

15. See John Winthrop, 'Reasons for Forsaking England' (1629) and the editor's note 'Genesis of the Bay Colony' in *The Puritan Tradition in America 1620–1730*, edited by Alden T. Vaughan (New York: 1972) pp. 25–35, 54.

16. Three central doctrines of Calvinism – the inherent sinfulness of the world and worldly possessions, predestination, and the calling – supplied the basis of the Protestant ethic and provided the bridges by which religious belief was linked to early capitalist practice. The first condemned 'covetousness' and urged the Puritan to deny himself the physical allurements of play and entertainment and to check sensual pleasure; the second led to the search for signs of one's election in one's daily activity; and the doctrine of the calling led 'to the position that not withdrawal from the world, but the conscientious discharge of the duties of business, is among the loftiest of religious and moral virtues'. Combined together they inculcated a 'worldly asceticism' in which hard work, thrift, self-discipline and rational foresight were heavily emphasised. Max Weber, *The Protestant Ethic and the Spirit of Capitalism*, p. 119 and *passim*. See also Tawney, op. cit., p. 239, Vaughan, op. cit., pp. 131, 133, 311, and Kitch, op. cit., pp. 156–8.

17. Hector St John de Crevecoeur, *Letters from an American Farmer* (1782, London: 1912), pp. 59, 220; Benjamin Franklin, *The Instructor; or Young Man's Best Companion* (1748), collected in *The Autobiography and Other Writings*, edited by L. Jesse Lemisch (New York: 1961) pp. 187, 186; Alexis de Tocqueville, *Democracy in America*, translated by George Lawrence and edited by J. P. Mayer and Max Lerner (London: 1968) II, p. 711. Not everybody accepted the strictures of the Protestant ethic without demur. In the 1840s Thoreau, in *Walden*, rejected the notion of labour as a calling and praised idleness as at times 'the most attractive and productive industry'.

18. Tawney, *Religion and the Rise of Capitalism*, pp. 229, 244; Franklin, *Autobiography and Other Writings*, p. 187; Weber, *Protestant Ethic*, p. 172.

19. Tocqueville, *Democracy*, II, p. 692; James Bryce, *The American Commonwealth* (1888, revised edition New York: 1911) II, p. 814; Simon

Notes and References

Kuznets, 'The Proportion of Capital Formation to National Product', *American Economic Review*, 42 (1952) 507–26.

20. Weber, *Protestant Ethic*, p. 71; Holbrook, *Age of the Moguls*, pp. 67, 113–4, 143, 155.
21. K. Samuelsson, 'Thrift and the Accumulation of Capital', in Kitch (ed.), *Capitalism and the Reformation*, pp. 172–5.
22. Crèvecoeur, *Letters*, pp. 42, 44.
23. Charles Beard in *An Economic Interpretation of the Constitution of the United States* (New York: 1935) attacked the notion of the homogeneous middle-class character of American society in the late eighteenth century, but Robert E. Brown in *Charles Beard and the Constitution* (Princeton: 1956) effectively demolished Beard's arguments and established that in 1787 American society was predominantly middle-class with few extremes of wealth and poverty and most men owning property.
24. Crevecoeur, *Letters*, p. 55.
25. Jefferson, 'Notes on the State of Virginia', reprinted in *The Portable Thomas Jefferson* edited by Merrill D. Peterson (Harmondsworth: 1977) p. 217; Crèvecoeur, *Letters*, p. 44.
26. Jeffersonian and, later, Jacksonian democracy were primarily political restatements of these doctrines of natural rights and unchecked freedom. The Jacksonians (in power in the 1830s and 1840s) believed deeply in *laissez-faire* and maintained that an over-development of governmental power crushed equality of economic opportunity and individual enterprise. His party's concern, Jackson said, was for 'the liberty of men owning independent means of livelihood'. Nye and Morpurgo, *Growth of the USA*, pp. 381, 403.
27. Tawney, *Religion and the Rise of Capitalism*, pp. 226–7, 253.
28. Tocqueville, *Democracy in America*, I, p. 5; II, pp. 652, 667.
29. 'Nature hath implanted in our breasts a love of others, a sense of duty to them, a moral instinct, in short, which prompts us irresistibly to feel and succour their distresses. ... The Creator would indeed have been a bungling artist, had he intended man for a social animal without planting in him social dispositions.' Jefferson, 'Letter to Thomas Law (1814)', reprinted in *Portable Jefferson*, p. 542.
30. Yehoshua Arieli, *Individualism and Nationalism in American Ideology* (Cambridge, Mass: 1964) p. 132.
31. Abraham Lincoln, *Collected Works*, edited by Roy P. Basler (New Brunswick, New Jersey: 1953) VII, p. 23.
32. Arieli, *Individualism and Nationalism*, pp. 24–5.
33. 'American social development has been continually beginning over again on the frontier. This perennial rebirth, this fluidity of American life, this expansion westward with its new opportunities, its continuous touch with the simplicity of primitive society furnish the forces dominating American character.' Frederick Jackson Turner, *The Frontier in American History* (1920, reprinted New York: 1962) pp. 2, 30; Bryce, *American Commonwealth*, II, pp. 590–1.
34. T. B. Bottomore, *Classes in Modern Society* (London: 1965) p. 42.
35. Bryce, op. cit. II, pp. 474–5.
36. Bryce, op. cit. I, p. 642; Morton and Lucia White, *The Intellectual Versus*

the City: From Thomas Jefferson to Frank Lloyd Wright (New York: 1977)
p. 149. See Holbrook, *Age of the Moguls*, and Josephson, *Robber Barons* for
accounts of the entrepreneurs' manipulation of the press and the political
machines.

37. Bryce, op. cit, II, pp. 811–12; Gabriel Kolko, *Wealth and Power in
America* (New York: 1962) p. 14; commentator quoted by Kolko, p. 99.
38. Tocqueville, *Democracy*, II, p. 652.
39. Arieli, *Individualism and Nationalism* p. 332.
40. Andrew Carnegie, 'Wealth', *North American Review* (June 1889), reprinted
in *Democracy and the Gospel of Wealth*, edited by Gail Kennedy (Boston:
1949) p. 1; William Graham Sumner, quoted by Richard Hofstadter, *Social
Darwinism in American Thought* (revised edition, Boston: 1955) p. 51.
41. Hofstadter, op. cit., pp. 201–4.
42. Weber, *Protestant Ethic*, p. 117; Thoreau, *Walden and Civil Disobedience*
(New York: 1960) p. 148; Franklin, *Autobiography*, p. 94; Emerson, 'Self-
Reliance', in *Selected Writings*, edited by Brooks Atkinson (New York:
1940) p. 148.
43. David Riesman, Nathan Glazer and Reuel Denny, *The Lonely Crowd*
(abridged edition, New Haven: 1961) pp. 14, 15, 111–12.

CHAPTER 2: THE LITERARY RESPONSE(i)

1. See Richard Chase, *The American Novel and its Tradition* (New York:
1957), for a discussion of the place of romance in the American novel.
2. Henry James, *Hawthorne* (1879, London: 1967) pp. 22, 23, 55, 110, 119.
3. T. B. Bottomore, *Classes in Modern Society* (London: 1965) p. 42.
4. Ian Watt, *The Rise of the Novel* (Harmondsworth: 1972) pp. 66, 78–9.
5. Dreiser describes the impact of his journalistic work on his conception of
society and literature in the second part of his autobiography, *A Book
About Myself* (1922, Greenwich, Conn: 1965); John A. Jackson draws
attention to the influence of journalism in 'Sociology and Literary Studies I,
The Map of Society: America in the 1890s', *Journal of American Studies*, 3
(1969) 103–10.
6. See Blanche Gelfant, *The American City Novel* (second edition, Norman,
Oklahoma: 1970), for a study of the city novel as a special genre, and also
Morton and Lucia White, *The Intellectual Versus the City*, for an
examination of the ambivalent responses of Howells, Norris and Dreiser
towards the city. Frank Norris's *The Octopus* (1901) is a notable exception
in taking an agrarian locale for its setting, though its subject – the futile
struggle of the independent farmer-businessman against the trusts – is a
socially representative one.
7. William Dean Howells, *A Hazard of New Fortunes* (London: 1965) p. 63.
8. Quoted by Edwin H. Cady, *The Realist at War: The Mature Years
1885–1920 of William Dean Howells*, (Syracuse: 1958) p. 52. Through
articles and reviews in *The Atlantic Monthly* and through his own novels
Howells waged a campaign against romance (of the degraded, sentimental
variety) and for realism throughout the 1880s and 1890s. He fostered the
young talents of Crane and Norris among others and became the man to

Notes and References

whom more youthful writers could look as the image of literary integrity and success. See Edwin H. Cady, *The Road to Realism: The Early Years 1837–1885 of William Dean Howells* (Syracuse: 1956) p. 222.

9. Howells, 'Criticism and Fiction', in Clara and Rudolf Kirk (eds), *Criticism and Fiction and Other Essays* (New York: 1959) p. 51.

10. Émile Zola, *Thérèse Raquin*, translated by L. Tancock (Harmondsworth: 1962) p. 22.

11. In *A Hazard of New Fortunes* Basil March, Howells's humane mouthpiece, contemplates the ruthless competition he has discovered in the metropolis: 'So we go on, pushing and pulling, climbing and crawling, thrusting aside and trampling underfoot; lying, cheating, stealing; and when we get to the end, covered with blood and dirt and sin and shame, and look back over the way we've come ... I don't think the retrospect can be pleasing' (p. 396).

12. See Stanislav Andreski (ed.), *Structure, Function and Evolution: A Selection of Spencer's Writings* (London: 1971) p. 121 and *passim*.

13. Collected in Theodore Dreiser, *Hey, Rub-A-Dub-Dub* (1925, London: 1931) p. 128.

14. Engels, 'Socialism: Utopian and Scientific', in Marx and Engels, *Selected Works* (London: 1968) p. 388.

15. Henry Brooks Adams, *The Education of Henry Adams* (private publication, 1906, Boston: 1918); Thorstein Veblen, *The Instinct of Workmanship* (1914, reprinted New York: 1964).

CHAPTER 3: THE RISE OF THE ENTREPRENEUR IN THE WORK OF HOWELLS, NORRIS AND DREISER

1. Edwin H. Cady, *The Road to Realism: The Early Years 1837–1885* of William Dean Howells (Syracuse: 1956) pp. 21, 34, 92; quotation taken from 'Criticism and Fiction' in William Dean Howells, *Criticism and Fiction and Other Essays*, edited by Clara and Rudolf Kirk (New York: 1959) p. 42.

2. Lionel Trilling, 'Manners, Morals, and the Novel', collected in *The Liberal Imagination: Essays on Literature and Society* (Harmondsworth: 1970) p. 212.

3. Howells, 'Criticism and Fiction', pp. 48–9.

4. Ibid., p. 62.

5. Franklin Walker, *Frank Norris: A Biography* (New York: 1963) pp. 8, 13–14.

6. Ibid., p. 276.

7. Walter Fuller Taylor, *The Economic Novel in America* (New York: 1973) p. 301.

8. Walker, op. cit., p. 293.

9. Frank Norris, *The Responsibilities of the Novelist, Complete Works* (Port Washington: 1960) VII, p. 16.

10. In *The Responsibilities of the Novelist* Norris championed the cause of the West and complained that the New England School did not represent the entire range of American fiction.

11. Theodore Dreiser, 'The American Financier', in *Hey, Rub-A-Dub-Dub* (London: 1931) p. 86.

12. Quoted in F. O. Matthiessen, *Theodore Dreiser* (New York: 1956) pp. 129, 135.
13. Donald Pizer, *The Novels of Theodore Dreiser* (Minneapolis: 1976) pp. 156, 162.
14. Frederick Engels, 'Letter to August Bebel (1893)', in *Marx–Engels Selected Correspondence* (Moscow: 1965) p. 429.
15. Pizer, *Novels of Theodore Dreiser*, p. 163.
16. Quoted in Matthew Josephson, *The Robber Barons: The Great American Capitalists 1861–1901* (London: 1962) pp. 336, 386.

CHAPTER 4: THE CONDITION OF THE POOR IN THE WORK OF HOWELLS, DREISER AND SINCLAIR

1. Frederick Engels, *The Condition of the Working Class in England* (London: 1969) p. 58. In his Preface to the 1892 English edition he wrote: '[American] manufactures are young as compared with those of England, but increasing at a far more rapid rate than the latter; and curious enough, they have at this moment arrived at about the same phase of development as English manufacture in 1844. With regard to America the parallel is indeed most striking.'
2. Edward and Eleanor Marx Aveling, *The Working-Class Movement in America,* second edition (London: 1891), quoting Bureau of Labor Reports, pp. 64, 77.
3. Ibid., p. 17.
4. Quoted in R. B. Nye and J. E. Morpurgo, *The Growth of the USA* (Harmondsworth: 1970) p. 628.
5. Quoted in Edwin H. Cady, *The Road to Realism: The Early Years 1837–1885 of William Dean Howells* (Syracuse; 1956) pp. 244–5.
6. Howells stood alone among prominent Americans in publicly defending the anarchists and in petitioning the Governor of Illinois for their death sentences to be commuted. Edwin H. Cady, *The Realist at War: The Mature Years 1885–1920 of William Dean Howells* (Syracuse: 1958) pp. 64, 79–80.
7. See George Warren Arms, 'Further Enquiry into Howells' Socialism', *Science and Society*, 3 (1939) 245–8; quoted in Cady, *Realist at War*, p. 91.
8. Cady, *Realist at War*, p. 105.
9. Henry James, *The American Scene* (1907, London: 1968) pp. 136–7.
10. Ibid., p. 86.
11. Cady, *Realist at War*, p. 105, thinks otherwise: 'It is Lindau who is the immediate, precipitating agent of Conrad Dryfoos' death; and he dies too, victim also of his irrational philosophy of violence.' This seems to me to be a misreading both of Howells's view of Lindau and of the presentation of the street violence.
12. The experience of his sister, Emma, and her lover, L.A. Hopkins, formed the basis for his account of Carrie and Hurstwood in Chicago, just as the experience of another sister, Mame, who was seduced by a prominent Terre Haute lawyer and had an illegitimate child, was used in the story of Jennie Gerhardt. Carrie's rise on the Broadway stage also paralleled the rise of his

brother, Paul, in the Broadway world of music, and to some extent in *Sister Carrie* Dreiser was fusing the story of his sister with that of his brother. Donald Pizer, *The Novels of Theodore Dreiser* (Minneapolis: 1976) p. 31.

13. See his autobiographical volume, *A Book About Myself* (1922. New York: 1965), in which he talks about his newspaper experience, e.g. pp. 113–14.

14. Quoted in F. O. Matthiessen, *Theodore Dreiser* (New York: 1956) p. 60.

15. See Sandy Petry, 'The Language of Realism, The Language of False Consciousness: A Reading of *Sister Carrie*', *Novel*, 10 (Winter 1977) 101–13, for an illuminating discussion of the coexistence of two styles within the novel.

16. Pizer, *Novels of Theodore Dreiser*, pp. 39–40.

17. The phrase 'literature of exposure' is Lenin's from his 1902 pamphlet *What is to be Done?*

18. Upton Sinclair, *The Autobiography of Upton Sinclair* (New York: 1962) pp. 108 – 10.

19. See Milton M. Gordon, 'The Immigrant in American Life and Thought', in *The Shaping of Twentieth-Century America*, edited by Richard M. Abrams and Lawrence W. Levine (Boston: 1965) p. 295.

20. James Bryce, *The American Commonwealth*, revised edition (New York: 1911) II, p. 477.

21. William Dean Howells, 'The Physiognomy of "The Poor"', *Harper's Monthly* (January 1903) reprinted in William Dean Howells, *Criticism and Fiction and Other Essays*, edited by Clara and Rudolf Kirk (New York: 1959) p. 343.

22. Bryce, *American Commonwealth*, II, p. 473fn.

23. Samuel P. Hays, *The Response to Industrialism 1885–1914* (Chicago: 1957) p. 151; Sinclair, *Autobiography*, p. 104.

24. Walter B. Rideout, *The Radical Novel in the United States 1900–1954* (Cambridge: 1965) pp. 35–6.

CHAPTER 5: SOFTWARE: THE ECONOMY, SOCIETY AND IDEOLOGIES OF CONSUMPTION

1. Louis J. Paradiso, 'Retail Sales and Consumer Incomes', Department of Commerce 1945, quoted in 'Consumption Economics: A Symposium', *American Economic Review*, 35 (May 1945) 52–4; H. T. Oshima, 'Consumer Asset Formation and the Future of Capitalism', *Economic Journal*, 71 (1961) 20–35; Walter Rostow, *The Stages of Economic Growth: A Non-Communist Manifesto* (Cambridge: 1961) pp. 10–11; see H. G. Vatter, 'Has there been a Twentieth-Century Consumer Durables Revolution?' *Journal of Economic History*, 27 (1967) for a criticism of the orthodox view and S. Juster and M. Lipsey, 'A Note on Consumer Asset Formation in the United States', *Economic Journal*, 77 (1967) for a counter-argument to Vatter.

2. Jim Potter, *The American Economy between the World Wars* (London: 1974) p. 37.

3. Stewart H. Holbrook, *The Age of the Moguls* (New York: 1953) p. 206.

4. United States Department of Commerce, *Historical Statistics of the United States: Colonial Times to 1957* (Washington: 1960) p. 462.

5. Charles H. Hession and Hyman Sardy, *Ascent to Affluence: A History of American Economic Development* (Boston: 1969) p. 619.

6. Rostow, *Stages of Economic Growth*, p. 76; Peter d'A. Jones, *The Consumer Society: A History of American Capitalism* (Harmondsworth: 1965) p. 282; Potter, op. cit., p. 64, also points to consumer-durable production as one of the marked features of the 1920s.

7. *Historical Statistics*, pp. 139, 601.

8. Quoted by Hession and Sardy, op. cit., p. 617.

9. Brookings Institute, *America's Capacity to Produce and America's Capacity to Consume: A Digest* (Pittsburgh: 1934) p. 31.

10. Jones, op. cit., p. 281.

11. Holbrook, op. cit., p. 209.

12. See Vance Packard, *The Hidden Persuaders* (Harmondsworth: 1960) p. 23 and *passim* for the use by manufacturers of 'psychological obsolescence' to avert a crisis of overproduction.

13. J. M. Gillman, *The Falling Rate of Profit*: Marx's Law and its Significance to Twentieth-Century Capitalism* (London: 1957) p. 131.

14. Hession and Sardy, op. cit., p. 624.

15. W. E. Leuchtenberg, *The Perils of Prosperity 1914–1932* (Chicago: 1958) p. 192.

16. Hession and Sardy, op. cit., p. 672; *Historical Statistics*, p. 526.

17. T. C. Cochran, *A Basic History of American Business* (Princeton: 1968) p. 68.

18. Leuchtenberg, op. cit., p. 200.

19. Cochran, op. cit., p. 83.

20. Potter, op. cit., p. 46.

21. Hession and Sardy, op. cit., p. 639. By 1950 the proportion had further decreased to 9.9 per cent.

22. Leuchtenberg, op. cit., p. 193.

23. Adolf A. Berle and Gardiner C. Means, *The Modern Corporation and Private Property* (reprinted New York: 1948) pp. 19, 31–3, 4.

24. *Historical Statistics*, p. 74; Potter, op. cit., p. 55; Gillman, op. cit., p. 93.

25. Potter, op. cit., p. 51.

26. *Historical Statistics*, p. 9.

27. Potter, op. cit., p. 51.

28. Lewis Mumford, *The Culture of Cities* (London: 1938) p. 226.

29. Between 1929 and 1933 all the economic indicators pointed to a sharp downturn in business activity and there was a steep decline in average income. See Potter, op. cit., p. 94. One factor in the economy which had been comparatively negligible in the 1920s but which after the Second World War was of enormous importance was the role of the Federal Government as consumer.

30. 'Consumption Economics: A Symposium', *American Economic Review*, 35 (May 1945) pp. 44, 55.

31. Rostow, op. cit., p. 79.

32. Oshima, 'Consumer Asset Formation'.

33. In 1958 the actual spending of consumers was 293 billion dollars compared with 215 billion dollars in 1948. Dexter M. Keezer and associates, *New Forces in American Business* (New York: 1959) p. 75; Harry Magdoff, 'Problems of US Capitalism', in *the Socialist Register 1965*, edited by Ralph

Miliband and John Saville (New York: 1965) p. 68.

34. Keezer, op. cit., p. 91.
35. Advertising figures, *Historical Statistics*, p. 526; see Packard, *Hidden Persuaders*, for the use of depth psychology in advertising.
36. Paul A. Baran and Paul M. Sweezy, *Monopoly Capital* (Harmondsworth: 1968) p. 374.
37. Keezer, op. cit., pp. 97, 118.
38. *Historical Statistics*, p. 74.
39. Keezer, op. cit., p. 77.
40. Hession and Sardy, op. cit., p. 785.
41. Magdoff, 'Problems of US Capitalism', p. 64.
42. Simon Kuznets, *Capital in the American Economy: Its Formation and Financing* (Princeton: 1961) p. 396.
43. David Riesman, Nathan Glazer and Reuel Denney, *The Lonely Crowd* (1950, abridged edition New Haven: 1961) p. 6; William H. Whyte, *The Organization Man* (London: 1957) pp. 4–6; David M. Potter, *People of Plenty: Economic Abundance and the American Character* (Chicago: 1954) p. 173; Daniel Bell, *The Cultural Contradictions of Capitalism* (London: 1976) pp. 21, 61, 64–5; Lewis Mumford also subscribed to the view that the United States had moved from a phase of scarcity into one of abundance, *The City in History* (Harmondsworth: 1966) p. 620; Talcott Parsons and Winston White, 'The Link Between Character and Society', in *Culture and Social Character: The Work of David Riesman Reviewed*, edited by Seymour Martin Lipset and Leo Lowenthal (Glencoe: 1961), take issue with Riesman and argue that the American value-system has not undergone any fundamental change.
44. Samuel P. Hays, *The Response to Industrialism 1885–1914* (Chicago: 1975) pp. 114–15; Robert S. and Helen M. Lynd, *Middletown in Transition: A Study in Cultural Conflicts* (New York: 1937) pp. 242–3.
45. Quoted in Hession and Sardy, op. cit., p. 669.
46. Bell, op. cit., pp. 71–2.
47. Thorstein Veblen, *The Theory of the Leisure Class* (1899, London: 1970) pp. 70, 82; David Riesman in *Individualism Reconsidered and Other Essays* (New York: 1954) p. 225, described Veblen's book as having fitted 'not too badly the American scene from the gay 90s to the not quite so gay 20s'.
48. Veblen, op. cit., pp. 37, 42–3, 218; Andrew Carnegie, 'Wealth', *North American Review* (June 1889), reprinted in *Democracy and the Gospel of Wealth*, edited by Gail Kennedy (Boston: 1949) p. 1.
49. James Bryce, *The American Commonwealth*, 2 vols (1888, revised edition New York: 1911) II, pp. 624–5; Lynd and Lynd, op. cit., pp. 247, 455.
50. See C. E. M. Joad, *Diogenes or the Future of Leisure* (London: 1928); Herbert L. Stewart, 'The Ethics of Luxury and Leisure', *American Journal of Sociology*, 24, 3(1918) 241–59; James Russell Lowell, 'Democracy', an Address delivered at Birmingham, England, 1884, collected in *Democracy and other Addresses* (Boston and New York: 1887) p. 28; C. D. Burns, *Leisure and the Modern World* (London: 1932) p. 148.
51. Riesman *et al.*, *The Lonely Crowd*, p. 118; Leuchtenberg, op. cit., p. 198.
52. Potter, op. cit., p. 23.
53. Whyte, op. cit., p. 68.
54. C. Wright Mills, *White Collar: The American Middle Classes* (New York: 1951) p. 86.

55. Whyte, op. cit., pp. 33–8.
56. Dale Carnegie, *How to Win Friends and Influence People* (1938, reprinted Tadworth, Surrey: 1953) pp. 24, 27; Riesman, *Individualism Reconsidered*, p. 31.
57. Whyte, op. cit., pp. 267, 350–65.
58. Mills, op. cit., pp. 252–3.
59. Ibid., p. 182.
60. Erich Fromm, *Man For Himself* (London: 1949) p. 68; Riesman *et al.*, *The Lonely Crowd*, pp. 19–22.
61. See Paula S. Fass, *The Damned and the Beautiful: American Youth in the 1920s* (New York: 1977) for the significance of the college-based youth culture.
62. David Riesman, *Faces in the Crowd* (New Haven: 1952) p. 6; Riesman *et al.*, *The Lonely Crowd*, p. 78.
63. Lewis Mumford, *The Culture of Cities*, p. 227.
64. Quoted by Vance Packard, *The Hidden Persuaders*, p. 13.
65. Fromm, op. cit., p. 72.
66. Riesman *el al.*, *The Lonely Crowd*, p. 139.

CHAPTER 6: THE LITERARY RESPONSE (ii)

1. F. O. Matthiessen, *Theodore Dreiser* (New York: 1956) p. 191.
2. Malcolm Cowley, *Exile's Return: A Narrative of Ideas* (New York: 1934) pp. 69–72.
3. Daniel Bell, *The Cultural Contradictions of Capitalism* (London: 1976) p. 64.
4. Cowley, op. cit., pp. 113, 238.
5. Bell, op. cit., p. 110.
6. See my 'John Dos Passos and the Visual Arts', *Journal of American Studies*, 15 (December 1981) 391–405.
7. Lewis Mumford, *The Culture of Cities* (London: 1938) p. 270.
8. John Dos Passos, 'Introduction' to the Modern Library edition of *The Forty-Second Parallel* (New York: 1937).
9. Recalling his period in the Norton-Harjes ambulance service, Dos Passos wrote, 'I was trying to divide all humanity into the useful people like cooks and farmhands and woodworkers and architects and engineers, who were always building up mankind, and the destructive people like politicians and bankers and college presidents and national propagandists, who spread illusions and destroyed civilisation as fast as the producers built it up. . . . Producers were good, exploiters were evil.' *The Best Times* (London: 1967) p. 44.
10. Dos Passos, 'Introduction', op. cit.
11. I am referring to the revised edition published in 1948. See Malcolm Cowley's note, *Tender is the Night* (Harmondsworth: 1955) p. 351.
12. See Daniel Aaron, *Writers on the Left* (Oxford and New York: 1977).
13. Arthur Miller, 'Introduction' to *The Collected Plays* (New York: 1957) p. 19.
14. Ibid., p. 23.

CHAPTER 7: CLASS AND THE CONSUMPTION ETHIC: DREISER'S *AN AMERICAN TRAGEDY*

1. Sergei Eisenstein, *Film Form*, edited and translated by Jay Leyda (London: 1951) p. 96. Eisenstein prepared a scenario of the novel for Paramount during his stay in the United States, but unfortunately it was turned down; see Irving Howe, 'Afterword' to the Signet edition of *An American Tragedy* (New York: 1964); F. O. Matthiessen, *Theodore Dreiser* (New York: 1956); Richard Lehan, *Theodore Dreiser: His World and His Novels* (Edwardsville: 1969); Ellen Moers, *Two Dreisers: The Man and the Novelist* (London: 1970); and Donald Pizer, *The Novels of Theodore Dreiser* (Minneapolis: 1976).
2. Theodore Dreiser, *An American Tragedy* (New York: 1964) p. 48.
3. Robert S. and Helen M. Lynd, *Middletown: A Study in American Culture* (New York: 1929) p. 134.
4. *An American Tragedy*, p. 169.
5. Ibid., p. 176.
6. See Paula S. Fass, *The Damned and the Beautiful: American Youth in the 1920s* (New York: 1977) for a discussion of the importance of the youth culture in the 1920s and its main elements of peer-group conformity, consumerism and changing sexual mores.
7. Thorstein Veblen, *The Theory of the Leisure Class* (London: 1970) p. 207.
8. Trigant Burrow, 'Social Images versus Reality', *Journal of Abnormal Psychology and Social Psychology*, 19 (1924) 230–5.
9. See Lauriat Lane Jr, 'The Double in *An American Tragedy*'. *Modern Fiction Studies*, 12 (1966) 213–20, for a discussion of the physical similarity between Clyde and Gilbert.
10. *An American Tragedy*, p. 233.
11. My contention that *An American Tragedy* registers changes and contradictions in the culture runs counter to Donald Pizer's belief that Dreiser's intention was 'to stress the continuity of American experience', *The Novels of Theodore Dreiser*, p. 218. In my view he lays too much stress on the persistence of repressive norms and is insufficiently alert to those new developments associated with a consumption-oriented capitalism that Dreiser carefully includes in the novel.
12. See Daniel Bell, *The Cultural Contradictions of Capitalism* (London: 1976) pp. 71–2 and p. 78: 'The new capitalism was primarily responsible for transforming the society, and in the process undermined the Puritan temper, but it was never able to develop successfully a new ideology congruent with the change, and it used — and often was trapped by — the older language of Protestant values.'

CHAPTER 8: THE RICH ARE DIFFERENT: SCOTT FITZGERALD AND THE LEISURE CLASS

1. F. Scott Fitzgerald, 'The Rich Boy' (1926), reprinted in *The Diamond as Big as the Ritz and Other Stories* (Harmondsworth: 1962) p. 139. 'The Diamond

as Big as the Ritz' (1922) is an imaginative fable about the arrogance and ruthlessness of the very rich.

2. F. Scott Fitzgerald, *The Crack Up and Other Pieces*, edited by Edmund Wilson (New York: 1945) p. 125 footnote. In his short story 'The Snows of Kilimanjaro' Hemingway wrote of him that 'he thought [the rich] were a special glamorous race and when he found they weren't it wrecked him, just as much as any other thing that wrecked him', *The Snows of Kilimanjaro and Other Stories* (Harmondsworth: 1963) p. 28. When the story was first published in *Esquire* in August 1936, Hemingway referred to Scott by name but he later changed the character's name to Julian after protests from Fitzgerald. John Peale Bishop, his old Princeton friend, apparently characterised Fitzgerald as 'an awful suck about the rich and a social climber', *The Letters of F. Scott Fitzgerald*, edited by Andrew Turnbull (Harmondsworth: 1968) p. 332.

3. Andrew Turnbull, *F. Scott Fitzgerald: A Biography* (Harmondsworth: 1970) pp. 11–26; Arthur Mizener, *The Far Side of Paradise* (London: 1969) pp. 9, 21; Letter to Mrs Harold Ober, 4 March 1938, quoted by Turnbull, p. 157.

4. Turnbull, *F. Scott Fitzgerald*, pp. 94–112.

5. 'Notebooks', collected in *The Crack Up*, p. 77.

6. E. J. Hobsbawm, in *Bandits* (Harmondsworth: 1962), has pointed out that bandits, the most rebellious members of peasant societies, had little intention of altering the social structure but only of altering their position within it.

7. George Orwell, *The Road to Wigan Pier* (Harmondsworth: 1962) pp. 108–9.

8. See Lionel Trilling, 'F. Scott Fitzgerald' in his *The Liberal Imagination: Essays on Literature and Society* (London: 1951); Marius Bewley, 'Scott Fitzgerald and the Collapse of the American Dream', in his *The Eccentric Design: Form in the Classic American Novel* (London: 1959); and Henry Dan Piper, 'Social Criticism in the American Novel in the 1920s', in *The American Novel and the Nineteen Twenties*, edited by Malcolm Bradbury and David Palmer (London: 1971).

9. '"I looked outdoors for a minute, and it's very romantic outdoors. There's a bird on the lawn that I think must be a nightingale come over on the Cunard or White Star Line. He's singing away —" Her voice sang: "It's romantic, isn't it, Tom?" "Very romantic," he said', *The Great Gatsby* (Harmondsworth: 1950) p. 22.

10. Letter to Maxwell Perkins, June 1940, *Letters of F. Scott Fitzgerald*, p. 310; Letter to Frances Scott Fitzgerald, undated late 1930s, *Letters of F. Scott Fitzgerald*, p. 119. C. W. E. Bigsby in 'The Two Identities of F. Scott Fitzgerald', in *The American Novel and the Nineteen Twenties*, interprets *Tender is the Night* in Spenglerian terms of cultural decline while ignoring its Marxian aspect and its class specificity.

11. 'Notebooks', in *The Crack Up*, p. 178.

12. *The Great Gatsby*, p. 126.

13. Ibid., p. 99.

14. Letter to Maxwell Perkins (January 1925), *Letters*, p. 195.

15. *The Great Gatsby*, p. 119.

16. Ibid., p. 168.
17. Letter to Maxwell Perkins (August 1924), *Letters*, p. 185, and Turnbull's footnote on the same page.
18. In 1919 he made 879 dollars; in 1920, 18 850; in 1921, over 19 000; in 1922, over 25 000; and in 1923, over 28 000 dollars; Turnbull, *F. Scott Fitzgerald*, p. 147.
19. Ibid., pp 162–3.
20. In a memorandum to himself, quoted by Malcolm Cowley in his 'Introduction' to his revised version of *Tender is the Night* published by Penguin Books (Harmondsworth: 1955), p. 13.
21. *Tender is the Night* (Harmondsworth: 1955) p. 101.
22. Ibid., pp. 122–3.
23. From his memorandum to himself, quoted by Cowley, p. 13.
24. Thorstein Veblen, *The Theory of the Leisure Class* (London: 1970), p. 21.
25. F. Scott Fitzgerald, 'Echoes of the Jazz Age', in *The Crack Up and Other Pieces*, p. 21.
26. *Tender is the Night*, pp. 168, 225.

CHAPTER 9: SATIRE AND SENTIMENT: SINCLAIR LEWIS AND THE MIDDLE CLASS

1. Mark Schorer, *Sinclair Lewis: An American Life* (London: 1961) pp. 264, 268.
2. See Horst Frenz (ed.), *Nobel Lectures: Literature 1901–67* (London: 1969) p. 280.
3. 'The shops show the same standardized nationally advertised wares; the newspapers of sections three thousand miles apart have the same "syndicated features"; the boy in Arkansas displays just such a flamboyant ready-made suit as is found on just such a boy in Delaware, both of them iterate the same slang phrases from the same sporting-pages, and if one of them is in college and the other is a barber, no one may surmise which is which.' *Main Street* (New York: 1961) p. 261.
4. See Malcolm Bradbury and David Corker, 'The American Risorgimento: The Coming of the New Arts', in *American Literature since 1900*, edited by Marcus Cunliffe (London: 1975).
5. As Howell Daniels points out in 'Sinclair Lewis and the Drama of Dissociation' in *The American Novel and the Nineteen Twenties*, edited by Malcolm Bradbury and David Palmer (London: 1971) p. 91. He does not elucidate the full significance of the myth, however.
6. Frederick Jackson Turner, *The Frontier in American History* (New York: 1962) p. 37.
7. *Main Street*, pp. 28–9.
8. Ibid., p. 197.
9. Schorer, op. cit., pp. 111–16, 178.
10. Samuel P. Hays, *The Response to Industrialism 1885–1914* (Chicago: 1957), pp. 146–8.
11. Schorer, op. cit., p. 166.
12. See Donald R. McCoy, *Coming of Age: The United States during the 1920s*

and 1930s (Harmondsworth: 1977) pp. 29–33. Mark Schorer in his 'Afterword' to the Signet edition of *Main Street* has drawn attention to the possible influence of Progressivism and its demise on the novel's mood.

13. Schorer, op. cit., p. 352.
14. See John McCormick, *American Literature 1919–32* (London: 1971), pp. 75–85, for a venomously critical account of Lewis, and for contrasting high praise, Maxwell Geismar, *The Last of the Provincials: The American Novel 1915–1925* (New York: 1959) pp. 67–150.
15. *Babbitt* (London: 1924) p. 143.
16. Robert S. and Helen M. Lynd, *Middletown: A Study in American Culture* (New York: 1929) pp. 278, 309.
17. W. E. Leuchtenberg, *The Perils of Prosperity 1914–1932* (Chicago: 1958) p. 198.
18. *Babbitt*, p. 99.

CHAPTER 10: UNDEMOCRATIC VISTAS: DOS PASSOS, MASS SOCIETY AND MONOPOLY CAPITAL

1. John Dos Passos, 'Statement of Belief', *Bookman* (September 1928) quoted by J. H. Wrenn, *John Dos Passos* (New York: 1961) p. 152; John Dos Passos, 'The Writer as Technician', in *American Writers' Congress*, edited by Henry Hart (New York: 1935), quoted by Blanche Gelfant, *The American City Novel* (Norman, Oklahoma: 1970) p. 137. In his 'Introduction' to the Modern Library edition of *Three Soldiers* (New York: 1932) Dos Passos also called the novelist 'an architect of history'.
2. I am drawing on the biographical narrative supplied by Townsend Ludington, editor of *The Fourteenth Chronicle: Letters and Diaries of John Dos Passos* (London: 1974) p. 9.
3. Ibid., p. 152.
4. Granville Hicks, 'The Politics of John Dos Passos', *Antioch Review*, 10 (1950), reprinted in *Dos Passos: A Collection of Critical Essays*, edited by Andrew Hook (Englewood Cliffs, New Jersey: 1974) p. 15.
5. *Three Soldiers* (Boston: 1921) p. 343.
6. Thorstein Veblen, *The Instinct of Workmanship* (London: 1914, reprinted New York: 1964) p. 311; *The Vested Interests and the Common Man* (London: 1924) p. 40.
7. In a letter to William H. Bond in 1938 he wrote, 'I read [Whitman] a great deal as a kid and I rather imagine that a great deal of the original slant of my work comes from that vein in the American tradition. Anyway I'm sure it's more likely to stem from Whitman (and perhaps Veblen) than from Marx, whom I read late and not as completely as I should like.' *Fourteenth Chronicle*, p. 516.
8. See Gelfant, op. cit., p. 134.
9. Lewis Mumford, *Sticks and Stones: A Study of American Architecture and Civilization* (New York: 1924, reissued 1955) p. 188.
10. See Morton and Lucia White, *The Intellectual Versus the City: From Thomas Jefferson to Frank Lloyd Wright* (New York: 1977).
11. In a letter to Rumsey Marvin in 1919, *Fourteenth Chronicle*, p. 254.

12. *Manhattan Transfer* (Boston: 1925) pp. 141, 175.
13. Ibid., p. 375.
14. Hicks, 'The Politics of John Dos Passos' op. cit., see also Daniel Aaron, *Writers on the Left* (Oxford and New York: 1977).
15. In a letter to John Howard Lawson in 1934 he wrote, 'I've been reading the Industrial Worker weekly with considerable pleasure — I still feel more in common with the wobbly line of talk than any other', *Fourteenth Chronicle*, p. 447.
16. John Dos Passos, *The Best Times* (London: 1967) p. 166.
17. Letter to Malcolm Cowley in 1932, *Fourteenth Chronicle*, pp. 403–4.
18. Thorstein Veblen, *The Vested Interests and the Common Man*, p. 160.
19. See his letter to Edmund Wilson in 1934, *Fourteenth Chronicle*, p. 443.
20. *USA* (Harmondsworth: 1966) pp. 812–13.
21. Edmund Wilson, 'Dahlberg, Dos Passos and Wilder' (1930), collected in *The Shores of Light: A Literary Chronicle of the Twenties and Thirties* (New York: 1952) p. 448.
22. Thorstein Veblen, *The Instinct of Workmanship*, pp. 33, 177.
23. Arnold Goldman, 'Dos Passos and his *USA*', *New Literary History* 1 (1970) 471–83, highlights the role of Moorehouse in the trilogy.
24. Dos Passos, *The Best Times*, p. 178; Interview in the *Paris Review*, 46 (1969), reprinted in George Plimpton (ed.), *Writers at Work*, Fourth Series (Harmondsworth: 1976) pp. 67–89.
25. *USA*, pp. 229, 718–19, 1130.
26. Jim Potter, *The American Economy between the World Wars* (London: 1974) pp. 23, 99, 126.
27. See John Dos Passos, 'The Situation in American Writing', *Partisan Review* (Summer 1939), reprinted in *Dos Passos: A Collection of Critical Essays*, edited by Andrew Hook, pp. 13–14.

CHAPTER 11: CONSUMER MAN IN CRISIS: ARTHUR MILLER'S *DEATH OF A SALESMAN*

1. C. Wright Mills, *White Collar: The American Middle Classes* (New York: 1951) pp. 164–5.
2. 'Thus it is that the forms, the accents, the intentions of the plays in this book are not the same from play to play. I could say that my awareness of life was not the same and leave it at that, but the truth is wider, for good or for ill. It is also that the society to which I responded in the past decade was constantly changing. . . . These plays, in one sense, are my response to what was "in the air".' *The Collected Plays* (London: 1967) p. 11.
3. Ibid., pp. 23–4.
4. Ibid., p. 180.
5. As Mills points out, op. cit., p. 180, the old manufacturer's representative who sold to retailers and wholesalers was supervised very little. He was his own in manner and territory, but as the organisation of the market became tighter, the salesman lost autonomy and became replaceable. The new commercial traveller became just one unit in an elaborate marketing organisation.
6. 'Introduction', *Collected Plays*, p. 28.

7. Erich Fromm, *Man For Himself* (London: 1949) p. 68.
8. David Riesman, *Individualism Reconsidered and Other Essays* (New York: 1954) pp. 59–60.
9. *Collected Plays*, p. 149.
10. David Riesman, Nathan Glazer and Reuel Denney, *The Lonely Crowd* (abridged edition, New Haven: 1961) pp. 240–4. Dennis Welland, *Arthur Miller* (London: 1961), has drawn attention to the relevance of *The Lonely Crowd* to the play, but he sees Willy's crisis in terms of a shift from inner direction to other direction.
11. 'Death of Salesman — A Symposium', *Tulane Drama Review*, 2 (1958) 63–9.
12. 'Introduction', *Collected Plays*, pp. 34–5.
13. Raymond Williams, 'The Realism of Arthur Miller', *Critical Quarterly*, 1 (1959) 140–9.
14. *Collected Plays*, p. 217.
15. 'Introduction' to *Collected Plays*, p. 30.
16. 'Death of a Salesman — A Symposium'; See also Arthur Miller, 'The Family and Modern Drama', *Atlantic*, 197 (1956) 35–41.
17. The continuity between these two characters has been commented on by Gordon W. Couchman, 'Arthur Miller's Tragedy of Babbitt', *Educational Theatre Journal*, 7 (1955) 206–11.
18. 'The play was always heroic to me, and in later years the academy's charge that Willy lacked the "stature" for the tragic hero seemed incredible to me.' 'Introduction', *Collected Plays*, p. 31.

SELECT BIBLIOGRAPHY

Only works central to the argument are listed. Place of publication is London unless otherwise stated. Date of original publication is given first.
ECONOMIC, SOCIOLOGICAL AND HISTORICAL SOURCES
Arieli, Y., *Individualism and Nationalism in American Ideology* (Cambridge, Mass., 1964); Bell, Daniel, *The Cultural Contradictions of Capitalism* (1976); Berle, Adolf A., and Means, Gardiner C., *The Modern Corporation and Private Property* (1932, reprinted New York, 1948); Brookings Institute, *America's Capacity to Produce and America's Capacity to Consume: A Digest* (1933, Pittsburgh, 1934); Bryce, James, *The American Commonwealth*, 2 vols (1888, revised edition, New York, 1911); Fass, Paula S., *The Damned and the Beautiful: American Youth in the 1920s* (New York, 1977); Franklin, Benjamin, *The Autobiography and Other Writings* (1750–90), edited by L. Jesse Lemisch (New York, 1961); Hays, Samuel P., *The Response to Industrialism 1885–1914* (Chicago, 1957); Hofstadter, Richard, *Social Darwinism in American Thought* (1944, revised edition, Boston, 1955); Holbrook, Stewart H., *The Age of the Moguls* (New York, 1953); Jones, Peter d'A., *The Consumer Society: A History of American Capitalism* (Harmondsworth, 1965); Josephson, Matthew, *The Robber Barons: The Great American Capitalists 1861–1901* (1934, reprinted 1962); Keezer, Dexter M., and associates, *New Forces in American Business* (New York, 1959); Kennedy, Gail (ed.), *Democracy and the Gospel of Wealth* (Boston, 1949); Kolko, Gabriel, *Wealth and Power in America* (New York, 1962); Kuznets, Simon, *Capital in the American Economy: Its Formation and Financing* (Princeton, 1961); Leuchtenberg, W. E., *The Perils of Prosperity 1914–1932* (Chicago, 1958); Lynd, Robert S., and Helen M., *Middletown: A Study in American Culture* (New York, 1929); Marx, Karl, *Capital*, 3 vols, I (1970), II (1971), III (Chicago, 1909); Marx, Karl, and Engels, Frederick, *Selected Works* (1968); Mills, C. Wright, *White Collar: The American Middle Classes* (New York, 1951); Potter, David M., *People of Plenty: Economic Abundance and the American Character* (Chicago, 1954); Potter, Jim, *The American Economy between the World Wars* (1974); Riesman, David, *Individualism Reconsidered and Other Essays* (New York, 1954); Riesman, David, Glazer, Nathan and Denny, Reuel, *The Lonely Crowd* (1953, abridged edition, New Haven, 1961); Rostow, W. W., *The Stages of Economic Growth: A Non-Communist Manifesto* (Cambridge, 1961); Tawney, R. H., *Religion and the Rise of Capitalism* (1926, reprinted Harmondsworth, 1938); United States Department of Commerce, *Historical Statistics of the United States: Colonial Times to 1957* (Washington, 1960); Veblen, Thorstein, *The Theory of the Leisure Class* (1899, 1970), *The Instinct of Workmanship* (1914, reprinted New York, 1964), *The Vested*

Interests and the Common Man (1919, 1924); Weber, Max, *The Protestant Ethic and the Spirit of Capitalism* (1905), translated by Talcott Parsons (1930, reprinted 1971); Whyte, W. H., *The Organization Man* (1957).

LITERARY, CRITICAL AND BIOGRAPHICAL SOURCES

Bradbury, Malcolm, and Palmer, David (eds), *The American Novel and the Nineteen Twenties* (1971); Cady, Edwin H., *The Road to Realism: The Early Years 1837–1885 of William Dean Howells* (Syracuse, 1956), *The Realist at War: The Mature Years 1885–1920 of William Dean Howells* (Syracuse, 1958); Cowley, Malcolm, *Exile's Return: A Narrative of Ideas* (New York, 1934); Dos Passos, John, *Three Soldiers* (Boston, 1921). *Manhattan Transfer* (Boston, 1925), *USA* (1938, Harmondsworth, 1966), *The Fourteenth Chronicle: Letters and Diaries*, edited by Townsend Ludington (1974); Dreiser, Theodore, *Sister Carrie* (1900, New York, 1958), *The Financier* (1912, reprinted New York, no date), *The Titan* (1914, reprinted New York, no date), *An American Tragedy* (1925, New York, 1964); Fitzgerald, F. Scott, *The Great Gatsby* (1925, Harmondsworth, 1950), *Tender is the Night* (1934, revised edition edited by Malcolm Cowley, Harmondsworth, 1955), *The Crack Up and Other Pieces*, edited by Edmund Wilson (New York, 1945), *Letters*, edited by Andrew Turnbull (1964, Harmondsworth, 1968); Howells, William Dean, *The Rise of Silas Lapham* (1885, New York, 1963), *A Hazard of New Fortunes* (1890, 1965), *Criticism and Fiction and Other Essays*, edited by Clara and Rudolf Kirk (New York, 1959); Lewis, Sinclair, *Main Street* (1920, New York, 1961), *Babbitt* (1922, 1924); Miller, Arthur, *Collected Plays* (New York, 1957); Mizener, Arthur, *The Far Side of Paradise* (1951, 1969); Norris, Frank, *The Octopus* (1901, New York, 1964), *The Pit* (1903, 1922); Pizer, Donald, *The Novels of Theodore Dreiser* (Minneapolis, 1976); Schorer, Mark, *Sinclair Lewis: An American Life* (1961); Sinclair, Upton, *The Jungle* (1906, Harmondsworth, 1965), *The Autobiography of Upton Sinclair* (New York, 1962); Taylor, Walter Fuller, *The Economic Novel in America* (1942, reprinted New York, 1973); Turnbull, Andrew, *Scott Fitzgerald* (1962, Harmondsworth, 1970); Welland, Dennis, *Arthur Miller* (1961).

INDEX